JOURNAL FOR THE STUDY OF THE NEW TESTAMENT SUPPLEMENT SERIES

32

Executive Editor, Supplement Series
David Hill

Publishing Editor
David E Orton

JSOT Press
Sheffield

Peter
and the
Beloved Disciple

Figures for a Community in Crisis

Kevin Quast

269-

Journal for the Study of the New Testament
Supplement Series 32

To Sandy, Kira and Graham

Published by JSOT Press
JSOT Press is an imprint of
Sheffield Academic Press Ltd
The University of Sheffield
343 Fulwood Road
Sheffield S10 3BP
England

Printed in Great Britain
by Billing & Sons Ltd
Worcester

British Library Cataloguing in Publication Data

Quast, Kevin
    Peter and the beloved disciple.
    1. Bible. N.T. Peter, the Apostle, Saint
    I. Title II. Series
    232.9'24

    ISSN 0143-5108
    ISBN 1-85075-217-6

CONTENTS

Chapter 1
INTRODUCTION AND BACKGROUND   7
  A. Introduction   7
  B. History of Interpretation   8
  C. Synopsis of Johannine Community History   13
  D. The Identity of the Beloved Disciple   16
  E. The Function of Anonymity in the Gospel   17
  F. The Representative Figures of the Fourth Gospel 21
    'The Twelve' in the Fourth Gospel   22

Chapter 2
PETER IN JOHN 1–12   27
  A. Introduction   27
  B. Jn 1.35-42   27
  C. Jn 6.60-71   41
  D. Conclusion   53

Chapter 3
PETER AND THE BELOVED DISCIPLE AT THE
LORD'S SUPPER   55
  A. Introduction   55
  B. Jn 13.21–30   57
  C. Jn 13.36–38   69
  D. Conclusions   70

Chapter 4
PETER'S DENIALS   71
  A. Introduction   71
  B. Jn 18.15-18, 25-27   71
  C. Jn 19.25-27   89
  D. Conclusions   97

Chapter 5
PETER AND THE BELOVED DISCIPLE
AT THE EMPTY TOMB   101
  A. Introduction   101
  B. Jn 20.1-10   102
    The Run to the Tomb   111
    Peter's Entrance into the Tomb   113
    Peter—Witness to the Empty Tomb 116
    The Beloved Disciple—The Response of Faith 117
    The Complementary Significance of the Partners 119
  C. The Commissioning of the Disciples   122
  D. Conclusions   122

Chapter 6
PETER AND THE BELOVED DISCIPLE IN JOHN 21   125
  A. Introduction   125
    The Provenance of Chapter 21   125
  B. The Basic Concerns of the Chapter   133
  C. Peter in John 21   137
  D. The Beloved Disciple in John 21   149
  E. Peter and the Beloved Disciple   153
  F. Conclusions   155

Chapter 7
CONCLUSION   157
  A. Introduction   157
  B. The Beloved Disciple   159
  C. Peter   162
  D. The Two in Relationship   164
  E. The Historical Context   167

Notes   171
Bibliography   207

Chapter 1

INTRODUCTION AND BACKGROUND

A. *Introduction*

The enigmatic figure of the Beloved Disciple occurs perhaps seven times in the Gospel of John, all during the final periods of the earthly life of Jesus. In all but one of those occurrences he is closely identified with Peter. This leads us to conclude that the evangelist wanted to convey a particular understanding of the relationship between Peter and the Beloved Disciple. It is imperative that this relationship is understood accurately, for a proper understanding of Peter and the Beloved Disciple is crucial to a proper interpretation of the whole Gospel of John. Writers have long recognized the unity that permeates the Johannine theological scheme—all its teachings are inter-related, so that one aspect of the Johannine perspective cannot be interpreted without its affecting the entire horizon of John's theology. One author has described it as 'a kaleidoscopic quality of the Fourth Gospel; its parts and the whole are so closely interdependent that a small shift in interpreting one element can cause all the others to revolve ever so slightly into a new and likewise coherent constellation'.[1]

What was the nature of the relationship between Peter and the Beloved Disciple that the evangelist was depicting? A consensus has developed that sees the evangelist portraying a rivalry between Peter and the Beloved Disciple in which Peter is subordinated to the hero of the Fourth Gospel because of the insight and intimacy the Beloved Disciple shares with Jesus.[2] It may be, however, that a straightforward rivalry is not intentionally portrayed—perhaps more complex dynamics are at work behind the depictions. This enquiry proposes to seek a more accurate understanding of the intended significance of the relationship that these two figures have in the Gospel of John.

To examine this question, an exegetical approach will be taken.

Operating with supportable conclusions regarding the basic nature of
the Johannine community and the representative functions of both
Peter and the Beloved Disciple, the present writer proposes to
examine pertinent passages in the Gospel of John in order to
ascertain whether or not there is a recurring pattern or purpose
behind the portrayals within the contexts of the various narratives.
Then, it may be possible to entertain the question of why these
figures are thus portrayed.

B. *History of Interpretation*

Suggestions concerning the historicity and identity of the Beloved
Disciple have gone full circle and one may only conclude that an
exact answer will always elude us.[3] Nevertheless, the result of such
studies has been the sharpening focus on the person and function of
the Beloved Disciple in the formation of the Fourth Gospel. Debate
still continues as to the historicity of the Beloved Disciple, the main
problem being the integration of the obvious paradigmatic significance
of this figure with his actual role in the authorship of the Fourth
Gospel and the formation of this particular circle of Christians.
While his actual role as evangelist requires qualification, a strong
case can be made that the Beloved Disciple served as a hero of a
particular Christian community, its link to Jesus and the symbol of
the individual in close, believing relationship to Christ as a model of
discipleship.

The relationship between the Beloved Disciple and Peter has been
interpreted variously by a wide range of scholars. Basic to most
approaches is the assumption that the Beloved Disciple (Johannine
Christianity) is heralded as superior by means of the relative
portrayal of Peter (Apostolic Christianity) within the Gospel of John.
Snyder speaks of the strong 'anti-Petrinism' of the Gospel of John
and even goes as far to state 'the figure of the Beloved Disciple, as
one more authoritative than the other disciples, especially those later
designated as apostles, is an absolute necessity to the structure of the
Gospel of John'.[4] Among scholars who see such a contrast are those
who attribute the same basic role or function to both Peter and the
Beloved Disciple with respect to their particular communities.[5]

For example, with both the Beloved Disciple and Peter cast as
teachers, the Beloved Disciple has been understood as the transmitter
of true original teaching in correction to the traditions associated

with Peter. 'We can hardly dispute those students of the Fourth Gospel, both ancient and modern, who see in it a subtle correction of the Petrine story, and understand the figure of the Beloved disciple to be introduced in connection with this purpose, to rectify what had been misunderstood'.[6]

Bultmann's interpretation of the Beloved Disciple as representative of Gentile Christianity in correlation to Peter's representation of Jewish Christianity is integral to his basic understanding of the Gospel. The contrast of the two figures reveals, according to Bultmann, the greater capacity for faith that the Gentiles have.[7] More recently, Pamment has restated the thesis:

> [Jn] 21.24 identifies the testimony of the Fourth Gospel as the testimony of the beloved disciple, of gentile Christianity, and assures readers of its truth. The picture of gentile Christianity presented in the portrait of the beloved disciple is not a picture of the passive reception of tradition, but of active and creative acceptance.[8]

In an equivalent contrast of loyalty to Jesus, the Beloved Disciple has been seen as the one who sticks to Jesus to the end in contrast to Peter.[9] Neirynck sees the Beloved Disciple duplicating and superseding Peter's role in the gospel traditions, although the substitution is never quite complete.[10]

The Beloved Disciple has been interpreted as being the authenticator and witness of tradition who makes an equal claim for his *Einzelkirche* as that which is made for the *Gesamtkirche*, represented by Peter.[11]

Going in a new direction, Minear has suggested that the Beloved Disciple represents Benjamin among Benjamite Christians who comprised the Johannine community. The contrast of Peter and the Beloved Disciple may well reflect, then, 'a corresponding suspicion of the Petrine community on the part of this Benjamite community'.[12] While Minear himself recognizes the speculative nature of his conjectures, he is on relatively solid ground compared to Edgar Bruns. Bruns has surpassed the imagination of Minear, and all other Johannine scholars, in linking the Buddhist figure of Ananda with the Beloved Disciple![13]

More reflective of the scholarly consensus are the positions of Watty[14] and J.J. Gunther[15] who see the rise of the status of the Beloved Disciple as a response to a developing Petrine tradition that was beginning to introduce negative or objectionable understandings of the gospel traditions. The portrayal of the anonymous Beloved Disciple was in

> ... response to a pastoral situation which seems to have necessitated a corrective to a developing Petrine tradition. 'Peter' stands for a negative strain in the gospel. The name focuses and highlights precisely what the evangelist wishes to correct. He goes out of his way to present a 'Peter of history' with warts and all, because, presumably the name bestowed by Jesus was assuming an inordinate importance.[16]

Gunther seeks to highlight the superiority of the Beloved Disciple in the Johannine tradition in terms of spiritual insight, perception and interpretation of the events of the life of Jesus.[17]

Some writers, such as Schuyler Brown, interpret the relationship between Peter and the Beloved Disciple as an equivalent contrast in the main part of the Gospel but discern a change in their portrayed relationship in ch. 21, perhaps in response to ecclesial concerns within the Johannine community.[18] The following statement of R.F. Collins exemplifies this position:

> The appearance of Simon Peter in John 21 assimilates somewhat the Johannine Peter with the Peter of the Synoptics... John 21, however, is a later redactional addition to the Fourth Gospel, an addition which some authors interpret as part of an ecclesiastical redactor's attempt to harmonize the last of the Gospels with the earlier Synoptic Gospels.[19]

Maynard agrees with the interpretation of a shift in attitude towards Peter in the last chapter of the Gospel, 'but in the body of the Gospel Peter is made to appear in a very bad light, indeed'.[20]

A second group of interpreters prefer to differentiate between the actual roles and functions of the Beloved Disciple and Peter while they still postulate some sort of rivalry. Kragerud sees the Beloved Disciple as the representative of a pneumatic circle (*Geist*) and Peter is taken to represent ecclesiastical office (*Amt*).[21] 'So ist L [the Beloved Disciple] als der Repräsentant eines kirchlichen Dienstes, und zwar eines "pneumatischen" aufzufassen'.[22] The functions of Peter and the Beloved Disciple are differentiated so that their 'rivalry' is not one of corresponding functions. In other words, ecclesiastical authority of Peter was recognized by the Johannine Christians, but they claimed didactic authority.

As the believer and disciple *par excellence*, the Beloved Disciple is also seen as the representative figure for all with respect to faith in

Christ. Next to him, Peter then serves as a subordinate spokesman, representing the Twelve in the common evangelical tradition. In this scheme, according to Collins, Peter is dependent upon the Beloved Disciple for his saving knowledge.[23]

R.E. Brown suggests that the Beloved Disciple is portrayed so as to offset the dominance of the Twelve in the developing church and to teach that 'ecclesiastical authority is not the sole criteria for judging importance in the following of Jesus'.[24] He sees an explicit contrast between these two figures by which the Johannine community symbolically counterpoises itself over against the Apostolic churches.

A number of scholars can be included in a third group which does not see a rivalry between the two figures at all. Indeed, many writers regard the role of the Beloved Disciple as symbolically significant without any necessary relationship to Peter. Perhaps the silence of many commentators with respect to a competitive relationship between the two in John can be taken as support for this position. However, it is not necessary to argue from this silence. For instance Schnackenburg sees a relationship of coordination and mutal recognition between the Beloved Disciple and Peter. He suggests that the association of the Beloved Disciple with Peter would result in the increased prestige of the lesser known disciple.[25] F.M. Braun maintains that the Beloved Disciple is not a rival to Peter, but the image of the believer in all his love, faith and attachment to Jesus.[26]

Cullmann is another scholar who belongs in this group, for he asserts that the Gospel of John

> ...nowhere attempts to deny directly the special role of Peter within the group of disciples. It only has the tendency to lessen this role, in so far as it seeks to show that beside the unique position of Peter there is the somewhat different special role of the 'Beloved Disciple'.[27]

In 1975 Mahoney published his dissertation *Two Disciples at the Tomb* in which he contested the generally held assumption that the Beloved Disciple is, himself, an important figure. Furthermore, he denied that there exists a Beloved Disciple–Peter contrast in the Gospel. He maintains that the Beloved Disciple and Peter are used as props in the dramas in which they are found. They are not contrasted in these narratives and as secondary figures or props, they have no abiding symbolic value.[28]

While there is considerable variation within the three general categories of positions just outlined, it can be said that the majority of scholars interpret the Gospel of John as reflecting a rivalry between the Beloved Disciple and Peter. Operating from this perspective, they have gone on to reconstruct the community history and the origins of the Christian church. In addition, their understanding of the relationship between the Beloved Disciple and Peter has, of course, influenced their understanding of Johannine theology, particularly in the areas of ecclesiology and revelation.

Bearing in mind this basic overview of the history of only one aspect of the study of the Beloved Disciple in the Gospel of John, Minear's words written in justification of his own unique thesis are well-taken:

> Over the centuries the search for the beloved disciple has been so intense and so wide-ranging that it is an act of consummate audacity to suggest a new thesis for consideration. Yet no one is wholly content with the present solutions to the riddle, and the issue is of such central importance that it would be wrong to call off the search entirely. That search requires the careful reexamination of every clue, however fanciful at first sight.[29]

It is hoped that this present work is not to be categorized as an act of 'consummate audacity', for the present solutions to the riddle are unsatisfactory to the writer for a number of reasons. The first, and perhaps most basic, problem with past approaches is that they have concerned themselves, for the most part, with the search for the identity of the Beloved Disciple, rather than the intended function of this anonymous figure within each of the narratives. It should be obvious that the evangelist intended the Beloved Disciple to remain anonymous. If centuries of intense and wide-ranging search for the Beloved Disciple have not satisfied anyone, then perhaps it is time to ask different questions of the text.

Second, those scholars who have noted a relationship between the Beloved Disciple and Peter have often too simply analyzed it as 'contrast' or 'rivalry'. It is not enough to stop there, especially when such a procedure is compared with the detailed analyses of redaction criticism of the parables, for example. The exegesis of the pertinent passages in the Gospel of John must be more specific to be accurate. It is hoped that the exegesis undertaken in this study will be specific—confining itself to the context, purpose and main thrust of each passage examined, and focusing the discussion upon what may be discerned as the specific function the evangelist/editor intended to give to either Peter or the Beloved Disciple.

Third, detailed and intricate reconstructions of Johannine Community history and the origins of Christianity in general are often built upon the assumed relationship between the two representative figures.[30] It may even be that imaginative historical reconstructions have dictated the manner in which the texts have been exegeted. Methodologically, this procedure is problematic. If a more accurate understanding of the roles and functions of Peter and the Beloved Disciple is developed it may help to arrive at a more accurate community history. Also, it would provide some sort of control by which to evaluate the work that has already been done in this area.[31]

Finally, it is hoped that the findings of this study may result in a further clarification of the theology of John in the areas of its ecclesiology, christology, pneumatology and eschatology. This examination will no doubt extend beyond sociological and historical considerations in its applications, but from the perspective of background and working presuppositions, the area of Johannine community history must be our starting point.

C. *Synopsis of Johannine Community History*

As much as scholars differ as to the nature of the background to the Gospel of John, with one voice they all assert 'the Fourth Gospel reflects to a large degree the history of a single community which maintained over a period of some duration its particular and rather peculiar identity'.[32] This, of course, is not only true of the Fourth Gospel. 'All the gospels must be read on two levels, as narratives of the ministry of Jesus and as reflections of the ecclesiastical contexts in which and for which they were written. . . Like any tool, redaction criticism is only as good as the judgment of the scholars who is using it'.[33]

Furthermore, the Gospel of John is understood as a literary work that has been composed over an extended period of time and thus reflects a continuous but developing Johannine tradition. For instance, Boismard has constructed an elaborate but carefully substantiated theory of the process of composition of the Gospel in which he isolates four stages of development, each one reflecting expansions and changes in context, theology and style.[34] N.E. Johnson has proposed an interesting hypothesis which he summarizes as follows:

> John, the son of Zebedee, apostle and Beloved Disciple, left behind
> him a document QJ which contained simple, eyewitness [Passion]
> narratives; this document was later worked into a theological
> gospel by a close friend and probable disciple of John the Apostle.
> Even later, more disciples of the apostle added the final chapter,
> still drawing upon their master's narrative.[35]

As a result certain periods of Johannine community history may be
discerned within the different 'strata' of the extended composition.[36]
Suggesting that 'the evangelist composed not one but three versions
of the farewell discourse',[37] Painter goes on to observe 'each version
reflects a particular situation of crisis in the history of Johannine
Christians'.[38]

It is apparent that from the earliest conception of the Johannine
community there were certain doctrinal chracteristics that served to
distinguish the Johannine Christians from other Christians. Not only
did they align themselves under the Beloved Disciple, but they
displayed a uniquely high Christology and a stress on the individual's
relationship with God through belief in Jesus that overshadowed any
ecclesiological developments. They were highly conscious of the
difference between their understanding of Christ and that of other
groups. 'In any reading of the gospel or epistles there appears a
sectarian consciousness, a sense of exclusivity. This sensibility is
sharper in 1 Jn (2.15-17) but it is also present in the gospel (3.16-17;
12.47; 17.9-14, 21, 23). . . . The sectarianism is without dispute'.[39]
This assertion—isolating the Johannine community—may be too
strong in light of the general tendency of Christian communities in
the New Testament era.

'The New Testament writings reveal, to the critical eye, a greater
pluralism than was tolerated by the orthodoxy which canonized
them. . . . the spectrum of religious belief and practice reflected in the
New Testament is every bit as broad as that which exists among
Christians today, and relations would scarcely have been uniformly
cordial. Moreover, in most books of the New Testament we find
explicit criticism of other Christians, whose teaching or conduct is
regarded as a threat to the community being addressed.[40]

The Johannine community built their faith around the traditions
of the Beloved Disciple concerning Jesus. They appealed to the Spirit
as the guiding authority in matters of faith, equating the Spirit
(Paraclete) with the abiding presence of the ascended Jesus.

> The Spirit appears prominently in many NT books, but the
> personal role of the Spirit in the Fourth Gospel under the title of

'Paraclete' is unique... The Johannine Jesus says to his disciples: 'It is for your own good that I go away, for if I do not go away, the Paraclete will never come to you' (16.7). It is the Paraclete, the Holy Spirit, who teaches the believer everything (14.26) and guides the believer along the way of all truth (16.13). And it is the Paraclete who bears witness to Jesus in coordination with the Johannine believer (15.25-26).[41]

A conclusion that is bearing the test of time and close scrutiny is the one that states that John reflects a historical conflict between the community and the synagogue.[42] Martyn is to be credited for bringing this to the fore. It is his thesis that the Fourth Gospel was written in response to the process of conflict with, and expulsion from, the synagogue community which the Johannine community, in particular, experienced. Pancaro builds upon this and points out that this development arose out of the struggle of Judaism to maintain itself after the destruction of the temple in AD 70. '... The measures taken against heretics by normative Judaism in the first century and up to the period in which the Church became "imperial" were directed against Hebrew Christianity. This is demonstrated not only by the *Birkat ha-Minim*, but also by the other measures taken by the synagogue in its self-defence'.[43] In commenting on Pancaro's work, Kysar states, 'his study is a definitive investigation of the concrete situation out of which the Fourth Gospel was written and evinces most forcefully how the conflict with the synagogue has shaped the thought of the Gospel'.[44] This observation has definite ramifications concerning the identity of the readership of the Gospel of John. It must be maintained that the Gospel is basically a work with Jewish concerns, and not primarily a tract for Gentile Christianity.[45] 'For all his hearers [i.e. John's],... a key problem was their own personal relation to the synagogue. His gospel was therefore designed to shape the subsequent conversations between those readers and their Jewish neighbours, both before and after any formal separation of church from the synagogue'.[46]

It is interesting to note that a Johannine 'school' is distinguished from the community by Painter. He does this by using the theological indexes of the Johannine Christology and the concept of the Paraclete. '... While the *Johannine school* was unified by the christology of the evangelist the *Johannine community* probably was not'.[47] A subjective appeal to pneumatic authority may have eventually led to the schism within the Johannine community that is evidenced in the Epistles (1 Jn 2.19).[48]

Based on a particular interpretation of John 21, Schuyler Brown remarks that 'the Johannine community's acceptance of apostolic authority, represented by Peter and its assimilation to Christian communities which appealed to this authority, seems to have been necessitated by dissensions within the community which were unleashed by the death of the beloved disciple'.[49] This crisis of authority may have been brewing relatively early in the history of the Johannine community and it may be reflected in the farewell discourses. 'The repeated prayer for unity suggests that there was already a real threat of schism but that this had not yet occurred'.[50]

Whatever the details are, the fact of the matter is that the Johannine community eventualy did find itself in a crisis of authority which may have definite ramifications in the interpretation of the significance of the Beloved Disciple–Peter comparison in the Gospel of John.

D. *The Identity of the Beloved Disciple*

There are sufficient indications to warrant the conclusion that he was an historical person, however the Beloved Disciple is to be identified. First, it is necessary to observe that, after the death of Jesus, it was the practice of different Christian groups to claim to possess the witness of a disciple of Jesus to lend authority to their particular beliefs and practices.[51] The Johannine Christians associated themselves with the witness of the Beloved Disciple.

> Later in community history when the Johannine Christians were clearly distinct from groups of Christians who associated themselves with memories of the Twelve (e.g., with the memory of Peter), the claim to possess the witness of the Beloved Disciple enabled the Johannine Christians to defend their peculiar insights in christology and ecclesiology.[52]

If the Beloved Disciple was not a real person, the appeal to his authority would have been worthless when juxtaposed with Peter, for example.[53]

Second, the anonymity of the Beloved Disciple itself suggests that he was a real person.[54] Cullmann notes, 'the very fact that the beloved disciple is anonymous does suggest that he was a historical figure. The apocryphal gospels tend to connect their legendary accounts with a known disciple rather than with an anonymous person'.[55]

Finally, Gunther makes the obvious comment, 'misunderstandings do not occur about the death of merely symbolic figures'.[56] In Jn 21.20-23, which is part of a later appendix to the Gospel, the writer relays confusion and disappointment in the community because of the Beloved Disciple's death.

Although a strong case can be made that the Beloved Disciple was a real person, his context in history is elusive. Traditionally, he has been regarded as one of the Twelve disciples of Jesus—John the son of Zebedee.[57] On the other end of this spectrum is the view that he was a second-generation Christian leader who became the hero of one particular community.[58]

> If the beloved disciple is, in fact, an anonymous Christian leader from the second generation, then we may suppose that just as the author of the epilogue has tried to make him the author of the gospel, so the author of the gospel has tried to make him the source behind his work. . .[59]

Mediating positions range from that of Lindars, who states that the Beloved Disciple is 'definitely one of the Twelve', but a 'faceless' one,[60] to the majority of scholars who hold that the Beloved Disciple is a contemporary of Jesus, one of his many disciples, but *not* one of the Twelve.[61] Schnackenburg sums up this perspective in stating, 'The anonymous figure introduced by the evangelist and the editors as the "disciple whom Jesus loved" and brought out at the last supper, is an historical person, an apostle, who, however, did not belong, to the circle of the twelve and was most likely to have been a man from Jerusalem'.[62]

E. *The Function of Anonymity in the Gospel*

Mention needs to be made of the anonymity of the Beloved Disciple, for it is this characteristic that has led to many problems, speculations and debates with respect to the background and interpretation of the Gospel. If indeed the Beloved Disciple was a real person, who presumably had a name, then his persistent anonymity throughout the Gospel must be significant and intentional, contrary to the assertions of some, such as Broomfield, who states,

> . . . it is a mistake to think that the Gospel was ever intended to be anonymous. The absence of the author's name from the Gospel, as we have it, does not imply anonymity. . . the Evangelist, in writing of his own part of the story, preferred to speak of himself as a

'disciple whom Jesus loved' but it does not follow that he intended his identity to be concealed.[63]

Such reasoning appears to be weak, especially in light of the fact that in all stages of the Gospel tradition the Beloved Disciple's anonymity is maintained. If the Beloved Disciple's anonymity was not intended to conceal his identity, then why was his identity not disclosed at some stage in the development of the Gospel tradition? It is more reasonable to state: 'The anonymity of this disciple loved by Jesus is, as we have seen, so striking and so insistent that we are forced to conclude that it was deliberately maintained by the author of the Gospel as we now have it. . . '[64]

When the attention to detail so characteristic of the Gospel of John is compared to its silence regarding the name of the Beloved Disciple, this anonymity should be regarded as very significant:

> . . . he [the writer] is at pains to prove that he knows who is who, what words, names and titles mean, what actually happened and where,. . . He goes out of his way in his desire to establish that his record of events is the reliable account of an eye-witness which can be tested and verified by lexicography, topography and family history.
> It is against this background of careful reporting, detailed description and precise identification that the prevalence of anonymity in the Fourth Gospel is all the more significant.[65]

Even if one agrees that the Beloved Disciple's anonymity is significant, the question still remains as to the function of such anonymity. Why is his anonymity so significant? In comparison with the function of naming, anonymity may signal the reader to identify more closely with the character in the narrative:

> . . . This is because a gospel, unlike a biography, is concerned as much with generalities which the reader can apply to himself, as with the particulars of individual historical events.
> . . . John is content to use descriptions rather than names in cases where the representative character of the individual or group is important, and where naming individuals would distract from the centre of interest in Jesus.[66]

It may be that the anonymity of the Beloved Disciple is not motivated by a desire to convey his representative nature but is simply a function of the historical context of the Beloved Disciple as a second-generation Christian leader. Schuyler Brown has suggested that the Beloved Disciple shares this trait with all the second generation leaders in the church, 'not one of whom is known to us by name'.[67] He goes on to observe that the Gospel of John is not the only truly anonymous gospel.

> All four gospels share in the anonymity which is characteristic of second generation Christianity. Not one of these works contains the name of its author. The titles by which they are now designated were added to the original works when they were brought together in a single manuscript, and it became necessary to distinguish them from each other.[68]

Except in the case of actual letters, such as Paul's, which by their specific and personal nature require the identification of the author, anonymity and pseudonymity are not only characterstics but also authenticating factors of our earliest Christian literature. Aland observes:

> In early Christianity Holy Scripture did not know any author in the modern sense... The one, who, in those days, instructed the Christian society did so according to the Spirit. He was but the pen moved by the Spirit. As soon as writings of this kind advanced beyond the pattern of the letter in the literal sense, they could not even mention the authentic author without attracting suspicion. In my opinion we do not have to explain or to justify the phenomena of anonymity or pseudonymity in early Christian literature. It is the other way round: we need an explanation when the real author gives his name.[69]

It should be pointed out that anonymity is not just a characteristic of second-generation Christian leaders but is also a trait of many disciples of Jesus who were contemporaries of the Twelve. Furthermore, one cannot directly compare the type of anonymity in the Fourth Gospel with that displayed in the synoptics. Only in John do we find an anonymous figure explicitly and centrally active in the narratives, independent of any questions of actual authorship of a document. This suggests to the present writer that even if the anonymity were due to an authenticating characteristic of second generation literary practices, its function extends well beyond that facet in the Gospel of John.

It has been suggested that the identity of the Beloved Disciple, in particular, was masked because 'his name did not evoke a universal esteem among potential readers which was commensurate with his excellence'.[70] In other words, anonymity was an instrument designed to elevate the underestimated authority of the Beloved Disciple. 'His authority to witness and explain was enhanced more by describing him, while leaving his identity obscure, than by citing his name'.[71] In one sense, this may have been part of the dynamic at work, especially if the Beloved Disciple had entered into the second-generation milieu of the Christian community.

On the other hand, his anonymity may have been pastorally motivated to promote unity rather than to promote his own authority. Watty has made some discerning observations in this respect, building upon the representative service of anonymity. The author of the Fourth Gospel, according to Watty did indeed 'straddle the generations' and had become peculiarly sensitive to the relative 'newcomers in the Church' and was concerned about the relationships between 'the earliest disciples and the larger body of believers'.[72]

> ... He therefore attempts to break up the magic circle which was in the making not so much by storming it from without as by dismantling it from within. 'Names' are rendered futile and superfluous so as to enable a unity and continuity in spite of the barriers of time and space. For the sake of solidarity with the unknown, he himself consents to remain incognito. As long as the beloved disciple remains unnamed, any disciple, however recent, however late, may be the disciple whom Jesus loved. . .[73]

It is most difficult to decide on the exact function the evangelist or editor intended to give to the Beloved Disciple's anonymity, but at least we can be sure that the anonymity was deliberate and as an anonymous figure he obviously carried substantial authority in at least one community. Furthermore, as a representative figure with whom the readers could identify, this anonymity does lend itself to the pastoral concerns of achieving unity among Christian communities struggling to maintain themselves beyond the first generation.

In summary, it would appear, on the basis of the evidence, that the Beloved Disciple was indeed an historical person. The question of whether or not he was a contemporary of Jesus is more difficult to answer with certainty. Further examination of some of the unique details in the pertinent texts will contribute to a tentative answer. In the meantime it should be noted that, for the purposes of this study, the actual identity of the Beloved Disciple can be left unresolved as it is the specific task of this book to focus on the function of the Beloved Disciple within the redaction narratives. What is important is the observation that this person bore symbolic and representative significance within the Gospel for the Johannine community. He is 'an historical person with paradigmatic significance'.[74] As an individual who lives on as a type, the Beloved Disciple is invested with a representative, symbolic nature':

> That the BD has a figurative dimension is patent. In many ways he is the exemplary Christian, for in the NT 'beloved' is a form of address for fellow Christians. Yet this symbolic dimension does not mean that the BD is nothing but a symbol. One may accept a symbolic dimension for Mary and Peter, as Bultmann does; but that does not reduce these characters to pure symbols. The obvious import of the passages in John that describe the BD is that he is a real human being whose actions are important on the Gospel scene.[75]

F. *The Representative Figures of the Fourth Gospel*

If the Beloved Disciple, as an actual person, could indeed assume symbolic significance in this Gospel, is he the only one to do so? John the Baptist, Nathanael, Nicodemus, the Samaritan woman at the well, the royal official whose son was healed, the healed lame man, the man born blind, Philip, Lazarus, Judas, Peter, Mary—the mother of Jesus, Mary Magdalen and Thomas have all been presented as representative figures in the Gospel of John.[76] From this list, Judas, Peter and Mary, the mother of Jesus have repeatedly surfaced in scholarship as representative figures and they will be further examined in the course of this particular study. It would appear that Peter, especially, serves as a symbol in the Gospel when one considers how Peter and the Beloved Disciple are strategically juxtaposed in chs. 13–21. It is not difficult to make a strong case for the representative function of Peter in the Synoptics and Acts. Cullman is able to conclude '. . . according to all three Synoptic Gospels Peter indubitably played the role of spokesman among the twelve disciples'.[77] The Gospel of John, in turn, does not deny Peter his role as representative of the twelve. Throughout the Gospel he is accorded this primary function. Leon Morris has summed it up well:

> Peter's primacy is just as clear in this gospel as elsewhere; consider his surname (1.43), his confession (6.68), his prominence at the footwashing (13.6), his defence of Christ (18.10), his waiting at the high priest's door (18.16), the fact that the resurrection message is brought to him (20.2), the fact that he first sees the signs that

Christ has risen (20.7), that he directs the group fishing (21.3), that he is the first to join Christ on the shore and chief in carrying out his command (21.7, 11), and that he receives the great commission (21.15ff.).[78]

Peter has become the representative of the twelve apostles in the entire Gospel tradition. Whenever the disciples have a question, a stylized Peter asks it. It is the same person who makes the confession of faith in their name. At the same time, when the disciples are to be rebuked, it is their spokesman, Peter who must receive the rebuke. Peter is the concrete character who is best known of Jesus' historical disciples, and, as such, he became the symbolical figure for the Twelve, regarded as their leader and spokesman.

1. 'The Twelve' in the Fourth Gospel

To be able to assert that Peter became the symbolical figure for the Twelve in the Gospel of John, of course, depends on whether or not the concept of Twelve disciples as a special group was indeed operative in the mind of the Fourth evangelist or redactor. The 'Twelve' are explicitly mentioned four times in the Gospel of John in only two contexts[79] and this paucity might, at first notice, suggest that the concept of the Twelve does not even figure in the Johannine scheme.[80] This is how James Dunn reads John:

> ... The small group left round Jesus after the tremendous sifting (crisis) of faith and loyalty do not form some hierarchy or particular office which sets them apart from other disciples; they are never called 'apostles' or 'the twelve' and presumably include some of the women who feature so prominently in the Gospel.[81]

Apart from the fact that Dunn is incorrect in stating that the small group which aligned itself with Jesus is never called 'the Twelve', he ignores the fact that it is precisely at the 'sifting' of disciples in ch. 6 that the Twelve are positively highlighted, with Peter acting as their spokesman.

At the other end of the spectrum is the reasoning that the group of Twelve is necessarily the central focus for all significant activity of the disciples. This has the effect of bringing the Beloved Disciple into the fold of the Twelve.

> The disciple's stature in the universal church and in the Evangelist's community suggests that he was among the least known of the Twelve. Anyone especially loved by Jesus would necessarily gravitate toward *membership* in the Twelve. Unless we are prepared

to dismiss the Fourth Gospel's portrait of his close kinship to Jesus as a mere 'sales pitch' undergirding the Gospel's credibility, we must assume that Jesus esteemed him enough to include him among the Twleve or perhaps to leave directions that he take Iscariot's place. . .[82]

To say that someone who was specially loved by Jesus would *necessarily* gravitate toward membership in the Twelve is to invest more significance and prominence to the Twelve than the Gospel of John, at least, (if not also the synoptic tradition) is prepared to give this group. Furthermore, such a supposition does not help much in the identification of the Beloved Disciple, since the constituency of this group is most difficult to define. Even a scholar who describes the Twelve as a 'closed' group of precisely twelve members, to which 'no further additions were ever made',[83] has to state:

> The lists of names of the Twelve in the Synoptic Gospels do not exactly correspond. The Fourth Gospel introduces the name of Nathanael; and other variants in the names occur in the uncanonical sources. All attempts to harmonize the lists are speculative.[84]

The category that John uses to speak of the closest followers of Jesus is not 'The Twelve', but rather 'the disciples'.

While the Twelve, in John, come from the larger group of disciples, they did not represent all of the disciples, or even the 'cream of the crop'.

> *hoi mathetai* are not simply the equivalent of *hoi dodeka*, the Twelve. This identification can only be observed in some parts of the tradition. The circle of the Twelve was both a symbolic representation of the twelve tribes of Israel, and thus the whole people of God, and also a section of the larger circle of disciples which Jesus summoned to discipleship from a still wider group of adherents. This is more probable than to suppose that there existed yet another separate circle of apostles alongside the circle of the disciples. It is no longer possible today to determine the precise limits of the circle of disciples. But it is clearly not a question with Jesus of an ascetic elite with a distinct ethic which Jesus was able to demand only of a few people. The disciples would have been a circle of immediate followers who were commissioned to particular service.[85]

The disciples were not a rigid group and the Gospel of John is certainly not exact in its categorization of the followers of Jesus. '. . .

the Evangelist allows for exceptions and overlappings in his general, loose groupings'.[86] These general groupings of disciples and the Twelve are distinguished from one another, as well as from other categories of people in the Gospel narratives.[87] R.E. Brown makes a strong case that Peter and the Twelve are to be distinguished from other groups of Jesus' disciples. He begins by appealing to Jn 6.60-69, where the contrast is explicitly highlighted between disciples of inadequate faith and the Twelve with Peter acting as their spokesman.[88] From this point he goes on to illustrate how Peter and the Twelve are meant to represent only one group of Christians which are separate from the Christians that comprise the Johannine community.

> But how do we know that Peter and the Twelve do not stand for *all* Christians, rather than for a group of Christians distinct from the Johannine community? The key to that question is the consistent and deliberate contrast between Peter and the Beloved Disciple, the hero of the Johannine community. In five of the six passages where he is mentioned, the Beloved Disciple is explicitly contrasted with Peter ... Such contrast cannot be accidental, especially since in several scenes John seems to have added the Beloved Disciple to establish the contrast.[89]

To summarize, the Twelve are a distinct group within the disciples of Jesus, but they are not portrayed as having an exclusive intimate relationship with Jesus. Because the Twelve, as a group, are distinguished from other groups in the Gospel of John it is likely that, through the representative nature of the figure of Peter, they carried symbolic significance for the Fourth Evangelist and his readership. At the present stage of this study, we are not in a position to isolate just exactly what Peter and the Twelve represented beyond the basic observation that they must have represented what has become labelled as the 'Apostolic' stream of the early Christian church.[90] While it is clear that the 'apostles' were not directly equivalent to the Twelve,[91] the two designations soon became closely identified.

> The identification of the apostles with the Twelve bears witness to a concern to root the activity of the church in the ministry and intention of Jesus, at a time when the founding fathers were passing from the scene.[92]

The observation that there arose a concern to root the activity of the church to Jesus through the apostles (represented by Peter) may be crucial to our understanding of the depictions of Peter and the Beloved Disciple in John.

In the next chapter, we will look at the depiction of Peter in the Synoptics and in the Gospel of John where he does not appear juxtaposed to the Beloved Disciple in order to have some measure of comparison and control of our evaluations of the two in relationship.

Chapter 2

PETER IN JOHN 1-12

A. *Introduction*

It is necessary to examine the picture painted of Peter by the fourth evangelist in places where he is not explicitly paired with the Beloved Disciple in order to set the stage for our considerations. If, in comparison with Synoptic parallels, the role of Peter is down-played or, on the other hand, enhanced, in John's accounts, this must be taken into account as we place him alongside the Beloved Disciple.

Peter does occur in a central role in two important places in the first half of the Gospel of John—Jn 1.35-42 and 6.60-71. The first passage recounts the calling of the first disciples and it can be compared with Mt. 4.18-22, Mk 1.16-20 and Lk. 5.1-11. There are some notable differences between John and the Synoptic parallels and some scholars have suggested that they are independent[1] and perhaps even describe different events altogether.[2] It may be, however, that the differences can be accounted for by the motives and structure of the evangelists.[3] In any case, the specific details in comparison with the Synoptic parallels will be discussed at some length and then we will be in a better position to make such a decision.

Chapter 6.60-71 can be linked to Peter's confession at Caesarea Philippi as found in Mt. 16.13-20, Mk 8.27-30 and Lk. 9.18-21, again, however, with significant differences in setting and context. This chapter will proceed by exegeting Jn 1.35-42 with attention to what is being said about Peter. This will be followed by a similar exercise with 6.60-71. A general conclusion will then be offered that will give us some control over our evaluations of Peter and the Beloved Disciple in the latter half of the Gospel.

B. *Jn 1.35-42*

From v. 35 we can gather that, according to the Gospel of John, the first disciples of Jesus were originally disciples of John the Baptist.

'... Τῇ ἐπαύριον πάλιν εἰστήκει ὁ Ἰωάννης καὶ ἐκ τῶν μαθητῶν
αὐτοῦ δύο'. The ablatival phrase ἐκ τῶν μαθητῶν can be understood
as an ablative of source or a partitive ablative. In either case, we have
here a description of two disciples leaving the ranks of the Baptist's
followers and aligning themselves with Jesus. Haenchen suggests
that they may have been the only disciples of the Baptist that were
present at the time, '... one must not assume from the construction
that other disciples were present. If only a pair out of a whole band of
disciples follow John's suggestion, that would be a paltry result'.[4]

The polemic the evangelist carries out against disciples of John the
Baptist has long been a recognized theme in the Gospel of John,[5] and
in light of this polemic Haenchen's reasoning becomes less convincing.
If only a pair out of the whole band of the Baptist's disciples followed
Jesus, then the Fourth Evangelist's negative sentiment towards that
group becomes understandable.

This observation is significant for our present considerations in
that it puts a perspective on the calling of the disciples—linking it to
the southern locale of Bethany, beyond the Jordan (rather than in
Galilee). Before Peter, or any of the other well-known disciples, is
called, two of the Baptist's disciples come to the fore in the Johannine
account of the calling of the first disciples.

In response to the witness of John the Baptist concerning Jesus,
'ἴδε ὁ ἀμνὸς τοῦ θεοῦ', the two disciples[6] follow (ἠκολούθησαν) Jesus.
The verb ἀκολουθεῖν can be interpreted in a variety of ways ranging
from the purely literal to the symbolical. ἀκολουθεῖν has been
understood as a description of the process of discipleship in the New
Testament[7] and there are those who would attribute such symbolic
significance to this occurrence in Jn 1.37. On the other hand, on the
basis of the use of the aorist tense, Bernard does not think that it is
possible to attach symbolic significance to the verb, as his comments
reveal:

> Here was no decision to follow Him throughout His ministry and
> attach themselves to His Person, for the aorist only indicates their
> action at one definite moment. Jesus had not yet 'called' them, or
> invited them to be His companions and disciples (cf. Mk. 1.17 and
> parallels); nor were they constrained to go after Him by anything
> that they had seen Him do.[8]

When the 20 occurrences of ἀκολουθεῖν in John are examined,[9] it
is seen that only one reference (11.31) is clearly to be understood
literally, and at least eight are intended to be taken figuratively.[10]

When this evidence is coupled with the observation that in the very context of the narrative of the calling of the first disciples here in John we encounter the phrase 'ἀκολούθει μοι' (v. 43) in Jesus' call to discipleship directed to Philip, the case for a figurative intepretation of the concept of 'following' throughout this chapter becomes strong.

Even when it is agreed that ἠκολούθησαν is to be interpreted figuratively, differences as to the implied symbolism arise. Is true discipleship being depicted, or just its precursor?[11] Does 'following' lead to 'remaining' (μένειν) with Jesus?[12] Is this a 'once for all' action? Morris tries to build the case for the decisive nature of the decision to follow Jesus:

> The verb 'followed' is in the tense appropriate to once-for-all action, which may be meant to indicate that they cast their lot with Jesus. They did not mean to make a tentative inquiry but to give themselves to him. . . . They walked down the path after Jesus and thus followed him. But they also symbolically committed themselves to Him.[13]

Perhaps it is not wise to make too much out of the specific use of the aorist tense, as both Bernard and Morris try to do, especially since the aorist tense can be used so ambiguously to describe simple action without reference to the quality or time of the action. It is reasonable to hold that the evangelist is indeed conveying the 'making' of the first two disciples of Jesus. However, speculation as to the *extent* of their understanding or allegiance to Jesus based on the tense and theological significance of ἠκολούθησαν is not warranted by the text.

The next few sentences of this narrative section that are of particular relevance to our discussion are those contained in vv. 40-42. Here one of the two disciples is identified while the other remains anonymous. Peter is not the first to be called, as he is in the Synoptic accounts, but rather he is placed in the midst of his peers, one of the many who are 'found'. Collins has summarized well the thrust of this narrative section:

> Jesus acts as the God-man from the very beginning by conferring upon Simon the name of Cephas. Peter himself, however, is placed *among* the disciples. He is brought to Jesus through the testimony of his brother Andrew. To this extent, he is a typical disciple.[14]

In other words, while this passage is significant for the attitude it displays toward Peter in comparison to some other disciples, it should be borne in mind that the *primary* thrust is *christological*. Jesus is confessed as the Messiah (v. 41) and he 'shows himself to be the θεῖος ἄνθρωπος, who recognizes and sees into the hearts of the strangers whom he meets'.[15]With that said, let us look at the pertinent details of these three verses:

Ἦν Ἀνδρέας ὁ ἀδελφὸς Σίμωνος Πέτρου εἷς ἐκ τῶν δύο τῶν ἀκουσάντων παρὰ ' Ἰωάννου καὶ ἀκολουθησάντων αὐτῷ.

Andrew is identified. The mystery of the identity of one of the disciples who appeared in v. 35, at least, is solved. But note how Andrew is identified—he is called ὁ ἀδελφὸς Σίμωνος Πέτρου. Peter, then, is the better known figure to the evangelist's intended readership.[16] Because we have an almost redundant reference to the relationship between Andrew and Simon in the next verse—τὸν ἀδελφὸν τόν ἴδιον Σίμωνα—it may be that the first phrase was a marginal addition to the text.[17] As rational as this may be, there is no supporting textual evidence for this suggestion. At best, the reference to Simon Peter in v. 40 directly anticipates the following two verses, which centre on Peter's first encounter with Jesus.[18]

Note the use of the full name Σίμωνος Πέτρου. The evangelist has an affinity for the full name, using it seventeen times in the Gospel, which is more than double the total number of times to be found in the Synoptics.[19] There are various explanations offered for this phenomenon. If the use of the full name grew in popularity at the end of the first century and into the second generation of the Christian church, this phenomenon in the Gospel of John may be a sign of a later date. However, the shorter designation of 'Πέτρος' is just as frequent in the Gospel.

It is possible to discern a stylistic pattern in the evangelist's use of the full name. 'Πέτρος is written only after the name Σίμων Πέτρος has occurred: the letter appears first in the context by way of reintroducing the disciple'.[20] J.K. Elliot has suggested that this pattern is a *bona fide* rule of Johannine style and the exceptions to this found in the Gospel are taken to be later textual additions.[21] On the other hand, the use of the full name can also be understood as 'slight, perhaps unconscious, swellings of emphasis',[22] especially in 13.9, 20.6 and 21.3, 7, 11, where these uses of the full name do not follow the 'rule' outlined by Elliott.[23] In any case, John preferred, more than any other evangelist, to use the full name of Σίμων Πέτρος in his descriptions of this important figure. At the same time, however, from this one narrative one can see that all priority is not automatically given to Peter. He is called through the mediation of his brother.

To whom does the priority in discipleship go, then? Sharing this honour with Andrew is the other disciple of John the Baptist, who remains anonymous. The evangelist may here be introducing his readers to the Beloved Disciple in a subtle way. Internal comparisons with other descriptions where the Beloved Disciple is unquestionably presented reveal similarities in structure, significance and function. It needs to be pointed out that the seemingly peripheral[24] presence of the 'other disciple' (another way of referring to the Beloved Disciple in Jn 18.15 and 20.2-10) is characteristic of John's narrative style and what we have here may be a typical Johannine foreshadowing. Maynard notes

> One of the literary characteristics of the Fourth Evangelist is to mention in a casual and almost off-hand manner ideas which he intends to develop later, and it therefore seems very probable that the unnamed disciple is identical with the later 'Beloved Disciple'.[25]

It appears, moreover, that the Johannine redactor responsible for ch. 21 of the Gospel sought to connect the unnamed disciple in ch. 1 with the Beloved Disciple, at least if the parallelism of description between the first and last chapters are any indication. 'He [i.e. the redactor of ch. 21] describes the Beloved Disciple in a situation closely resembling what we have here [i.e. 1.35-43]'.[26] Note some of the parallels: Peter and the other disciple (the Beloved Disciple?) both respond to Jesus' call to follow; in both instances Jesus and Peter carry out a significant dialogue pertaining to Peter's identity and future; only in these two instances is Simon called 'son of John' (Ἰωάννου);[27] and, the other disciple, who in both cases is depicted as following Jesus silently but surely, is presented as having remained or abode (μένειν) as a disciple *before* Peter came on the scene and *after* his departure.

The other possible identification we can make is that the unnamed disciple is actually named in v. 44 as 'Philip, from Bethsaida, the city of Andrew and Peter'. This interpretation is suggested by Boismard and Schnackenburg, among others.[28] 'Si Philippe est avec André l'un des deux disciples du Baptiste, aux vv. 35-39, plusieurs détails du texte johannique prennent leur pleine signification'.[29] Some of the détails that Boismard finds clarified by this hypothesis are: the evangelist's parallelism between the calling of Simon through

Andrew and the calling of Nathanael through Philip; the theme of
'finding' (1.41, 45) further unifies the whole narrative if Andrew and
Philip are the ones saying 'We have found. . . ' (1.41); and the πρῶτον
of 1.43 becomes more understandable. Andrew becomes the first of
the two to find another disciple, the πρῶτον implying that Philip
follows suit. 'Ils étaient deux: André et Philippe; André, en premier,
mène Simon à Jésus; ensuite Philippe joue le même rôle à l'égard de
Nathanaël'.[30]

However, the great weakness of this reconstruction is that, as R.E.
Brown observes, '. . . 1.43 seems to introduce Philip for the first time
and makes it difficult to believe that he has already been mentioned'.[31]
Even Boismard admits this when he states, 'Toute la difficulté vient
donc du v. 43, où nous voyons Jésus appeler directement Philippe.
C'est ce verset qui rompt la chaîne du témoignage et bouleverse la
rigoureuse structure des vv. 35-51'.[32]

Although it is difficult to discern which came first—the idea that
v. 43 is a redactional addition or that Philip was the unnamed
disciple—it is argued that v. 43 probably does not belong to the
original narrative.

> The mention of another day. . . and the remark that Jesus was
> about to set off for Galilee are not important for the context; they
> are so vague that they may have been deducted from 2.1. Other
> points (cf. 'he [Jesus] met. . . ', with v. 41 and v. 45; the mention of
> Jesus by name in the second part) suggest that v. 43 is an addition
> of the redaction.[33]

This hypothesis has the effect of tying verses 40-42 to v. 44,
thereby linking the second (unnamed) disciple with Philip. 'If v. 44
was originally intended to describe the doings of the second disciple,
hitherto unnamed (vv. 37-39), the πρῶτον of v. 41 becomes
intelligible'.[34]

Verse 41 reads: εὑρίσκει οὗτος [i.e. Andrew] πρῶτον τὸν ἀδελφὸν
τὸν ἴδιον Σίμωνα καὶ λέγει αὐτῷ, εὑρήκαμεν τὸν Μεσσίαν, ὅ ἐστιν
μεθερμηνευόμενον χριστός. If πρῶτος is read rather than πρῶτον,
then the previously unnamed disciple, Philip, may be being described
as the *second* person to find his brother, following the example of
Andrew, who was the *first* (i.e. πρῶτος). As a matter of fact, there are
three variant readings of this word and each one is significant in its
effect upon our understanding of the sentence.

The commonly accepted reading is πρῶτον, which can be
interpreted either as an adverb—meaning Andrew found Peter before

Andrew did anything else[35]—or an accusative adjective modifying τὸν ἀδελφὸν τὸν ἴδιον Σίμωνα—meaning Peter was the first person that Andrew found. If in v. 43 Andrew is the subject of εὑρίσκει, meaning that Andrew found Philip in the second place, then πρῶτον is a correct and necessary reading. Some scholars have made even more of the adjectival interpretation, suggesting that this indicates Peter has 'first place'.[36]

> In this reading [πρῶτον] Peter receives the honourable rank of 'the first one', yet only in so far as he is the first to be found and led to Jesus by his brother, the former disciple of the Baptist... Here also, it seems, the evangelist did not intend to deny the pre-eminent position of Peter, but he did wish to show how the unnamed disciple is 'first' in another respect, in the way he became Jesus' disciple.[37]

The second, relatively well attested, reading—πρῶτος—could not only be read to imply that Philip was the second one to find a new disciple for Christ, as outlined above, but it also has been taken by the early church to refer to the Evangelist. In effect then, John is said to be following the example of Andrew, who was 'the first' to act in this missionary capacity, by going to bring his brother to Jesus also. Haenchen criticizes this, suggesting that if πρῶτος is the reading that is accepted, the unnamed disciple could have more easily been James

> The ancient church saw in this a concealed self-reference of the modest author (John the son of Zebedee), without stopping to ask whether modesty and concealed self-reference comport with each other. Of course, the unnamed companion of Andrew—if one permits the thought patterns of the early church—could also be James, the other son of Zebedee, who is almost always named before his brother John in the Gospels; only in Luke 8.51 and 9.28 do the readings vary.[38]

Another twist to the interpretation of πρῶτος is offered by Bultmann, '... if we read πρῶτος, then it follows that the second one, the "other one" found Philip'.[39]

The third possible reading, that of πρωί, has little textual support, but is actually suggested by some Old Latin manuscripts, which have the word *mane* (in the morning).[40] Bernard, who accepts this reading, postulates that the more widespread reading of πρῶτον arose (presumably *very* early) through the dropping of one letter and a consequent case of dittography;

An original ΠΡΩΙΤΟΝΑΔΕΛΦΟΝ would readily be corrupted to ΠΡΩΤΟΝΑΔΕΛΦΟΝ, which leads to ΠΡΩΤΟΝΤΟΝΑΔΕΛ -ΦΟΝ. We conclude that πρωί is the true reading. Jn. uses this form (not πρωια) again at 18.28 20.1; and it gives excellent sense here.[41]

Indeed, the meaning of πρωι does give excellent sense, for then the scenario is clarified—Andrew goes to see where Jesus is staying, he stays there overnight and then, early the next morning, he goes to get his brother Simon. The problem is that it is easy to understand how such a reading could have been purposely put into the text for clarification, which is more likely to happen than to have the text undergo the accidental process outlined by Bernard above.

> ... It is equally arguable that this has arisen by haplography from *proton ton adelphon*; if John would have really meant to say the next day, he would surely have written *te epaurion*, as in verses 29, 35 and 43.[42]

So, the possibilities are many, varied and interrelated. Andrew first finds his brother Simon before going to see where Jesus stays, or Andrew first finds Simon and then he finds Philip, or Andrew finds Simon and then the unnamed disciple either finds Philip or else he finds his brother, or Andrew first finds Simon and then Philip finds his brother Nathanael, or Andrew first goes to stay with Jesus and then, the first thing next morning, he goes to get Simon!

Confronted with these choices, we can only employ some sound methodology and go with the reading that demands the least speculation and is supported by the strongest external evidence.

The first thing to state is that v. 43 must be preserved in the text—there are no solid grounds for considering it a scribal addition. This allows us to remove any likelihood that Philip is the unnamed disciple who is the implied second person to find his brother.

Second, the weight of the textual evidence favours πρῶτον as the original reading. It has the earliest single witness (p[66] 2nd-3rd cent.) and the great majority of other early witnesses. It has the widest geographical distribution[43] yet its major attestation is from the generally reliable Alexandrian tradition. In light of the fact that the external evidence does heavily favour πρῶτον with the earliest support, superior in quality and quantity and diversified geographical distribution, this reading should be preferred as the original.

Third, when the three variants are compared to one another and the possible relationship between them is reconstructed, it is seen that πρῶτον is the most difficult reading to interpret, which could explain why the others arose. The nominative reading, πρῶτος, would not present any sort of problem—grammatically, theologically or otherwise—to warrant its revision to πρῶτον, so it is difficult to imagine the change going in that direction. As most scholars point out regarding the reading of πρωι, 'the adverb is an "easy reading" and may be a scribal attempt to clarify the obscure πρῶτον'.[44]

Fourth, the subject of εὑρίσκει in v. 43 is most naturally Jesus (and not Andrew or the unnamed disciple). If this is admitted, then the grounds for an adjectival interpretation of πρῶτον (i.e. Peter was the *first* person found) are significantly lessened.

What remains is the adverbial interpretation of πρῶτον suggesting that before Andrew did anything else after deciding to follow Jesus, he went and found his brother Simon. What effect does this have on our considerations? We are able to conclude that Andrew was the only one who went and found another disciple in that first encounter with Jesus. As far as we can tell, the unnamed disciple, whoever he was, did not go and bring anyone to meet Jesus.[45]

Another relevant conclusion that we can make is that Peter is not highlighted in any significant way as 'first' or pre-eminent, contrary to the assertions of Cullmann. On the other hand, we are able to place his encounter with Jesus quite early, even before the two other disciples went to stay with Jesus at his abode that evening. This has the effect of placing Peter with these two in the presence of Jesus from the first day of their discipleship. If this is indeed the case, then it is understandable how the Synoptists could make the case that Peter was the first to be called—after all, he was *among* the first few who followed Jesus on that first day. The Fourth Evangelist makes it clear, for whatever purpose he had in mind, that Peter was *not* the first disciple in the strict sense. Furthermore, it may be symbolic that 'Peter was not called directly by Jesus, but by his brother'.[46] His purpose for this presentation is of particular interest to the present writer and we will delve into the possibilities in a later chapter.[47]

The second half of v. 41 records a confession made by Andrew; εὑρήκαμεν τὸν Μεσσίαν, ὅ ἐστιν μεθερμηνευόμενον χριστός. This messianic confession is vaguely comparable to the confession of Peter at Caesarea Philippi 'Σὺ εἶ ὁ χριστός' (Mk 8.29 and parallels). Apart from any literary relationships that may or may not be present, both Peter's confession in the Synoptics and this confession of Andrew in John represent the *first* articulation of belief in Jesus' messiahship in their respective Gospels. Clearly John has radically departed from the Synoptic presentation and unless the whole list of messianic confessions in Jn 1.41-50 are to be understood as early 'expressions of an enthusiasm which became dulled',[48] we are confronted with another Johannine statement that may reflect how the evangelist regarded the traditions surrounding Simon Peter. In the Gospel of John, Peter is no longer the first to express belief in Jesus as the Christ.

However, almost to balance the confession of Andrew, we do see that Peter and Jesus participate in a very significant interchange as early as the next verse (i.e. 42). The change of Simon's name is taken by Ellis to be the focus of the complete passage of 1.19-51. He justifies this by outlining an indistinct chiastic structure. 'The centre (c) concentrates on Simon Peter and foreshadows his mission as the 'Rock', the vicar of Christ'.[49] This account of the naming of Simon has a parallel much later on in the 'story line of Matthew'.

> All the evangelists know that Simon bore the sobriquet of Peter, but only Matthew and John mention the occasion on which he received it... In John the change of name takes place in the beginning of the ministry; in Matthew it takes place more than halfway through the ministry.[50]

In order to account for the different settings of the naming of Simon in Mathew and John, we must seek to discern *what* they are trying to convey to the readers by placing this event where they have in their Gospels.[51] Also, the intended effect of the naming itself in John must be established.

It is quite possible to harmonize the accounts of the naming in John and Matthew if the future tense κληθήσῃ in John is taken in a predictive sense, so that what we see in John can be understood as Jesus' foretelling of what will happen later (i.e. Mt. 16).[52] Bultmann calls this verse a 'prophecy that Simon will some day bear another name'.[53]

> ... this does not mean that Simon receives a new name from Jesus *now*. For this reason 1.42 cannot be taken as the Johannine form of the tradition found in Mk. 1.16-18 or 3.16. Rather Jn. 1.42 *foretells* such a scene, which however, the Evangelist did not need to retell afterwards, because he could assume that it was well known.[54]

On the other hand, the combination of a messianic confession, the call of Simon and the change of his name to Peter are common to both accounts, so one suspects that the accounts are actually parallels in the true sense of the term. The use of the future tense, then, is better understood as an imperative or volitive future.[55] Brown has offered a telling evaluation of Bultmann's understanding of the tense:

> Bultmann's interpretation of the future tense is certainly dubious, for the future tense is part of the literary style of name changing, even when the name is changed on the spot. The future is used in the LXX of Gen. xvii. 5 and 15 even though the author consistently uses the new name from that moment on. Seemingly, then, John's account means that Simon's name was changed to Peter at his first encounter with Jesus.[56]

If this is indeed the case, John's placement and use of this pericope is deliberate and significant.[57]

Given the theme of Jesus' divine insight that runs through this chapter[58] we can get a clue to perhaps at least one of the functions of this narrative in the Johannine framework. Note how the naming of Simon is prefaced in v. 42: ἐμβλέψας αὐτῷ [i.e. Simon] ὁ Ἰησοῦς εἶπεν, σὺ εἶ Σίμων ὁ υἱὸς Ἰωάννου, σὺ κληθήσῃ Κηφᾶς, ... The word ἐμβλέψας has been given theological import by a number of interpreters.[59] The same word is used a few verses earlier when the Baptist looks (ἐμβλέψας) at Jesus and then exclaims 'ἴδε ὁ ἀμνὸς θεοῦ'. As Bernard observes; 'This verb has already (v. 36) been used of the Baptist's earnest look at Jesus, it is used by the Synoptists of the piercing, scrutinising gaze of Jesus (Mt. 19.26, Mk 10.21, Lk. 20.17), and of His "looking" upon Peter after his denial'.[60]

That the theme of the divine knowledge of Jesus is truly a central concern of the evangelist is substantiated by the observation that this motif occurs throughout the Gospel after being introduced here in ch. 1.

> The same motif occurs in vv. 47f; 2.24f.; 4.17-19. The idea is widespread in pagan and Christian Hellenism; the ability to recognize and to read the thoughts of those whom one meets characterizes the θεῖος ἄνθρωπος. ... [this motif] is not the decisive element in the Gospel; for Jesus' omniscience is not based on any particular talents which enhance his humanity, but on his unity with God, which he enjoys in his full humanity.[61]

Thus, in essence, we can see how the Fourth Evangelist takes traditional material and sets it in the context that best suits his theological purpose. 'We have here a clear example of the Johannine narrative approach, which is to take facts known from tradition and place them in a certain light—above all Christological'.[62]

If the person of Jesus is the focus of this narrative, with an emphasis highlighting the 'high christology' for which John is noted, then are we justified in reading any more significance into the process of the naming of Peter, especially with regard to the person of Peter? An interesting explanation for the name change is offered by Roth, who has made the case that during 'the first century and perhaps for some time afterwards the use of the name Simon was deliberately avoided by the Jews, whether from symbolic or patriotic or superstitious reasons, or even out of sheer nervousness'.[63] Simon Peter, then, would be no exception to this tendency. 'The name Kaipha (= Peter) was thus left. At a later stage, this change was naturally given a more elaborate explanation'.[64]

Fitzmyer has responded to this thesis by suggesting that the use of the name was not avoided at all, but rather it was so popular it had to be further qualified.

> ... Since Simon or Simeon was such a commonly used name, the patronymics or nicknames were frequently used as a means of distinguishing those who bore the name of the tribal patriarch of old. Even though we do not have a complete listing of all the names of Jewish males in the Roman period, the evidence which has come to light in the various areas seems all to point in the direction of the great frequency of the name Simon.[65]

Certainly the process of renaming here in 1.42 must have considerably more meaning beneath the surface for it to have any meaning even as a christological account. After all, the evangelist deliberately and explicitly offers the translation of the name Κηφᾶς himself.

The dynamic of naming in the ancient world demands that we attach theological significance to this narrative. The naming of Peter here points to the authority that Jesus was claiming and perhaps also the character that is divinely ordained to Peter. Morris comments

> This must be understood in the light of the significance attaching to the name in antiquity. It stood for the whole man. It summed up his whole personality. The giving of a new name when done by man is an assertion of the authority of the giver (e.g. II Kings 23.34; 24.17). When done by God it speaks of a new character in which the man henceforth appears (e.g. Gen. 32.28).[66]

Bernard suggests that this naming marks the beginning of Peter's new relationship with God:

To give a new name in the O.T. history sometimes marked the beginning of a new relation to God; e.g. Jacob was called Israel (Gen. 32.28), and Abram became Abraham (Gen. 17.5), after a spiritual crisis (cf. also Isa. 62.2; 65.15). When adult converts from heathenism are baptized, they are given a new name for a similar reason.[67]

If there is an element of this understanding being conveyed to the evangelist's readers, then we have an even deeper christological statement being made. By entering into a new relationship with Jesus, Simon Peter is beginning a new relationship with God, the Father. This is very compatible with Johannine theology, but, at the same time, it is assuming too much of the unexpressed symbolism of the narrative.

While Matthew is clear concerning the significance of the naming, suggesting that Peter is the foundation stone of the Church, John leaves the final interpretation unsaid. The most common interpretation of the naming of Simon in John is the one which holds that the nickname Κηφᾶς or Πέτρος reflects either Simon's innate personality or his prospective change in character.[68] A few scholars, such as Westcott and Schnackenburg, suggest that we have in John the same relationship between Peter and the Church reflected as we do in Matthew. 'The title appears to mark not so much the natural character of the Apostle as the spiritual office to which he was called'.[69]

Indubitably nearly every interpretation of this naming involves a certain amount of 'grasping at straws' because the evangelist does not provide any leads. At most, following what we have in John alone, the meaning of the name Πέτρος (= Aramaic כיפא) suggests a trait of solidness or hardness. 'Neither *Petros* in Greek nor *Kepha* in Aramaic is a normal proper name; rather it is a nickname (like American "Rocky") which would have to be explained by something in Simon's character or career'.[70]

Fitzmyer has noted that contrary to Brown's statement that *Kepha* was not a proper name in Aramaic, it was used as early as 416 BC in an Aramaic text from Elephantine.[71] Nevertheless, it was certainly uncommon and its use is likely to have been linked to the idea of 'rock' or 'crag'.

The least one can say is that *kp'* is not unknown as a proper name and that Peter is not the first person to have borne it... the existence of it as a proper name at least makes more plausible the

suggestion that a wordplay in Aramaic was involved. . . He or some
aspect of him is to be a crag/rock in the building of the
ἐκκλησία.[72]

Perhaps the evangelist purposely avoided making the interpretation
of the naming explicit because he was not entirely in agreement with
it or else he realized that any interpretation offered did not actually
stand the test of time in Peter's life. Barrett makes this suggestion:

> He [i.e. John] gives no interpretation of the name, neither
> Matthew's (Peter the foundation stone of the Church), nor that
> commonly accepted here (a prospective change in Peter's character).
> Perhaps, he was aware that Peter's subsequent career would bear
> out neither interpretation.[73]

Going even a step further, Agourides twists the evidence and reads
far too much into the text when interpreting the naming of Peter in
ch. 1 as actually having a negative impact on the presentation of this
character by highlighting Peter's instability:

> . . . Whereas such an important disciple is left anonymous, in the
> same passage, concerning the gathering of the first disciples around
> Jesus, there is a reference to the change in the name of Simon
> Cephas. This exception among the first disciples I do not think is
> accidental or indeed flattering for Peter. It is a comment on Peter's
> character and foreshadows a change in it.[74]

Maynard's evaluation of the text in John, if it is indeed intentionally
removed from an original setting similar to that found in Matthew, is
more sound, for he states that 'the renaming of Simon as Peter is
moved early in the Gospel and dissociated from the giving of
ecclesiastical power (to loose and to bind) to him'.[75] However, such
an argument stands or falls on the assumption that Matthew does
reflect the original setting of the naming, whereas it may be just as
possible that Matthew has joined the tradition of the naming of Peter
with an account of the investiture of ecclesiastical authority.

In summary, then, this naming of Peter has an ambivalent effect
upon the image of this important figure. In comparison to the
Synoptic parallel, Peter has less prestige and position accorded him,
but at the same time in the context of the first chapter of John, it
could be argued that Peter is singled out for 'special treatment'.
'Since the evangelist has passed over in silence Jesus' conversation
with the first disciples, Peter is distinguished by the words addressed
to him and the prediction of his future rank'.[76]

In the final analysis, it is best to state that the naming of Peter in the Gospel of John has primarily a christological function and it serves a secondary purpose of highlighting the 'rock-like' character or role that Jesus intended Peter to assume in the Christian community. As the evangelist is no more explicit in his motives or interpretation of the traditions involved, we are likewise limited.

The naming of Peter is merely one aspect of the whole narrative of Jn 1.39-42 which reflects some of the Johannine attitude towards this central figure. Basically, Peter does not stand on the pedestal he was evidently placed on in some circles. But, at the same time, he may have been lifted up in other circles as a result of these passages. Peter is not the first disciple to follow Christ, but rather two disciples of John the Baptist are, and one of these disciples may be the Beloved Disciple. Yet, Peter is placed among the first three that are called, and it is evident that the evangelist's readers know this 'Simon Peter' better than they know his brother Andrew. Peter is not the first to make a messianic confession, that honour belongs to another. Yet Peter is the only one who is given a new name by Christ, although the naming probably is intended to say more about Christ than about Simon Peter.

On the basis of our analysis of the evidence, we must conclude that Peter is certainly not disparaged in this initial chapter in the Gospel of John. Some of his position and prestige in the earliest traditions can be discerned here. On the other hand, at this point at least, he is definitely denied any primacy of discipleship and leadership that other circles had accorded him.

C. *Jn 6.60-71*

In Jn 6.60-71 we find mention once more of Simon Peter. Here he assumes a central role as spokesman for the Twelve at a very crucial point in the ministry of Jesus. At this point in the Gospel story John is highlighting the separation of the true disciples of Jesus from those who lack faith and understanding as to the nature of Christ. It is most important, then, for our considerations, to see how Peter fares at this strategic stage in the evangelist's portrayal of the development of the Christian community.

While we will see that this particular passage has its own problems in terms of context and placement, we must first consider the greater context and placement of the whole sixth chapter. This entire chapter presents itself to even the most cursory reader as being set apart from its surrounding context of chs. 5 and 7, both in terms of geography and sense. Both chs. 5 and 7 are set in Jerusalem, while ch. 6 is set in Galilee. Chapters 5 and 7 share a conflict atmosphere between Jesus and the Jews, while ch. 6 rises above the heat of the conflict to present a highly theological self-revelation of Jesus as the Bread of Life. Consequently, it has been proposed by generations of scholars[77] that ch. 6 be removed from the midst of chs. 5 and 7 and be placed somewhere else in the first half of the Gospel, the most common suggestion being that it rests immediately before ch. 5.[78] While this displacement alleviates some of the difficulties with the traditional ordering, it is not entirely satisfactory. Mary Shorter, who places ch. 6 between 10.21 and 22, cites at least three reasons for placing the chapter later, rather than earlier, in the Gospel. Chapter 6 is rather early for a discourse. It is also early to contain the last account of a Galilean ministry in a Gospel of 21 chapters. The opening statement of ch. 7 indicates that there are further events in Galilee to come. The break between 10.21 and 22 is chosen because the narrative there jumps from the Feast of the Tabernacles to the Feast of Dedication. Moreover, the words ἐν τοῖς Ἱεροσολύμοις seem otiose without the insertion of chapter 6.[79] The effect of the insertion of ch. 6 is positive in that the Good Shepherd becomes a fitting prelude to the feeding of the multitude of ch. 6. The confession of Peter thus comes to serve as a fulcrum in the shifting emphasis of the Gospel.[80] Peter declares the allegiance of himself and the rest of the Twelve to Jesus Christ at a time when Jesus is preparing to devote the rest of his earthly ministry to revealing his glory to true disciples only.

Shorter's arguments are attractive. However, as neat and tidy as they may be, there is little evidence to justify any rearrangement. Moreover, all attempts at rearranging the ordering operate under the assumption that the evangelist is bound to logical, thematic, historical or geographical structure in his theological presentation. Strachan expresses proper reserve regarding attempts to improve the structure of the itinerary recorded in the Gospel of John:

> This evangelist is not interested in itineraries. In other cases [*i.e. other than John 6*] where it is contended that the sequence of thought is improved by rearrangement, the argument is even more precarious. The evangelist has a habit of interrupting the immediate flow of his thought. Note the two sudden references to the Baptist in the prologue.[81]

In light of such considerations, it may be best to assume that the traditional order of chs. 5–7 was indeed the intended order of the evangelist, although his reasons for the order are not readily apparent. In spite of the difficulties present readers may have with the order, the fact remains that this is the order of the text and there is no textual evidence to suggest that it may originally have been otherwise.[82]

As previously mentioned, the particular passage of 6.60–71 has also been subject to criticism regarding its place in the chapter (and even its place in the Gospel apart from the rest of ch. 6). Bultmann contends 6.60–71 'has been divorced from its original context, which must be sought in another part of the Gospel altogether'.[83] He goes on to suggest that this section belonged originally between chs. 12–13, signalling the change in audience from the crowds to the community of disciples. What can be said about removing the whole of ch. 6 from its present context can also be said of similar attempts to remove 6.60–71 from the rest of ch. 6. Smith, who painstakingly analyzes Bultmann's argument is able to conclude with reference to this particular passage.

> It is my view that the text may be interpreted with sufficient clarity and coherence to warrant leaving it as is. Its incongruities or inconsistencies may be attributed to the evangelist as easily as to the redactor. They are perhaps a sign of the gulf that separates our way of thinking from his.[84]

The incongruities and inconsistencies Smith refers to include the exhortation to eat the flesh and drink the blood of the son of Man in 6.51–58 and the disparagement of the flesh in 6.63. While this appears as a lack of continuity to some, it must be maintained that the continuity (or lack thereof) depends to a considerable extent on the interpretation of both of these sections and their eucharistic overtones. Suffice it now to say that the description of Jesus' words as being 'hard' (σκληρός) itself suggests inconsistency or incongruity, or at least difficult to accept.

Jn 6.60–71 is similar to the Synoptic accounts of the rejection of Jesus in the synagogue of his home territory (Mk 6.1-6; Mt. 13.54-58; Lk. 4.16-30), the confession of Peter in Caesarea Philippi (Mk 8.29; Mt. 16.16; Lk. 9.20), and the prediction of the betrayal of Judas Iscariot (Mk 14.18; Mt. 26.21; Lk. 22.21).[85] The Fourth Evangelist has taken his sources, whether they be the Synoptics or some source common to the Synoptics and John, and presented them in such a

way as to call attention to the process by which the true disciples of
Jesus were sifted from unbelievers.

This is no doubt reflects the historical situation which gave rise to
this section of the Gospel.

> The evangelist is certainly convinced that in Galilee there was a
> falling away, that the people ceased to follow Jesus. This is what he
> has emphasized and dramatized in terms of his historical and
> theological outlook... The whole section relies on historical
> memories, but it is given a theological structure based on the theme
> of unbelief and faith and a second focus in the community's
> attitude to faith.[86]

That second focus that Schnackenburg refers to may indeed be a
response to the secession within the Johannine community.[87] If we
read the true context of the evangelist and his readers, then whatever
is said about Peter may be taken to reflect their attitude (or at least
his attitude) towards the apostle in a context of the sifting of
disciples, both at the time of Jesus and as the different Christian
communities developed at the time of writing.

The first five verses of this pericope set the stage for the actual
portrayal of Peter in 6.66-71, so they will be dealt with in a summary
fashion, focusing only on the exegetical issues that are relevant to our
particular concerns.

Verse 60 begins by speaking of πολλοὶ ἐκ τῶν μαθητῶν αὐτοῦ. As
vv. 66-67 will indicate, this is a larger group of disciples than the
Twelve, yet they cannot be equated with ὁ ὄχλος (6.24) or οἱ
Ἰουδαῖοι (6.41), although they may have been part of that larger
audience.[88] μαθητῶν in this sense is derived from primitive Christian
terminology in which all believers are disciples (cf. Jn 4.1; Lk.
10.1).

> The number of Jesus' disciples and the term 'disciple' as used here
> betray a theological interest deriving from the writer's own
> situation. In the disciples of the past the evangelist is thinking of his
> readers too... [he] wants to speak to the later disciples of Jesus, the
> members of his community, who are similarly threatened by
> shocks to their faith. In Judea too the 'disciples' of Jesus are
> contrasted with 'the Jews' (cf. 7.3 with 7.1); the 'Jews' represent
> unbelievers in general, while the 'disciples' are still uncommitted
> followers of Jesus'.[89]

The disciples are reported to have described Jesus' words as 'hard'
or 'rough' (σκληρός). Most commentators point out that this does

not mean that the words are difficult to understand, but rather that they are hard to receive or believe. The sense of the words being offensive, intolerable or incredible is conveyed. Barrett suggests, 'It is parallel to ὑμᾶς σκανδαλίζει in the next verse'.[90] τίς δύναται αὐτοῦ ἀκούειν; may be translated, 'Who is able to listen to him?' or, 'Who is able to listen to it [i.e. his word]?' Both Barrett and R.E. Brown suggest that ἀκούειν carries the same force as שׁמע, thus allowing the meaning 'obey'.[91] The 'word' which is 'hard' is either that contained in vv. 35-50 (the καταβαίνειν of Jesus) or vv. 51-58 (eating the flesh and drinking the blood of Jesus). It is not possible to rule out either concept as being referred to in ὁ λόγος οὗτος.[92]

The scandal, or cause for stumbling among the disciples is obvious to Jesus. Verse 61 implies a supernatural knowledge, which we have seen to be a characteristic of the Johannine picture of Christ.[93] Jesus responds to the hesitancy to accept his teaching by proposing a further consideration in v. 62: ἐὰν οὖν θεωρῆτε τὸν υἱὸν τοῦ ἀνθρώπου ἀναβαίνοντα ὅπου ἦν τὸ πρότερον;... This conditional sentence lacks the apodosis. The reader is forced to decide for himself; will the offence be greater or will the offence dissipate? What was Jesus implying?[94] Due to the critical point of this narrative, in which the true disciples of Jesus are sifted from the unbelieving, the evangelist was purposely ambivalent in order to elicit the dynamics of such a separation even within the minds of the readers.

> It would seem that John has deliberately left the meaning open with an incomplete sentence so that the ambivalence of all that takes place concerning the Son of Man might be left unqualified. For those who believe, the ascension would ease the present talk about Jesus being the living bread who gives his flesh for men to eat; to those who do not believe the ascension would be a further cause of grave difficulty on the plane of physical happenings.[95]

The next verse, 63, begins with a typical Johannine statement referring to the life-giving Spirit. However, it is what is set up as its antithesis—the flesh—that causes interpretive problems. How can Jesus say that the flesh is of no profit after having exhorted his disciples to eat his flesh in order to live forever?[96] It would appear that, in the final analysis, the evangelist is simply but graphically calling for a full recognition of the spiritual realm as being the source of the eternal life Jesus offers.[97]

The second part of 6.63 has Jesus attributing the qualities of the Spirit and life to the words he has spoken to his disciples. Scholars are divided on their understanding of what words Jesus is referring to when he says 'τὰ ῥήματα ἃ ἐγὼ λελάληκα ὑμῖν. . .' (6.63). It may be a reference to the preceding discourse(s).[98] On the other hand, both Barrett and Lindars prefer the interpretation that the Johannine Jesus is here referring to the whole of his teaching.[99] Schnackenburg's reconstruction perhaps offers the best context for limiting the reference, '. . . after 63a Jesus makes a short pause. He considers the whole of what he has just said (λελάληκα, cf. the ending in 8.20), which the disciples described as "hard", (60) and tells them that, on the contrary they mean spirit and life. . .'[100]

The emphasis on unbelief in 6.64 is reminiscent of 6.35-47 and the charge in 36 is repeated here in 64. Further, as 6.36 is followed by the teaching that only those who are drawn by the Father believe in Jesus, so 64 is followed by the same teaching in 65. In the sequence of 63-65 it is seen that 'the life contained in the words of Jesus is received on the basis of faith'.[101] Continuing the Johannine pattern that equates believing in Jesus and coming to him (as a disciple) is again spelled out (cf. 6.35, 37, 45). What is significant is that belief in Jesus has become the watershed for eternal life and the category of discipleship is not identical to the category of those who believe. Belief 'inevitably divides the hearers of Jesus into two parties, which, however, do not necessarily correspond with visible groups, since even among those who are reckoned to be μαθηταί there are unbelievers'.[102] So, in the Johannine scheme, those who are considered 'disciples' may still not have the necessary belief. This evidently could even include members of the 'Twelve' (6.70). Consequently, the idea that even Peter may not have the belief John talks about is, as yet, a distinct possibility.

Again, here in v. 64 an emphasis on Jesus' omniscience is found. Here the temporal aspect is highlighted with the phrase ἐξ ἀρχῆς. Jesus' omniscience extends into the realm of foreknowledge. Barrett cautiously suggests that ἐξ ἀρχῆς may be equated with the ἀρχῇ of Jn 1.1 since in this Gospel 'all things are commonly traced back to their origin in the eternal counsels of God'.[103] Taken in its immediate context of unbelievers among the disciples, ἐξ ἀρχῆς need only mean 'from the beginning of His connection with individuals'.[104] In other words, Jesus' awareness of the unbelief of some of his disciples existed even from the beginning of his ministry or of the disciples' call, and it may have been mentioned here as 'an editorial attempt to prevent any misconception which might imply that Jesus had made a mistake'.[105]

Because of the unbelief the disciples were practising among themselves (v. 64a) Jesus found it necessary (διὰ τοῦτο, v. 65) to prepare those believers who witnessed this lack of faith by explaining the divine initiative which underlies faith. He states οὐδεὶς δύναται ἐλθεῖν πρός με ἐὰν μὴ ᾖ δεδομένον αὐτῷ ἐκ τοῦ πατρός. Compare this to Jesus' statement to Peter in Mt. 16.17. Terminologically, there is not any significant correlation, except perhaps the reference to the 'Father', but nevertheless there may be some common background or relationship between these two passages, given the fact that they share a context of Peter's confession.[106]

Verse 66 describes the actual division of the group of disciples which began with the questioning in 60 and was made explicit in 64. The phrase ἐκ τούτου can carry either temporal (i.e. 'from this time') or causal (i.e. 'because of this') force. While ἐκ is used temporally in 6.64b, the only other place where ἐκ τούτου is used, a causal sense is implied.[107] Because of both the dynamics of divine initiative and the 'hardness' of Jesus' teaching, many disciples could no longer align themselves with Jesus.

The division, then, reflects a contrast between the Twelve, who remain faithful, and those who retreat in disappointment and unbelief. In its historical context, this scene may be reflecting the lack of success of Jesus' ministry in Galilee, as reported in the parallel Synoptic scenes of the rejection of Jesus in Nazareth. R.E. Brown concludes:

> It is not surprising, then, since the Synoptic account of the ministry in Galilee ended on a tone of disbelief, to find this same tone in John vi 66. The Twelve believe, but the majority of people do not.
> .. It is interesting to compare John vi 65-66 with Mt. xi 20-28. In Mt xi 20-24 Jesus issues a judgment on the Galilean cities which have refused to believe his mighty deeds; even so in John vi 66 the disciples do not believe him. In Mt. xi 27, which is part of the 'Johannine logion' found in Matthew and Luke, we hear: 'All things have been given over to me by my Father. No one knows the Son except the Father, and no one knows the Father except the Son and anyone to whom the Son chooses to reveal Him'; this is quite like John vi 65.[108]

He would suggest that these disciples who fall away are not to be included among the ranks represented by the Twelve, nor are they to be included originally within the Johannine community, if this is to

be read in a later context of community concerns. He goes on to
assert that these apostate disciples are most likely Jewish Christians
outside both the Johannine and Apostolic streams whose faith was
deficient from the start.

> Some would interpret this scene in light of the internal struggle
> portrayed in 1 John. . . However, the whole context in John 6
> concerns the outsider groups ('the Jews'; the Twelve representing
> the Apostolic Churches), so that I assume this is an outsider group
> too.[109]

However, if John is describing a falling away in Galilee with
particular and specific applicability to the community of his own
readers, it may be that those who fall away in unbelief are to be
regarded as 'insiders' in the same way the secessionists were in 1 Jn
2.19.

As mentioned earlier, Jn 6.67-71 is the Johannine equivalent to the
confession of Peter at Caesarea Philippi. It is most similar to Luke's
account in that Peter's confession, in both narratives, follows the
feeding of the five thousand.[110] It is noteworthy that neither Luke
nor John identify Peter with Satan in this narrative, while Matthew
and Mark do.[111]

Verse 67 is the first direct reference to the 'Twelve' disciples in the
Fourth Gospel. Only once again is the term δώδεκα used—in 20.24.
What is most significant here is that the evangelist, in spite of a lack
of earlier direct references, 'takes for granted that his readers know
about them [i.e. the Twelve] as a special group among the disciples,
though he has not mentioned the call of more than five men'.[112] The
significance of this observation lies in the fact that it shares with the
Synoptics a recognition of the authority inherent in the representation
of the Twelve in the development of the Christian church.[113] This is
the case even though the Fourth Gospel is unique in its stress on the
role and function of the Beloved Disciple in comparison to the
Twelve (as represented by Peter).

Since Peter and the Twelve do not represent all Christians in the
Fourth Gospel, but just a group of Christians distinct from the
Johannine community,[114] then it must be maintained that the
Johannine attitude towards Peter and the Twelve was basically
positive. While the passage of 6.60-71 which has been examined had
dealt with the gradual falling away of 'outsiders' to the faith, it would
be a mistake to include the Twelve, as portrayed by John, among
those who were not true disciples and who were in danger of falling

away. 'The preceding sections of this chapter have shown how first the multitude and then some of His disciples were repelled. Now comes the big test. What will the Twelve do?. . . '[115]

The wording of Jesus' question betrays the positive attitude of the evangelist towards the faith of the Twelve. The use of μή indicates a negative answer to the question of whether or not the Twelve will also forsake Jesus.[116] In effect, the evangelist is suggesting that, *of course* the Twelve will not turn away in unbelief. Could it be that the evangelist is trying to build up the attitude of his readers with respect to the Twelve? Jesus may have asked the question of the Twelve in such a way so as to confirm their faith and perhaps even to gladden himself after experiencing the falling away of other disciples.[117] The evangelist is probably also addressing the question to his community of readers who were likely experiencing similar crises of faith in their midst. 'Questions from Jesus which insist on a choice help other people in John's gospel to clear the solemn confessions (9.35-38; 11.26-27). With the Twelve the readers are also questioned, and called on to think about their faith'.[118] Jesus poses the rhetorical question for the Twelve, and the one who consistently serves as their spokesman in all four Gospels, Simon Peter, speaks out on behalf of the Twelve.

As Schnackenburg points out, although the hero of the Gospel is the Beloved Disciple, rather than Peter, the role of Peter as the primary witness to Christ is not denied but recognized.

> Though he [i.e. Peter] is surpassed in loyalty and faith in the passion (19.26) and at the empty tomb (20.8) by 'the disciple whom Jesus loved' the confession to Jesus at this historic moment is not denied him, and indication of the fixed tradition to which the fourth evangelist also feels committed.[119]

Verses 68 and 69 make up Peter's three-part answer, which begins with another rhetorical question in response to Jesus' rhetorical question. Peter responds, κύριε, πρὸς τίνα ἀπελευσόμεθα. While Dods has interpreted this question to imply that the disciples feel they 'must attach themselves to someone as teacher and mediator of divine things' and they really could not think of anyone better than Jesus,[120] Schnackenburg is probably closer to the spirit of the reply when he writes, 'The question form is not meant to express the disciples' bewilderment at the thought of finding a better leader, but to prepare the way for the next sentence and confession'.[121]

The next sentence continues Peter's reply,. . . ῥήματα ζωῆς

αἰωνίου ἔχεις. These words echo the words of v. 63b; τὰ ῥήματα ἃ ἐγὼ λελάληκα ὑμῖν πνεῦμά ἐστιν καὶ ζωή ἐστιν.[122] The all-embracing life-giving quality of Jesus' words are obvious to the disciples and, in spite of their difficulty (c.f. σκληρός ἐστιν ὁ λόγος οὗτος) the Twelve have decided to listen to his words and accept them rather than turn away from them and Jesus.

> The words of Jesus are words which are in themselves living, deal with the subject of eternal life, and convey eternal life to those who believe. Those who have once become aware of the meaning and possibility of eternal life can take refuge with no other.[123]

Verse 69 completes Peter's response with a 'solemn declaration of belief'.[124] Peter says, ἡμεῖς πεπιστεύκαμεν καὶ ἐγνώκαμεν... The ἡμεῖς is emphatic, and this is probably stressed in order to contrast the Twelve with the unbelieving disciples as described in vv. 60-66. The evangelist is drawing clear lines to distinguish Peter and the Twelve from unbelievers. The use of the verbs πιστεύω and γινώσκω together are characteristic of John[125] and they exist in either order, so it is unadvisable to make a case that here a definite development is being described.[126] It is much easier to assert that the two verbs are practically synonymous in John, and they are often used interchangeably in close contexts to one another.[127] The fact that the verbs are put in the perfect tense in this confession suggests that they be understood in their fullest sense (i.e. 'We have come to faith and continue in it. We have acquired knowledge and retain it').

What Peter confesses, on behalf of the Twelve, is that they believe and know that Jesus is ὁ ἅγιος τοῦ θεοῦ. Peter prefaces this title with the simple words directed to Jesus σὺ εἶ. Schnackenburg suggests that these two words are meant to correspond to the ἐγὼ εἰμί sayings of Jesus himself which in turn are Jesus' way of identifying himself with God, as God reveals himself in the Old Testament.

> The ἐγὼ εἰμί sayings are striking in Chapter 6 (20, 35, 48, 51); the σὺ εἶ of Peter's confession could be a counterpart to them... Peter's confession is therefore the appropriate responsory (σὺ εἶ) to the revelatory formula ἐγὼ εἰμι which John transfers from God to Christ, who reveals himself to the Father.[128]

The title that Peter gives to Jesus—ὁ ἅγιος τοῦ θεοῦ—is noteworthy in that it appears only one other time with reference to Jesus. In that case, it is on the lips of a demonic spirit.[129] Snyder capitalizes on this comparison to suggest that, in John, Peter's 'corporate confession is tainted with the demonic',[130] so that John is here seen to be carrying out 'a sly attack on the validity of Peter's confession'.[131] He points out that the title is not used anywhere else in John to speak of Jesus and that it is used of Jesus by demons in Mk. Then he goes on to assert, 'Armed with this knowledge the next verse becomes a shock. Jesus replies to the confession of Peter, "Did I not choose you, and one of you is a devil?"'[132]

There are a number of problems with Snyder's interpretation of the force of this confession. First of all, the same word (i.e. ἅγιε) is used by Jesus to address the Father in John 17.11, which suggests that the word itself is most certainly to be associated with the divine rather than the demonic. Second, as Bultmann points out,

> If John knew the Synoptics it would have to be admitted that he consciously changed the conclusion of the scene in Mk 8.27-33, in that in place of the saying of Jesus that rebuked Peter as Satan (Mk 8.33; Mt. 16.23) he set the description of Judas as a devil.[133]

In other words Peter comes out in even a more positive position in the Johannine account as compared to the Synoptic, in that he is not explicitly identified with Satan as he is in the Synoptics. 'Instead of a humiliation of Simon Peter, he [i.e. the evangelist] echoes the synoptic report by including a derogatory report about the traitor'.[134]

Instead of Peter being identified with Satan, it is Judas who is the devil.[135] This deliberate change would have been necessitated by the exemplary role Peter assumed in vv. 68-69. Peter's entire tri-partite response within these two verses embodies the process by which one becomes a believer and true disciple as characterized by the Fourth Gospel. Lindars has described Peter's response well:

> He comes, as one drawn by the Father, he recognizes that the teaching of Jesus is 'spirit and life', and accordingly he entrusts himself to him in faith and can make acknowledgement of Jesus from personal experience. Thus at this point Peter typifies the kind of response John hopes that his readers will be led to make.[136]

In light of this picture of Peter, the identification with Satan had to lie with someone else. After all, how could a true believer also be a devil? Barrett suggests that the Johannine evangelist may have felt constrained to correct Mark at this point by insisting that the real devil is Judas and not Peter.[137]

Perhaps closer to the truth than the idea of *correcting* another evangelist is the idea of adjusting the characters of the story to fit in with the highly symbolic scheme of the Fourth Gospel. 'John has transferred this element from Peter to Judas, because he likes to use characters symbolically, and Judas represents Satanic influence in the Gospel story'.[138] Note that John is displaying the dynamics of unbelief and false discipleship as operative even among the inner circle of disciples. Among the carefully selected circle of men, individually chosen by Jesus,[139] there is not complete loyalty. One may understand that even within the close Johannine community there are false disciples. The evangelist may not only be pursuing his point about unbelief among disciples to its logical end, but he may very well also be reacting to the objection raised by incredulous Jews that Jesus himself (mistakenly or ignorantly) called the traitor to be a member of his inner group of disciples. 'The Johannine Jesus takes the sting from the reproach by announcing his knowledge of the traitor'.[140] One more time the theme of Jesus' supernatural knowledge presents itself.[141]

In conclusion, it can be said that Jn 6.60-71 presents a most enlightening picture of the development of the Christian church from the time of Jesus' earthly ministry as well as hinting at that development after his death among the peculiar branch of Johannine Christianity. We see the evangelist's attempt to deal with the historical phenomena of a falling away of many half-hearted followers of Jesus in Galilee. A similar threat in the Johannine community to which this Gospel is directed may also be detected.

This passage offers a heterogeneous picture of the disciples of Christ. Not all disciples share in the eternal life Jesus gives, because not all disciples remain attached to Jesus in faith. Some disciples can be described as followers yet uncommitted. Belief in the life-giving words of Jesus becomes the deciding factor in man's destiny. Peter's confession typifies the response of faith.

This brings us to the point of being able to make some conclusions regarding the Johannine attitude toward Peter and the Twelve. Operating from the understanding that the Gospel and Epistles of John reflect a community mentality that identifies strongly with the Beloved Disciple and that the figures of the Beloved Disciple and Peter are used symbolically to represent the Johannine community and Apostolic Christianity, it is necessary to qualify the degree of exclusiveness the Johannine community nurtured. While a strong case can be made that the Johannine community considered themselves distinct from the Apostolic type of Christianity represented by Peter and the Twelve, it is still an open question as to whether the Johannine Christians viewed their Apostolic brethren negatively in any way, and, if so, in what areas?

From this passage one must conclude that the Johannine evangelist (*at least*) displays a positive attitude towards Peter beyond simply according him the honour of his confession (as he may have been forced to do by common knowledge anyway). In contrast to the picture of Peter in the Synoptics, the Johannine Peter is not identified with Satan. Peter is the symbolic spokesman for the Twelve. He remains a true, faithful disciple in the midst of apostasy. He recognizes the divine self-revelation of Jesus for what it is. It is most difficult, in light of the evidence examined, to maintain that Peter is disparaged in any way in Jn 6.60-71 as compared to the Synoptic picture of him, although his stature seems heightened in the Matthean account at Caesarea Philippi in that it is associated with ecclesiastical authority.

D. *Conclusion*

We have examined the first half of the Gospel of John in order to ascertain what the Johannine attitude towards Peter might be independent of his relationship to the Beloved Disciple. Even though Peter does not appear any more than two times in John 1-12, in both of those cases he is placed in a strategic point in the Gospel narrative. The two treatments of Peter are compatible in that he is neither disparaged nor given inordinate status as compared to any other disciple of Jesus. Some of his position and prestige in the earliest traditions is evident in both passages, yet John presents him as one *among* the disciples of Jesus. He acts as spokesman for the Twelve and his faith is seen to be exemplary. It is seen as exemplary, not in the sense that it is the deepest, truest, most insightful and most loving, but in the sense that it exemplifies what John understands to be the faith that is necessary for anyone to become a true disciple of Jesus. It exemplifies the level at which John understands 'the Twelve' to be, however/he might compare that faith and insight to his own and that of his community.

If the evangelist is purposely portraying Peter in the way we have outlined above, we must guard against automatically assuming that the evangelist's understanding of Peter is one which he shares with the rest of the Johannine community. Could it be that he is seeking to present a picture of Peter that is to serve as a corrective to the actual sentiment the Johannine community was nurturing with respect to this figure? This is a question that we must keep in mind as we seek to compare the roles and functions of Peter and the Beloved Disciple in the various narratives that follow in John 13–21.

Chapter 3

PETER AND THE BELOVED DISCIPLE
AT THE LORD'S SUPPER

A. *Introduction*

Regardless of how scholars construct their analyses of the structure of the Gospel of John, they are generally agreed that John 13.1 begins a new section of the Gospel. Apart from the prologue (1.1-18) and appendix (21.1-25), the tendency is to divide the Gospel into two parts.[1] The first part, 1.19–12.50, presents the public ministry of Christ. In this section Jesus is portrayed as offering signs to his own people to reveal his Father. In recognition of the central role of σημεῖον in this section it has been titled 'The Book of Signs'.[2] The crisis of faith initiated by these signs leads some to believe and others to reject the claims of Jesus, as we have seen in our examination of Jn 6.60-71.

The second major section shifts emphasis. It no longer seeks to elicit belief through signs, but rather it proceeds to manifest the glory of Jesus through his ὥρα of crucifixion, resurrection and ascension to those who have become his disciples through belief.[3] The purpose of Jesus' ὥρα is 'that he may give the Spirit to those who believe in him and thus beget them as children of God'.[4] It must be kept in mind that this section of 13–20 is directed to the limited audience of believers. The Johannine emphasis of discipleship comes into its own now as a prevalent theme. 'Discipleship is the primary Christian category for John, and the disciple *par excellence* is the Disciple whom Jesus loved'.[5] In light of this, it is natural to find the first explicit reference to the Beloved Disciple in 13.23. Lindars states, 'He comes into the Gospel here for the first time, because John is preoccupied with the problem of true and false discipleship in his presentations of the Last Supper traditions'.[6] Minear has made the insightful distinction between three levels of response to the revelation of Jesus to his disciples that he sees outlined in ch. 13. He outlines the three representations:

The blackest light falls upon Judas as a tool of Satan, a Jewish disciple who betrayed his Master. He stands in the lowest echelon of the Johannine cast, much more culpable than secret believers and more culpable even than unbelievers in the synagogues. Simon Peter represents quite a different type: well-meaning, but dull and slow, if not stupid. He requires help from others to know what is going on; he cannot fathom the footwashing (xiii 6, 7) nor grasp the intent of Scripture (xiii 18). His lack of the gift of prophecy makes him dependent upon the disciple who had it. The latter, i.e. the unnamed disciple, was in a position to ask Jesus and to relay his reply (xiii 25).[7]

It may very well be that John is operating with the full representative function of these figures in mind, but judgment on the specific qualities of these 'types' needs to be withheld until a closer look at the evidence is conducted.

Immediately preceding 13.21-30 is the description of the foot-washing. Both the foot-washing and the disclosure of the betrayer are placed in the greater context of a meal.[8] John's account of the Last Supper omits the story of preparation and the words of the institution that are found in the Synoptics.[9] This account of the footwashing and the long Last Discourse (13.31–17.26) are not found in the Synoptic tradition. Not only does this suggest a certain amount of Johannine independence from the Synoptic tradition,[10] but it also illustrates the thematic selectivity of John. 'The words of institution are not included because they are not relevant to the theme of the homily'.[11]

The significance of the foot-washing poses interpretive problems that are not particularly pertinent to this thesis, but, nevertheless, certain elements should be discerned. In the midst of Jesus' actions and words in this scene are veiled references to Jesus' awareness that Judas is going to betray him (13.10, 18, 19). When this is coupled with the introduction of 13.2, τοῦ διαβόλου ἤδη βεβληκότος εἰς τήν καρδίαν ἵνα παραδοῖ αὐτὸν ῾Ισκαριώτου..., it becomes apparent that the stage is being set for Jesus to reveal his foreknowledge of his betrayal.

That such a purpose lies behind 13.21-30 does not mean it holds no value as a statement of the relationship between the Beloved Disciple and Peter in the greater context of discipleship and the Christian community. However, it is wise to keep in mind that such information must be evaluated in light of the main purpose of the pericope, which is to declare to the reader that Jesus did indeed know of his forthcoming betrayal and consciously initiated his own final hour.

B. *Jn 13.21-30*

As in the Synoptics, in Jn 13.21-22 Jesus solemnly declares that one of his own will betray him, which understandably causes confusion and consternation among the disciples. 'All the evangelists agree that this startling annoucement was made for the first time at the Last Supper—even then Jesus gave no clue as to who the traitor was . . .'[12] From this point on (13.2), however, John departs from the Synoptics and it is here that one may discern a peculiar Johannine message.

For the first time in the Gospel of John the Beloved Disciple is explicitly singled out, yet he is not named. It has been suggested that the evangelist has purposely refrained from presenting the Beloved Disciple before in order to contrast noticeably the Beloved Disciple with Judas (and not Peter, as some might suspect). 'Perhaps the reason we have not heard of him before is that the evangelist wished to introduce him as an antithesis to Judas, showing the good and bad extremes of discipleship'.[13] The Beloved Disciple, claims Lindars, is depicted here as 'all that Judas is not'.[14] However, his very anonymity has been interpreted by Mahoney to be the evangelist's way of keeping him 'a secondary figure, in the background'.[15] The problem with this interpretation is that this figure is not just *anonymous*, he is explicitly and specifically called 'ὅν ἠγάπα ὁ Ἰησοῦς', as he is in other strategic places in this latter half of the Gospel. His description has become a title and it is maintained that he carried substantial authority in at least one Christian community. Furthermore, his particular description had become invested with a representative, symbolic nature so that it is very difficult to understand why the evangelist would introduce the Beloved Disciple into the scene at such a prominent position and still maintain that he is intended to remain in the background.[16] Surely there must be some significance here, and given the infamous but important role that Judas plays, it is reasonable to assume that the Beloved Disciple may have an antithetical role.

The Beloved Disciple is said to be lying close to the breast of Jesus. The reference is obviously one of proximity, although it probably also implies intimacy. The phrase ἐν τῷ κόλπῳ τοῦ Ἰησοῦ may be a deliberate allusion to John 1.18, where Jesus is described as εἰς τὸν κόλπον τοῦ πατρὸς. While most interpreters see in John 1.18 a reference to the intimate communion that Jesus enjoyed with the Father, translating the phrase '. . . the only Son who is *in the bosom* of the Father. . .', Moloney has proposed an interesting alternative translation. He makes the case that κόλπος 'refers only to the external part of the body, be it man (chest) or woman (chest–breast). There is no reference to some sort of inner space within which something or someone may dwell, be kept, or held'.[17] From this conclusion he proceeds to make a distinction between the Johannine use of εἰς with the accusative and the use of ἐν (as we find in 13.23). He maintains that εἰς reflects 'some sort of dynamic relationship'[18] that exists between Jesus and the Father. In the final analysis, he understands the phrase in 1.18 to mean 'turned towards the Father' rather than 'in the bosom of the Father'. If we were to transfer that interpretation to the use of the similar phrase in ch. 13, it would make excellent sense. Because the Beloved Disciple was 'turned towards Jesus', Peter beckoned him to ask the question. However, the problem with such an approach is that even if we were to accept Moloney's understanding of John 1.18, we would be stretching his argument too far in applying it to 13.23, since in ch. 13 we find ἐν used instead of εἰς and much of his argument depends on a particular understanding of the use of εἰς. In any case, Moloney does not do justice to the tender, physical closeness and intimacy that is implied in all other occurrences of this word in the Biblical literature. We must allow for some sort of parallel between the intimacy of the Jesus–Father relationship and Beloved Disciple–Jesus relationship. Readers of the Gospel could not have avoided coming to this conclusion themselves.

A number of scholars have gone as far as to suggest that the use of this phrase in John 13.23 may signal the special revelatory role the Beloved Disciple plays.[19] As Sanders wonders, 'Is this meant to suggest that as only Christ can reveal the Father, only the Beloved Disciple can reveal the Christ?'[20] This somewhat cautious suggestion cannot stand, for as we shall see, the Beloved Disciple does not reveal anything to anybody in this narrative or in any other narrative in which he appears in the Gospel. R. Meyer, in the *Theological Dictionary of the New Testament*, interprets κόλπος, as indicative of 'membership of the community',[21] whether that community be of a familial or religious nature. When used in the context of a meal, such as the 'feast of the blessed' in religious literature, it has been used to designate 'the place of the guest of honour', and therefore can be understood figuratively 'to express an inward relationship'.[22]

Although one must be wary of building too much upon such a veiled reference, even the physical proximity of the Beloved Disciple to Jesus is enough to enable one to discern the intended message of the evangelist. It certainly is not reading too much into the description to conclude that the evangelist is here conveying the 'notion of tender relationship' by the use of this phrase, as this is general metaphorical use of the phrase throughout the Biblical Literature.[23] The Beloved Disciple is in the closest of relationships to Jesus.

The seating arrangements and the respective honours of the designated spots at this meal have been the object of much speculation among scholars. Some have said that the highest honours belong to the one on the left,[24] others maintain honour belongs to those on the right.[25] Some have suggested that Judas was the honoured guest of the host, Jesus.[26] Others assert that the Beloved Disciple was the honoured guest of Jesus.[27] To complicate matters further, it has been proposed that it was the Beloved Disciple who was the host and Jesus occupied the place of the honoured guest. Sanders and Mastin suggest

> ... It is probable that either Jesus himself or the Beloved Disciple acted as host, for it is difficult to think that if Jesus was not the host, he was not the principal guest. The latter could have been the case if the meal took place in the house which afterwards became the apostle's headquarters, that belonging to Mary, the mother of John Mark (Acts xii. 12), and if John Mark himself is the Beloved Disciple.[28]

Any and all interpretations allow for relative significance of the Beloved Disciple in the scene. It can be observed that those at the meal were reclining, propped up on their left elbows, as was the custom for Passover and other formal meals.[29] If the Beloved Disciple was to the immediate right of Jesus in this position, he would have been able to turn his head back to Jesus' chest and have a quiet conversation with him. No one else would have been in the position to address Jesus so intimately.

The physical mechanics of the situation alone could dictate why the evangelist describes Peter as beckoning to the Beloved Disciple to ask Jesus who it was that was to betray him. Peter himself was in a

less convenient position that made it difficult for him to ask Jesus on
his own. Peter may have been 'at a distance and did not want to
shout aloud such a question'.[30] Whether Peter said anything at all to
the Beloved Disciple, or just motioned to him to ask Jesus is a
question of textual variation. Textual critical study seems to point to
an original reading of πυθέσθαι τίς ἄν εἴη περὶ οὗ λέγει. The
variants of this reading are many, but the major difference between
this and the others is that the others depict Peter as actually talking
to the Beloved Disciple (e.g. καὶ λέγει [Peter] αὐτῷ, Εἰπὲ τίς ἐστιν
περὶ οὗ λέγει). This second reading does not have the age and
diversity of manuscript support that the first reading does.[31]

The first reading has greater geographical distribution, incorporating
Byzantine, Alexandrian, Ceasearean and Western text types. To a
limited extent, it is also better supported by the age and character of
its witnesses. The division of Alexandrian support between the first
and second reading, along with the conflated reading found in Codex
Sinaiticus, nevertheless shows that antiquity of support is a valid
claim for both the first and second readings.

In considering internal evidence, it can be maintained that the first
reading is to be preferred as both the 'hardest' and shortest, although
the second reading has the ambiguous advantage of being in the
Johannine style of direct discourse. It is best, in light of an analysis of
these variants, then, to conclude that the original reading was simply
'Simon Peter beckoned him' and the later variants represent scribal
misunderstandings and attempts at explanation and conflation.[32]

The case is strong that silence reigned at this point in the
narrative. K.G. Kuhn has attempted to explain the silence by
drawing a parallel between this meal and the communal meal of the
Essenes. He quotes 1QS 6.10, 'No man shall interrupt the speech of
the other before his brother has finished speaking. Nor shall he speak
out of his rank. . . '[33] This possibility seems unlikely since no one
appears to have been speaking at the time and few would 'outrank'
Peter, if indeed they even regarded such a protocol of rank. Barrett
observes that the manner of conversations in chs. 14–16 do not
depict such a custom,[34] but then his argument is severely weakened
by the observation that these three chapters, in all probability, are
not original to the context.[35]

Perhaps in this dramatic scene we are to imagine that the
emotional declaration of Jesus left the disciples shocked and
confused, at a loss for words. Consequently, in the vivid picture
painted by the evangelist, Peter directly urges the Beloved Disciple to

ask Jesus the answer to the question that was in the minds of all the disciples.

Was Peter asking on behalf of all the disciples, or just to satisfy his own curiosity? While, according to the Gospel accounts, it was not exactly characteristic of Peter to act discreetly, it is entirely in character for him to be the first to pose a question. In fact, this is not the first time in this chapter of the Gospel that we see this illustrated, for Peter is singled out in the foot-washing scene in 13.1-20. It would be wise to examine briefly this account in preparation for our interpretation of the role of Peter in 13.21-30.

Before reclining for the meal, Jesus lays aside his garments, girds himself with a towel and proceeds to wash the disciples' feet. When he came to wash Peter's feet, who, interestingly enough, was apparently not the first one to be washed, Peter questions the actions of Jesus. σύ μου νίπτεις τούς πόδας; (13.6). Verses 7-10 go on to highlight the fact that Peter is totally misunderstanding the significance of Jesus' actions.

Jesus tells him that in order for Peter to have a part in him, he must allow himself to be washed (ἐὰν μὴ νίψω σε, οὐκ ἔχεις μέρος μετ᾽ ἐμοῦ). This verse gives us an indication of the main theological thrust of the passage. Traditionally, the whole foot-washing scene has been interpreted as an admonition to humble service after the example of Jesus.[36] Bearing in mind that this scene replaces the words of the institution of the Lord's Table, with all of its sacramental overtones that we find in the Synoptics, it is probably more accurate to understand this passage *first* as the assimilation of the self-giving Jesus in the lives of his disciples. The ethical example that is being set becomes secondary.

If this is the theological thrust of the passage, then scholars such as Snyder and Maynard may be correct in their interpretation of the episode as 'the final "sifting" of the disciples'.[37] Referring to verse 13.20, Maynard suggests that Judas is sifted out, and Peter comes dangerously close to the same fate.

> The crux of the passage is the last verse, as is so often the case in the Fourth Gospel: 'Truly, truly I say to you, he who receives any one whom I send receives me; and he who receives me receives him who sent me'. Judas fails the test and is 'sifted out', and Peter almost fails!. . . At the very best, Peter appears in a bad light in the passage, almost refusing to accept the Life that Jesus offers.[38]

Snyder has set this interpretation in the context of the debate over

true discipleship versus apostleship which he sees underlying the
Gospel of John. Crucial to his thesis is his translation of John 13.16—
ἀμὴν ἀμὴν λέγω ὑμῖν, οὐκ ἔστιν δοῦλος μείζων τοῦ κυρίου αὐτοῦ
οὐδὲ ἀπόστολος μείζων τοῦ πέμψαντος αὐτόν. Rather than the
usual translation of ἀπόστολος in this context (i.e. *the one sent*), he
translates it: 'Truly, truly I say to you, a slave is not greater than his
lord, nor is an *apostle* greater than the one who sent him'.

> The question is: has primary apostleship been established by seeing
> the resurrected Lord and by dying a martyr death, or is primary
> apostleship established by being loved by Jesus, and then, in turn,
> loving and feeding the sheep? I believe 13.16 intends to say that
> Christianity emanates from the life of the Son, not from apostles
> who saw the risen Lord. The author wants to say that the church
> depends on those who received the love of Jesus and not on those
> whose lives were changed by the resurrection.[39]

Snyder's understanding merits recognition for it fits in well with
what we know of the Johannine community and its theology.
Certainly John would have his readers believe that true discipleship
and eternal life hinge on 'remaining in Jesus', in a loving relationship
of faith rather than on being an actual witness to the risen Lord. The
danger of Snyder's interpretation is that it focuses much too sharply
on the specific person of Peter. Snyder is not the only one to focus
this narrative upon the specific person of Peter. Agourides also sees
Peter as the central individual in the foot-washing, and he applies its
significance directly to Peter's ecclesial functions in the later
church.

> I think that in the scene of the washing of the disciples' feet in John,
> the refusal of Peter to have his feet washed is not intended to show
> his humility in distinction to the other apostles; it rather hints at
> Peter's difficulty in understanding the meaning of this act of Jesus.
> His original reluctance to have his feet washed by Jesus and his
> final wholehearted acceptance seem to prefigure his denial of Jesus
> and his restoration to the apostolic office.[40]

It is granted that Peter does surface as a prime character in this
narrative, but certainly Judas deserves top billing among the
disciples here. Also, the corporate, representative nature of the figure
of Peter leads us to conclude that John is speaking of apostleship in
general, and Peter is presented as expressing the confusion, misunderstanding and status of the whole group. Note that in 13.10 Jesus
switches from the second person singular when he is addressing Peter

to continue in the second person plural, so as to suggest this very dynamic.

Thus in considering 13.1-20 and recalling where we left off with the discussion of 13.21-30, we can see how Peter invariably verbalizes what is on the minds of the other disciples. It is almost impossible to differentiate between Peter the individual and Peter the stylized representative of the disciples, especially in such strategic scenes in the Gospel as this one. It can justifiably be maintained that in this scene Peter is acting on behalf of the Twelve as their representative.

Due to the physical mechanics of the situation, not withstanding any intended symbolism, Peter is constrained to query the Lord through the Beloved Disciple. In close intimacy the Beloved Disciple is able to ask κύριε, τίς ἐστιν; He was asking Peter's question, he was asking the question of the Twelve (13.22) and, not insignificantly, he was asking his own question with these words. The deeper understanding of Christ and his work presupposed by the Johannine Christians finds no support here. If the Beloved Disciple was supposed to know who the betrayer was, why did he not disclose his identity directly to Peter rather than having to ask Jesus the question?

In other words, this text itself cannot be understood as introducing the Beloved Disciple as 'having a special knowledge of Jesus'.[41] At most, it suggests a special intimacy or relationship to Jesus. An interesting fact that should be observed now is that this is the last reference to either Peter or the Beloved Disciple in the whole pericope. This indicates the secondary role both play in the scene relative to Jesus and Judas. Whatever other significance they may have, Peter and the Beloved Disciple may be regarded as props which enabled the story to proceed with the desired effect. Mahoney refers to the role in this way:

> No further indication will be given in this text to tell us his role includes any more than having asked κύριε, τίς ἐστιν; in order to lead in 13.26f. with the degree of discretion the evangelist desired.[42]

The interaction between Peter and the Beloved Disciple is included to provide adequately for the continued unenlightened state of the disciples as evidenced in vv. 28-29. 'The details then of verses 23-25a seem inserted to prepare for and support verses 28f.'[43] The evangelist utilized the anonymity of the Beloved Disciple in the process of revealing the identity of the betrayer to the readers, while at the same time preserving the tradition that none of the disciples knew that Judas was about to betray Jesus. Pamment attributes no more significance to the role of the Beloved Disciple than Mahoney does: 'The impression created is that the beloved disciple participates in the supper with Jesus, but that nothing he says or does affects the events. He seems to be both present and absent, so to speak'.[44] However, the somewhat peripheral involvement of both Peter and the Beloved Disciple in this scene should not be taken as an indication that they are insignificant. As Neirynck notes, with reference to 18.15-16, 'the incidental character is a rather common feature of all mentions of the Beloved Disciple'.[45] That the characters are thus employed still allows for a somewhat symbolic interpretation of their roles. The question can still be asked, 'Why were these two figures specifically chosen?' Before attempting to answer this question, the remainder of the story must be allowed to unfold, for it offers more clues as to a proper interpretation.

Verse 26 focuses solely upon the actions of Jesus by beginning with the words ἀποκρίνεται [ὁ] Ἰησοῦς. For the purposes of clarity, one would wish that the evangelist would have explicitly stated to whom the answer was given. That this response of Jesus immediately follows the question of the Beloved Disciple makes it reasonable to assume that Jesus was giving an answer to the Beloved Disciple, probably in the same quiet manner in which the question was asked. However, it could very well be possible that the evangelist intended this to be obscure. It was not his intention to suggest to the readers that anyone except Jesus and Judas knew what was about to transpire. At any rate, one cannot assume as Barrett does, that 'it is plain from the narrative that the beloved disciple must have understood that Judas was the betrayer'.[46] Gunther goes as far as to say that the Beloved Disciple purposely kept the answer to the 'private' question secret, thereby indicating that he was on particularly close and trusted terms with Jesus.[47]

It was common courtesy of table etiquette for the host to dip the food and offer it to a guest. 'What John describes is a basic gesture of Oriental hospitality, as can be seen from Ruth ii 14'.[48] An illuminating emphasis can be detected in this passage when it is compared with its Synoptic counterparts. In Mk 14.20 Judas is described as dipping in the same dish as Jesus and the others. In John, it is Jesus himself who dips the bread for Judas and hands it to

him. 'Mark has brought out the enormity of Judas' evil intention by
drawing attention to the fact that he dips in the common dish. But
John has taken the idea a step further by suggesting that Jesus, as the
host of the meal himself dipped a tasty morsel in the dish and gave it
to Judas. . .'[49] N.E. Johnson has suggested that the evolution of
tradition has gone the other direction with the Johannine account
reflecting the original eyewitness material while the Synoptics reflect
a later, more general saying. After outlining the differences between
the accounts, he states:

> From this it would seem that the Beloved Disciple communicated
> his Master's saying verbally, at first to the disciples, but through
> oral transmission this became distorted to a more general saying;
> this form was used by the Synoptic writers, since they were
> unaware of the existence of QJ. It remains then that the original
> saying occurs only in the Fourth Gospel and could have come only
> from the Beloved Disciple.[50]

Whatever the direction of change between John and the Synoptics,
the direct action of Jesus in John is noteworthy. Jesus is obviously
communicating something by his actions and words. To Judas he
could be communicating his awareness of the intentions of the
betrayer. His motive for doing so could be an appeal to Judas to
reconsider, or he could just be doing his part to facilitate the process.
Sanders suggests, 'Jesus may have chosen this course as a last
reminder to Judas of the heinousness of betraying one with whom he
had eaten—and not having been unmasked publicly, Judas could still
change his mind'.[51] This psychological dynamic extends beyond the
evidence and does not fit in with the train of thought in the text.
Perhaps closer to the actual dynamics involved is R.E. Brown's
description:

> This sign of Jesus' affection, like the act of love that brought him to
> the world, brings Judas to the decisive moment (see iii 16-21). His
> acceptance of the morsel without changing his wicked plan to
> betray Jesus means that he has chosen for Satan rather than for
> Jesus.[52]

Jesus is communicating his understanding and his love to Judas to
elicit a decision and subsequent action on the part of Judas. It is a
distinct tenet of Johannine theology to have Jesus present a choice to
his hearers and call them to a decision,[53] and it may very well be
operative here in this narrative. Provoking the crisis of commitment
that calls for a decision, Jesus then says to Judas, ὅ ποεῖς ποίησον

τάχιον. In turn, Judas does respond; λαβὼν οὖν τὸ ψωμίον ἐκεῖνος ἐξῆλθεν εὐθύς. ἦν δὲ νύξ. The reference to the night is not purely a reference to the time of day. One scarcely need be reminded of the prevalence of the light versus darkness motif in the Johannine writings.[54] With the recognition and even permission of Jesus behind him, Judas is embraced by Satan and enters into the power of darkness.

This may be made clear to the readers, as the evangelist intended it to be, but, returning to vv. 28-29, it is seen that no one at the meal understood the bleak significance of Jesus' words and deeds. Verse 29 reports in an incidental manner how the disciples interpreted Jesus' command to Judas. This further substantiates the claim that the others were ignorant—but other than that, it probably has no deeper significance. In this sense, verse 29 has been compared with vv. 23-25 as a prop that supports the main story.[55] However, Lindars has made the interesting comment that 13.29 may point to a factor in Judas' failure in discipleship; that is, his greed. In other words, v. 29 is

> . . . intended to convey to the reader a hint of the reason for Judas' failure of discipleship. John has already referred to the motif of avarice in the growth of Judas' legend, when he introduced the idea into the story of the anointing at Bethany. He here reproduces the same material.[56]

Collins, in an article dealing with several representative figures in the Gospel of John, outlines the general picture of this infamous figure:

> The Evangelist has borrowed from the common tradition of the early church that Judas was the betrayer (even though the Christology of the Fourth Gospel renders a 'betrayal' in the strict sense somewhat unnecessary). To this common trait the Johannine tradition adds a further characterization. Like Nicodemus, Judas is the figure of the night (John 13, 30). He can be described as a thief who usurps that which is not properly his own (John 12, 6; 13, 27-30). More specifically, Judas is the one into whom the devil has entered (John 13, 2; cf. 13, 27).[57]

Turning our attention from Judas to Peter and the Beloved Disciple, we must pose the problem that if the symbolic nature of these two were prevalent in the writer's mind, one would expect that some sort of explanation would be offered pertaining to their understanding (or lack thereof). It is precisely because the roles of Peter and the Beloved Disciple are foremost in the minds of the present day interpreters that explanations are offered on behalf of the evangelist.[58] For example, Sanders seeks to rationalize the apparent unresponsiveness of the disciples; 'All but the Beloved Disciple were unaware of what had been happening and he can be forgiven if he did not realize that Jesus was bidding Judas put his plan into effect, and did not know what to do'.[59] To enter into such speculation is to go beyond the bounds of the narrative. 'In all events, the evangelist is in 13.28 no longer *thinking* of the anonymous disciple in 13.23-25'.[60]

Nothing is said about the Beloved Disciple's or Peter's special positions or intimate understanding, because that is not the point of the passage. Bearing in mind that this is the beginning of the section of the Gospel which reveals Jesus' glorification in his hour to his true disciples, it must be concluded that *Jesus* is the central character of this drama and the prediction of his betrayal is the central thrust of the action. Furthermore, when the Synoptic parallels are compared to John 13.21-30, a significant difference is noted. It is Jesus who actively singles out Judas and sends him on his way.

> The resulting pericope is not simply Jesus' prediction of his betrayal, as in the Synoptics, but proleptically in Judas the actual beginning of Jesus' passion. The time of this beginning is not fixed by Judas, not by Satan, but by Jesus.[61]

This emphasis on Jesus' full consciousness of being sent from his Father for a definite mission and his own participation in bringing it about is typical of the high christological themes reflected in the Johannine writings, as we have already noted in our examinations of chapters one and six of the Gospel.

The evangelist wanted to mark the beginning of Jesus' hour and he wanted to illustrate Jesus' full participation in its initiation.[62] To do so, he uses the figures of the Beloved Disciple and Peter. Therefore, these two were not important for their own sake, that is, standing in isolation. Each one was a means to the evangelist's end, 'enabling or facilitating the dramatic expression of a point'.[63] Their significance is derived from both the context and their inherent profile in the minds of the readers.

Therefore the very fact that these two figures were explicitly employed is enough to establish some significance. If the Beloved Disciple is the hero with whom the readers would identify, and if he is to be understood as the embodiment of true discipleship, then here he may be used to make a statement about that discipleship. Indeed, Lindars asserts, 'In the present context he performs an essential function for the mechanics of the story, and at the same time provides a sharp antithesis to Judas Iscariot'.[64] Barrett echoes these words; 'It is better to say, with Lindars, that the chapters are about discipleship—with which, we may add, its blessedness and shame'.[65] If the Beloved Disciple symbolizes true discipleship in intimate relationship to Jesus as contrasted to Judas, then what is said about Peter, individually, and the relationship between Peter and the Beloved Disciple?

It is tempting to conclude that this passage puts Peter in a lesser position than the Beloved Disciple, dependent upon the insight and mediation of the Beloved Disciple, which is afforded him by virtue of his loving intimacy with Jesus. Snyder comes to four conclusions along these lines after discussing this passage:

> 1) Peter acts and speaks for the disciples; 2) Peter's position is inferior to that of the Beloved Disciple; 3) the Beloved Disciple is not included in that group for which Peter speaks; 4) the Beloved Disciple mediates between Peter and Jesus; 5) the Beloved Disciple stands on the side of Jesus rather than on the side of the disciples.[66]

Peter certainly does act and speak for the disciples and it is an open question whether or not the Beloved Disciple is included in that group for which Peter speaks, although evidence seems to suggest that he indeed was not part of the 'Twelve'.[67] Peter could have very well been speaking on behalf of *all* who were present. There is no proof that would limit the participants in this meal to the Twelve, exclusively. This is an assumption all too often made and then used as a foundation for important arguments centring on the place of the Twelve in the development of the early Church. Maynard is guilty of doing this to the denigration of Peter:

> Peter is presented here as having to go through an intermediary in order to get his question to Jesus. There is no way that we can assume that this was physically necessary. A group of thirteen people eating cannot be conceived as being so far apart that the verbal spokesman for the group cannot make himself heard by the leader... The Evangelist knew the tradition that Peter was the spokesman for the twelve, but he wants to show that he is a bungling spokesman who fails to understand and—can I add—who therefore has no claim to leadership in the later church.[68]

Hawkin counters the argument that the Beloved Disciple does serve as a mediator between Jesus and Peter:

It can hardly be cogently maintained that the purpose of the pericope is to represent the Beloved Disciple as the 'mediator' between Peter and the disciples. This is simply not true to the text. Nothing is mediated to Peter! Peter is mentioned only once in the pericope in verse 24. Certainly nothing of significance is said about the relation of Peter to the Beloved Disciple.[69]

Interestingly enough, while Raymond Brown seeks to make a case for the significance of a Beloved Disciple–Peter comparison in the Gospel of John, he states, 'There is nothing symbolic in Peter's signal to ask him about the betrayer'.[70] The present writer is inclined to agree with this position. All that this passage reflects of Peter is that he may indeed be regarded by the evangelist as the spokesman for the Twelve and an historical witness to the event. To the extent that all the disciples were ignorant and confused concerning the impending events in Jesus' life and their significance, Peter reflects this. It must also be recognized that, by comparison, Peter does not enjoy the intimacy and loving relationship with Jesus that the Beloved Disciple (as his very title implies) enjoys. But that is not to say that one figure is highlighted above the other consistently in all areas of an equivalent contrast. Clearly, Peter and the Beloved Disciple should be allowed to stand on their own respective terms. We do not do justice to the intricacy of the evangelist's style and symbolism if we merely construct an equivalent contrast between the two.

When Peter is placed alongside the Beloved Disciple introduced in this passage the result is by no means a contrast, or even a competition. They do reflect different and supplementary roles used in harmony to be supporting roles in the greater drama of the unfolding hour of Jesus.

Jn 13.36-38
One other passage in this chapter has been noted as a further example of the fourth evangelist's 'anti-Petrinism', that is, Jn 13.36, which describes how Peter insists that he is willing to follow Jesus even to the point of laying down his life for his Lord. Jesus then responds, 'Will you lay down your life for me? Truly, truly, I say to you, the cock will not crow, till you have denied me three times'. Except for the prediction of Peter's denials, which will be discussed in the next chapter, a cursory reading of 13.36-38 suggests anything but criticism of Peter. After all, he is alone in maintaining his allegiance to Jesus until the end. The point that is picked up on,

however, is that Peter is *alone* in maintaining this. Maynard comments

> ... It may be significant that whereas in Matthew and Mark the other disciples join with Peter in their willingness to die for Jesus, John leaves this out. It may well be that he wants it to appear that only Peter misunderstands his Lord. .. As a prediction of betrayal, Peter inevitably stands in a bad light, but his position is made worse by the Fourth Evangelist's failure to follow the Synoptic suggestion that the other disciples shared his plight.[71]

The fact that this interpretation rests solely on an argument from silence needs to be recognized, although the reference to Peter's denials is certainly to be taken as a serious allegation that puts Peter in a bad light. Because Peter is a representative figure for the twelve, it is possible, and even probable, that Peter's attitude and actions here are to be taken as representative of the eager but ignorant commitment of the twelve who were yet to understand the dynamics of Jesus' forthcoming arrest and crucifixion. In this case, then, John's account differs little in its effect from that contained in the Synoptics.

D. *Conclusions*

We see that the Fourth Evangelist does not dispute the leadership/ spokesman role that Peter assumes in the greater Christian tradition. It is not going beyond the evidence to maintain that the Beloved Disciple *followed* the lead of Peter and acted *under* his direction when he asked Jesus about the identity of the betrayer.

On the other hand, from this narrative the reader is able to see that the Beloved Disciple, and hence the Johannine community, can and *does* enjoy a direct, intimate relationship with Christ. He does this to a level unequalled by his peers—yet he does this while still being a part of the wider fellowship and structure of Christian disciples.

What would the evangelist be trying to convey to his community by his depictions of these two characters and the inter-relationship displayed? Perhaps the two are purposely being brought together in the same manner the evangelist sees the need for the Johannine and Apostolic communities to be brought together—i.e. as partners in the greater drama of the unfolding 'hour' of the Church? We will have to forego making such conclusions until all the evidence is in hand.

Chapter 4

PETER'S DENIALS

A. *Introduction*

It is the purpose of this chapter to examine Peter's denials of association with Jesus during the events immediately preceding the crucifixion as recorded in Jn 18.15-18, 25-27. Moreover, because the Beloved Disciple has been linked to this event as John describes it, we will continue our considerations to include Jn 19.24-26. Since the account of Peter's denials is common to all four Gospels, the Johannine account will be compared with the Synoptic accounts in the hopes of arriving at some source-critical conclusions. In turn, the particular Johannine style and content having been isolated, an attempt will be made to ascertain the Johannine perspective in this tradition. The theological purpose of the Fourth Evangelist in including this tradition and handling it the way he does will be sought.

B. *Jn 18.15-18, 25-27*

While verbal similarities in comparative accounts are necessary to establish literary relationships, conceptual similarities are also important as indicators of common underlying literary and oral traditions. Therefore, conceptual similarities are worthy of our attention, since we are concerned with the specifically Johannine treatment of the figure of Peter in comparison with the Synoptics.

In v. 15 only two words have synoptic counterparts: ἠκολούθει and αὐλήν. The first of these, ἠκολούθει, is common to all four Gospels. It is a frequently used word, occurring ninety times in the New Testament, twenty of those occurrences being in the Gospel of John. As noted in Chapter 2 above, the term often signifies 'discipleship' but it is difficult to assign such a specific interpretation to this context. It is evident that John also uses ἀκολουθεῖν in the more general sense in other narratives (cf. Jn 11.31). The commonness of ἀκολουθεῖν may be sufficient to override the postulation of a

literary dependency in this case. After all, it is difficult to think of a
more appropriate word to convey the idea of *following* which is
necessary in this context. The fact that a single verb is used with a
plural subject[1] should not be taken as proof of careless interpolation
of a second subject (i.e. the anonymous disciple). As in Hebrew and
other Greek precedents, the verb legitimately covers both subjects.[2]

The second term, αὐλήν, is relatively rare in John and in the New
Testament. Eleven of its twelve occurrences are in the Gospels (it
occurs once in the Apocalypse). It occurs three times in John, but in
the other two places John uses the word to refer to the sheepfold (10,
1, 16). It appears that here in 18.15 John uses it in the same way that
it is used in the Synoptics. 'The Greek word αὐλή, the equivalent of
the Latin *aula*, can in fact mean either the palace or the court. It can
refer to the building as a whole as well as to the people to be found
there or the central courtyard of the palace'.[3]

Before any conclusion can be made regarding the similarity of this
verse to its Synoptic parallels two differences need to be noted
(besides the obvious difference of the presence of an anonymous
disciple). While John accords with the Synoptic tradition that Peter
followed Jesus after his arrest, he is alone in using the full name
Σίμων Πέτρος. As observed in an earlier discussion,[4] this can be
regarded as no more than a Johannine stylistic characteristic—Peter
is introduced for the first time here in this narrative. In light of this
we should not attempt to attach any source-critical or theological
significance to the use of the full name. The second observation that
can be made is that while the Synoptics describe Peter as following
from a distance (μακρόθεν), John does not give this impression.

Verse 16 continues the narrative by relating some difficulty Peter
experienced in entering the courtyard. As R.E. Brown states, 'none of
the Synoptics indicate that Peter had trouble entering the court'.[5]
The only feature that this verse has in common with the Synoptic
account is the *concept* of Peter *going in*. εἰσήγαγεν in this verse may
have as its subject ὁ μαθητὴς ὁ ἄλλος (i.e., the other disciple
introduced or brought in Peter) or τῇ θυρωρῷ (i.e., the female
doorkeeper *brought in* Peter) The translation depends upon what
meaning is attached to the verb. In the former translation, the other
disciple is given an active role in the entire process of gaining Peter
entry whereas in the latter translation, the doorkeeper does the
'letting in'. The θυρωρῷ of John's account may be equivalent to the
maid (παιδίσκη) introduced in Lk. 22.56 (Mt. 26.69 and Mk
14.66).

Continuing on in verse 17, it can be further noted that both the terms παιδίσκη and θυρωρός are used to describe this person at the door of the courtyard. The term παιδίσκη is common to all four gospels, but only in John is this person given a function. Bultmann and others doubt that the θυρωρός would be a woman. He interprets it as a harmonization of the gatekeeper of v. 16 with the παιδίσκη of the Synoptics.[6] The addition of θυρωρός corroborates (for Lorenzen) the redactional character of v. 16.[7] Dauer says that this shows the combination of two stories: the story with ὁ (or ἡ) θυρωρός (the intervention of the other disciple) and the story of Peter's first denial (with the question of the παιδίσκη):

> Diese Beobachtungen lassen vermuten, dass hier zwei—ursprünglich verschiedene—Berichte ineinander—gearbeitet worden sind: einer, dem zufolge Petrus durch die Intervention des 'anderen Jüngers' bei dem (oder der) θυρωρός in den hohepriesterlichen Hof kam— ein anderer von der Verleugnung des Petrus, der eingeleitet wurde durch die Frage einer παιδίσκη. Das Ergebnis dieser Kombination war dann, dass aus dem (oder der) θυρωρός eine (ἡ) παιδίσκη ἡ θυρωρός wurde und dass die erste Verleugnung berits am Eingang zum Hof stattfand.[8]

While John is the only account which has the maiden ask a question, all four gospels convey the accusation that Peter was *with* someone (Mt. and Mk use μέτα while Lk. uses σύν). John does not use μέτα or σύν, but the ablative construction ἐκ τῶν μαθητῶν. It is noteworthy that all four Gospels use καὶ in the sense of 'also' or 'too' in the accusation/question. This is relevant because then it is not possible to apply *automatically* καὶ here in John as a reference to the 'other disciple', although this is possible in its immediate literary context.

Peter's reply in Jn 18.17 differs from that attributed to him in the Synoptics. The three other gospels report that Peter explicitly *denied* (ἠρνήσατο) something.[9] The Synoptics also give a longer response of Peter characterized by the words οὐκ (or οὔτε—Mk) οἶδα. In John, Peter simply states οὐκ εἰμί, which is significant for a number of reasons in its reflection of Johannine concerns and theology. These will be discussed later, but it can be noted now that John may be *softening* Peter's denials for some reason. This certainly would take away from the interpretation that John has a lower view of Peter than the Synoptists.

To summarize, it can be seen that John shares a few phrases with the Synoptic accounts. The presence of the παιδίσκη and the wording of the accusation (i.e. σύ καί) are notable. On the other hand, John differs in that the παιδίσκη is given a function (θυρωρός). She asks a question of Peter, using the preposition ἐκ instead of μέτα or σύν. Peter is not said to deny anything, and his response is comparatively brief. One may conclude that there are not enough grounds to establish any literary dependency but perhaps there may be a common underlying tradition behind the mention of the παιδίσκη and her accusation.

Verse 18 goes on to describe Peter warming himself with a group of slaves and officers at a fire. In common with the Synoptics, John speaks of the presence of the ὑπηρέται (cf. 18.3, 12). To these, John adds the δοῦλοι. If anywhere in this narrative John's language is to be characterized as 'strikingly similar'[10] to Mark's, it should be here. Note the two instances of the verb θερμαίνομαι.[11] It is found in this context only in Mark and John. The fact that it occurs in these two gospels may signify a literary relationship. It may be, as Boismard postulates, that the Fourth Evangelist was acquainted with a pre-Markan tradition.[12] Regarding the double occurrence of the verb in John, R.E. Brown suggests, 'Since it occurs twice in this verse, one occurrence may represent a scribal addition'.[13]

Mark assumes a fire where Luke and John describe the making of a fire. Luke 22.55 uses the word περιαψάντων[14] and John uses the word πεποιηκότες. Mark uses the word φῶς, Luke πῦρ and John ἀνθρακίαν. The use of this word may suggest an independent source behind this account, as we will discuss later when we focus upon the unique Johannine treatment of the narrative of Peter's denials. John also adds the explanatory remark ὅτι ψύχος ἦν.

Upon examination, then, the conceptual similarities with both Luke and Mark have been isolated. The mention of a fire is shared with both Mark and Luke. Both Luke and John describe the preparation of a fire, but in different terms. Verbal correspondences can be noted regarding the terms ὑπηρέται and θερμαίνομαι (the latter being conspicuously similar to Mark). Again, one can only conclude a common tradition with Mark and Luke. The fact that some of the similarities are not appearing to be unique to John and Mark (or else John and Luke), suggests that there may have been several distinct traditions circulating, all based on a common (oral?) tradition.

While the Synoptics continue their narration of Peter's denial uninterrupted, John interrupts his account with an account of Jesus' interrogation in vv. 19-24. All the Synoptics suggest the passing of time, but John is not specific concerning the passage of time. On the other hand, the opening words of v. 25 seem to tie it directly to v. 18, thereby conveying the sense that this was all happening simultaneously with Jesus' interrogation. This simultaneous construction will prove to be significant in the discussion of the theological thrust of John's account of Peter's denials.

A source critical comparison of vv. 25-27, the account of Peter's second and third denials, with its Synoptic parallels reveals only limited verbal similarities. Like the Synoptics, John uses the verb ἀρνεῖσθαι to describe Peter's second denial. John also offers the same terse response of Peter that Luke presents (i.e. οὐκ εἰμί). It is difficult to discern who would be dependent upon whom in this case, but the fact that Luke has these words weakens any attempt to assign particular theological significance to the negative counterpart of ἐγὼ εἰμί so distinctive throughout the Gospel of John. Nevertheless, one may compare it with Christ's own christological confessions, especially since the two figures are being contrasted by the structure of this narrative.

Verses 26 and 27 display one verbal similarity with the Synoptics, that of ἀλέκτωρ ἐφώνησεν. About the only consistent similarity throughout the four Gospels is the *concept* of the immediacy of the cock crow after the third denial. John may indeed have the same source as the Synoptics, which Luke has in turn modified to suit his style. However, there are notable differences between John and the Synoptics in the record of this third denial. There is no reference to time passing in John. John is uniquely specific in his description of the accuser. And finally, in describing Peter's actual reply, only John uses the word ἠρνήσατο. Note also that John is alone in not giving any words to Peter. It is in this third denial that all three Synoptics give Peter his most elaborate responses.[15]

In light of the verbal similarities worthy of note[16] it is wisest to conclude that there is not enough evidence to trace any literary dependency that runs throughout the narrative. There is some similarity with Mark (i.e. use of θερμαινόμενος), but, given the uniquely Johannine details (i.e. ἀνθράκιαν and ὅτι ψῦχος ἦν), John does not appear to build upon Mark. Rather, to some extent, the Fourth Gospel parallels the most basic account behind the Synoptics. There exists in the Johannine pericopes nothing in particular that is shared with Luke, except maybe the use of οὐκ εἰμί.

At this point, then, the most one can conclude is that John is sharing a common tradition that there was a servant-girl who questioned Peter in an αὐλή, where ὑπηρέται were present. Further, all the Gospels agree that the last denial of Peter was immediately following the crowing of a cock. Such reductionistic conclusions do not do justice to the rich theological import infused into this event as described in the Gospel of John. Therefore, it is necessary to turn attention to the specific Johannine treatment of this common tradition. We want to comprehend the general purpose and theology the Fourth Evangelist is presenting. Also, we want to isolate what, if anything, is being said about Peter, the 'other disciple' and their relationship.

As a result of the preceding comparison with the Synoptic accounts, the following details have appeared as potentially significant in discerning the theological import of the event as John narrates it:

1. The mention of another disciple (ἄλλος μαθητής) who was known to the high priest (v. 15).
2. The description of the female doorkeeper (vv. 16-17).
3. The 'οὐκ εἰμί' as descriptive of Peter's denials (vv. 17, 25).
4. The inclusion of δοῦλοι in the courtyard (vv. 18, 26).
5. The stipulation that the fire in the courtyard was a charcoal fire (ἀνθρακιάν—v. 18).
6. The explanation ὅτι ψῦχος ἦν (v. 18).
7. The construction of the narrative around the interrogation of Jesus and the lack of any references to the passing of time.
8. The specific reference to the person of Peter's third accuser as 'a relative of the one whose ear Peter had cut off' (v. 26).
9. The two references to events in the garden during the third denial (in addition to the above reference, Peter is asked if he was in the garden; v. 26).

Of these details, the first one on the list, the mention of another disciple, is the most conspicuous and also the most pertinent to this thesis. This figure is not mentioned by any other Gospel and in John his identity is obscure. However, students of the Fourth Gospel consistently identify this anonymous disciple with the Beloved Disciple, who is present in other key narratives in John. Barrett offers his concise evaluation of this interpretive problem: 'It is quite possible to identify him as the disciple "whom Jesus loved", but there is no definite ground for doing so'.[17]

A number of scholars resist the identification with the Beloved Disciple, basically due to the limited function given to the other disciple in this narrative and the lack of a more specific description given to this figure. Bultmann states,

> Who the ἄλλος μαθητής is cannot be divined. There is no basis for identifying him with the 'Beloved Disciple' (as C A pl. do by the addition of the article), and in particular his appearance with Peter is no reason for it; for the two figures do not appear here, as in 20.3-10 and 21.1-23, as rivals or as contrasted types. . .[18]

Apart from the fact that Bultmann is here using a questionable conclusion (i.e. that the Beloved Disciple and Peter are always contrasted as rivals when they are juxtaposed in John) as a criterion for his judgment, one could conceivably argue that the two are indeed contrasted by their actions in this narrative.

Lindars also refers to the manuscripts which have the article,[19] thereby hinting that the other disciple was understood by many scribes as the Beloved Disciple, but he contests this interpretation:

> . . . the identification is unlikely, because elsewhere John gives adequate description to avoid confusion (cf. 19.26), and also has a definite purpose in mentioning the Beloved Disciple. Here the absence of the article in the best textual authorities, and the fact that the disciple has no part to play once he has gained entry for Peter into the court, tell strongly against it.[20]

Gunther cannot reconcile the attitude and actions of the anonymous disciple with what he knows of the Beloved Disciple. Here in ch. 18, the disciple with Peter is stupid, disloyal and unloving, hardly the picture we would have of the Beloved Disciple

> The hypotheses that the beloved disciple appears in 18.15-17 and was himself a Jerusalem priest, presupposes that he who was most perceptive in understanding Jesus was stupid enough to bring Peter into mortal physical and spiritual danger, and disloyal enough to associate with the forces of the unbelieving world at the moment of conflict. This disciple performs no act of love. Nothing in his role or character is suggestive of the Evangelist's portrait. Peter and the beloved disciple stand in a very different relation than that assumed in 18.15-17.[21]

According to other interpreters, such as Haenchen,[22] Dauer[23] and

Barrett, the other disciple in this description has been introduced merely to get Peter into the courtyard of the high priest. 'It is not impossible that John was aware of an objection to the traditional narrative, that Peter would not have been admitted to the scene of the trial, and introduced the other disciple to answer it'.[24] There may be more of a purpose for the inclusion of another disciple than the rather mechanical one of transporting Peter into the courtyard, but aside from questions of the other disciple in 18.15, we only need to remind ourselves of the same apparently incidental physical function of the Beloved Disciple in the narrative we examined in the last chapter. To argue against identifying the other disciple here in ch. 18 with the Beloved Disciple on the basis that he has little part to play in the actual story line only serves to strengthen the argument for the identification, since the Beloved Disciple does not do much in any narrative where he is found. Potter finds difficulty in the identification with the Beloved Disciple because she does not think that any one who would have been undoubtedly a disciple of Christ would have been free enough to enter into the courtyard so easily. On this basis, the anonymous disciple must have been one of the 'crypto-Christians' we find in the Gospel, she reasons:

> The real difficulty is to see how one of the twelve could approach the high priest's entourage at this point in the gospel story, when Jewish hostility was exacerbated. So the 'other disciple' of 18.15 may be one of the leading people who believed in our Lord but not openly, the crypto-Christians of the time (cf. Jn 12.42); if this is so we can suggest Nicodemus or Joseph of Arimathea who came to the fore at our Lord's burial.[25]

Dauer adds to the arguments against the identification of the other disciple with the Beloved Disciple by suggesting that it is most improbable that the Fourth Evangelist would describe the Beloved Disciple as one who is known to the high priest. 'Es ist recht unwahrscheinlich, dass Johannes einen "Bekannten des Hohenpriesters", des grössten Gegners Jesu und Repräsentanten der ungläubigen "Welt" mit dem "Jünger, den Jesus liebte", gleichsetzen wollte'.[26] There have been various attempts to explain the nature of such a relationship between the Beloved Disciple and the high priest, ranging from the suggestion that John (i.e. the Beloved Disciple) had priestly family connections[27] to the suggestion that the acquaintance being described is not strictly with the high priest, but with some members of the household.[28] The force of γνωστός has also been debated. On the one hand, Schlatter argues that it carries a very weak force.[29] On the other hand, most scholars agree that the force of γνωστός in this context cannot be taken lightly. Other uses of the term in varying contexts suggest a rather close relationship. Barrett comments

> In the LXX it sometimes represents the Pu'al participle of ידע ('to know'; m^e *yudda*'), which seems to be used for 'familiar friend'; see 2 Kings 10.11, and especially Ps. 54(55).14. It was thou, a man my equal, my companion, and my *familiar friend*. The collateral form, γνωτός, may mean 'Kinsman' or even 'brother' (e.g. Iliad xv, 350, γνωτοί τε γνωταί τε, 'brothers and sisters').[30]

In light of the precedents set for an understanding of the force of γνωστός it is reasonable to recognize a *bona fide* acquaintance between the 'other disciple' and the high priest as being intended by the evangelist, even if it be that this relationship is being created for literary reasons. It is questionable whether or not it is legitimate to attach a negative evaluation to such a relationship, as Dauer does.[31] It is not wise to make any assumptions about the Johannine attitude toward such things as the high priesthood and then apply those assumptions as governing factors in the interpretation of what may be simply circumstantial details, especially if this reference is no more than a device to insert the Beloved Disciple into the story. 'A theology of the high priest lies beyond the intention of the evangelist'.[32]

Following other lines of reason, Gunther has proposed that Judas Iscariot is the anonymous disciple, painting a bleak and sinister picture of the motives of Peter's companion. Having betrayed Jesus, Judas goes on to betray his disciples

> The disciple who brought Peter into the courtyard had the sinister, devilish function of betraying Peter. Though he posed as a friend doing Peter a favour, he may have been setting a trap for Cephas as the potential ringleader of Jesus' disciples... such a negative role and unavoidably sinister motives befit Judas Iscariot.... He who entered with Jesus and his captors and who was known to these captors and the door keeper had sided with the ruler of this world. Once he had let Peter into a trap, he disappears inside (among the witnesses against Jesus—?), leaving Peter on his own.[33]

Gunther's speculations are unwarranted by the evidence. As Giblin points out

Nothing in vv. 15-16 suggests that he endangers his associate by
enabling him to enter into the palace courtyard, much less that he
tests him by leading him in. If anything, the contrary is true; *he
facilitates his co-disciple's contact with Jesus.* What ensues is not his
doing, but Peter's.[34]

A better account of what evidence we do have has led many scholars
to identify this anonymous disciple with the Beloved Disciple. The
fact that this has been the traditional understanding has influenced
some commentators to presume the identification.[35] Westcott is
categorical in his statement, 'The reader cannot fail to identify the
disciple with St. John'.[36] However, the popularity of a particular
position, or its affinity with the oldest and most traditional
understanding are not sufficient criteria to establish the accuracy of
such an interpretation.

Neirynck has estalished what can be considered as sufficient
criteria to make the association between the 'other disciple' and the
Beloved Disciple in a thorough study on Jn 18.15-16.[37] His article
compares the Johannine and Synoptic parallels, as well as focusing
upon other Johannine descriptions of an anonymous disciple and the
Beloved Disciple. The association of this other disciple with Peter in
18.15-16 shows notable similarity with 20.3-8 and consequently
Neirynck concludes that 18.15-16 should be assigned to the same
layer of Johannine tradition as 20.3-10. The source behind both
narratives can be found in a Synoptic 'Peter story', and in both,
maintains Neirynck, the role of Peter is duplicated and superseded by
the ἄλλος μαθητής. Note the continuing series of parallel literary
constructions which have the effect of equating the Beloved Disciple
(τὸν μαθητὴν ὃν ἐφίλει ὁ Ἰησοῦς) and the other disciple in John 20
with ἄλλος μαθητής in John 18:

18.15	ἠκολούθει δὲ τῷ Ἰησοῦ Σίμων Πέτρος καὶ ἄλλος μαθητής
20.3	ἐξῆλθεν ὁ Πέτρος καὶ ὁ ἄλλος μαθητής
	‒‒‒‒‒‒‒‒
18.15c	καὶ συνεισῆλθεν τῷ Ἰησοῦ εἰς τὴν αὐλὴν τοῦ ἀρχιερέως
20.6b	καὶ εἰσῆλθεν εἰς τὸ μνημεῖον
	‒‒‒‒‒‒‒‒
18.16a	ὁ δὲ Πέτρος εἱστήκει πρός τῇ θύρᾳ ἔξω
20.5b	(ὁ ἄλλος μαθητής) οὐ μέντοι εἰσῆλθεν
	‒‒‒‒‒‒‒‒
18.16b-d	ἐξῆλθεν οὖν ὁ μαθητὴς ὁ ἄλλος... καὶ εἰσήγαγεν τὸν Πέτρον
20.8a	τότε οὖν εἰσῆλθεν καὶ ὁ ἄλλος μαθητής[38]

The equation of the Beloved Disciple with the 'other disciple' in Jn 20.2 and the parallel construction of 20.3a and 18.15 is the telling focal point for his thesis. It would be a reasonable inference, in light of the work of Neirynck, to understand the 'other disciple' of 18.15-16 as the Beloved Disciple, as described in 20.3-10. Of course, the question is then raised as to whether or not the 'Beloved Disciple' of ch. 20 (using the word ἐφίλει) is to be equated with the 'disciple whom Jesus loved' (using the word ἀγαπᾶν) in other Johannine texts.[39] Boismard distinguishes between the use of ἀγαπᾶν and φιλεῖν. He attributes the use of φιλεῖν to the redactor who identifies the 'other disciple' with the Beloved Disciple.[40]

Brown, as well, sees the two titles as representing two stages of composition. Referring to the passage in ch. 20, Brown comments, 'The textual witnesses show variation in the clause "the one whom Jesus loved"; it is almost certainly a parenthetical editorial insertion, for in vv. 4 and 8 this man is called only the "other disciple", the more original designation'.[41] In any case, it is sound to assume that the text of the Fourth Gospel as it stands displays what is very probably intended to be an equation of the other disciple with the Beloved Disciple, the hero of the Johannine community.[42]

Assuming the identification, one is then forced to consider why this figure was included in the Johannine narrative. In stark contrast to Peter, the other disciple (i.e. Beloved Disciple) follows Jesus unhesitatingly into the courtyard. The word used here is συνεισῆλθεν. This word is used only in John, and in the Gospel it is found twice. In 6.22 Jesus is pictured as entering (συνεισῆλθεν) into the boat *with his disciples*. Although there may be some significance in the context of intimacy and discipleship, there are hardly enough grounds to conclude this. As in Jn 13.23-25, the Beloved Disciple's closeness to Jesus is highlighted here. It is not doing justice to the description to ignore the implied closeness of his intimacy and loyalty to Jesus and suggest that his only function in this narrative is to get Peter into the courtyard. '. . . This other disciple has virtually no other function in the narrative but to lead Peter inside. His only special qualification is that he can enter because he is known, and is known well enough to gain entry for still another'.[43]

A certain amount of contrast, coupled with a certain amount of cooperation, between the two is created when the Beloved Disciple serves as the instrument of Peter's entry into the courtyard. In this respect, it is interesting to note that the two have similar roles to play in relationship to each other in comparison with their interaction in ch. 13. Verse 16 of the narrative here in ch. 18 is the last time the other disciple is mentioned. In this verse he is described again (somewhat redundantly) as ὁ γνωστός τοῦ ἀρχιερέως.[44] After the Beloved Disciple introduced Peter to the maid who kept the door, attention focuses on the actions of Peter. It is important for us to examine fully the rest of the narrative even though the Beloved Disciple has faded into the background, because it will offer a clearer picture of the evangelist's portrayal of Peter.

Peter's first denial comes in response to a question from the doorkeeper. As was noted earlier, John is alone in referring to the ἡ θυρωρός. Consequently, Bultmann suggests that the feminine form is secondary and is the result of harmonization with the παιδίσκη of the Marcan tradition or due to a misunderstanding of the Aramaic text.[45] In the first section of this chapter, the possibility of this text being a combination of two stories was presented, as outlined by Dauer.[46]

We note that only in John does the maiden ask a question. The Synoptics report accusations. Furthermore, the question put to Peter by the doorkeeper uses the particle μή, which normally anticipates a negative answer. It is possible to understand the use of μή here as expecting a negative answer, indicating that the doorkeeper may not have believed that Peter was virtually one of the trouble-makers associated with Jesus, since he was a friend of the Beloved Disciple, who was in turn known by the High Priest. However, if the question is to be understood in this way, then again one is faced with the expectation of a negative response to the question put to Peter by others in 18.25. Given the fact that a positive answer is undoubtedly expected to the question that leads to the third denial in 18.26 it may be that the μή is to be understood with a slightly different nuance than the expectation of a negative response. Indeed, it may be that μή has lost a greater part of its force in Johannine questions. In Jn 4.29 the Samaritan woman whom Jesus met at the well asks the members of her community, μήτι οὗτός ἐστιν ὁ χριστός, and she honestly believes that he *is* the Christ. The use of μή in this has been characterized as the 'μή of cautious assertion'.[47] The use of μή may be associated with the incredulity of the situation in both instances cited (e.g. 'I don't believe it, but it appears as if. . . '). In any case, the Johannine account of Peter's 'interrogation' is easier on Peter and his image than the accusations of the Synoptics are.

Note further the use of καί with the sense of 'also' in the maiden's question. What the καί refers to is a matter of interpretation since it could refer to the Beloved Disciple (thereby giving it a particularly Johannine context) or it could refer to the disciples of Jesus in general (thereby giving it a context similar to that of the Synoptic accounts). Because καί is found in the Synoptic accounts as well as in John, it would be prudent to interpret it as referring to the disciples of Jesus in a general sense, rather than attaching any specific Johannine slant to it. If it were to refer to the Beloved Disciple, then we are faced with the problem of the maid *knowingly* allowing a disciple of Jesus into the courtyard after his arrest, although this may not have been as much of a problem as some might assume. We must remember that *Jesus* is on trial, not the disciples, not the followers of Jesus. This being the case, it may not have been as dangerous for Christians to be in the courtyard as we often assume. Agourides states:

> The question asked of Peter by the young lady, 'Are you not one of this fellow's disciple [*sic*]', and the similar questions later in the court, indicate that those asking the questions found it very natural to find some of the disciples of Jesus in the court, like John, for instance, who was known to the High Priest.[48]

To the maid's question, Peter responds 'οὐκ εἰμί'. In essence, then Peter is denying that he is a disciple of Jesus. Given the emphasis on discipleship in the last half of the Gospel, one may wonder whether or not the Fourth Evangelist is making his own statement about Peter and true discipleship. Only John uses the phrase οὐκ εἰμί to describe Peter's first denial, although Lk. 22.58 shares the phrase with John in Peter's second denial. Grundmann suggests that the οὐκ εἰμί of Peter's denials is to be understood in contrast to the positive ἐγώ εἰμι spoken by Jesus in 18.5 and 8. '... die Verleugnung des Petrus, bei Johannes als Selbstverleugnung gestaltet, indem den zweimaligen ἐγώ εἰμι Jesu (xviii 5, 8) das zweimalige οὐκ εἰμί des Petrus (xviii 17, 25) gegenübertritt...'[49]

This connection is entirely in keeping with the apparent thrust of the Johannine denials of Peter. The juxtaposition and resultant comparison of Peter and Jesus are further highlighted by the ἐγώ εἰμί/οὐκ εἰμί contrast, especially since it is clear that at least once the ἐγώ εἰμί has more than usual significance in this eighteenth chapter of John.[50]

It becomes strikingly obvious that the Fourth Evangelist is comparing Peter and Jesus in this passage when attention is paid to

the descriptive details of vv. 18 and 26. The very fact that the
mention of δοῦλοι occurs in both vv. 18 and 26, but in none of the
Synoptic parallels, causes the perceptive student to compare the two
verses. Indeed, this may have been the intention of the evangelist, for
v. 18 serves to set the stage for the transition to the second and third
denials, which are separated from the first denial by the interrogation
of Jesus in vv. 19-24. The mention of the slaves in v. 18, then, is
probably a preparation for v. 26, where one of the slaves puts the
final question to Peter.

John is not alone in describing the making of a fire, but he is most
specific in his description. He uses the word ἀνθρακιάν, which,
according to Liddell and Scott, refers to 'glowing pieces of charcoal'.[51]
This term is found in only one other place in the New Testament,
and that is in Jn 21.9, which describes the charcoal fire prepared for a
breakfast meal with Jesus and the disciples.[52] We will see that the
description in ch. 21 is probably intended to strengthen the ties
between Peter's experiences here in ch. 18 with his three-fold
'interrogation' in ch. 21.

One explanation of this detail runs along the line that John is
building in dramatic realism in order to bring a climax to his
scenario.[53] On the other hand, it is quite possible that a coal-fire was
described because that is exactly what it was, and hence we have an
account here that is based on an eyewitness source.

> This historical value of details peculiar to one or the other pre-
> Gospel traditions is not to be discounted quickly, although there is
> greater possibility that such details stem from the theological or
> apologetic concern of the respective tradition . . . Yet the acceptance
> of the thesis of an independent, early tradition underlying John
> should make us cautious about assuming too quickly that the
> doctrine, apologetics and drama *created* the raw material basic to
> the scenes involved. In our opinion John's genius here as elsewhere
> consisted in re-interpreting rather than inventing.[54]

All that can be said regarding the use of ἀνθρακιάν can also be
said regarding the explanatory phrase ὅτι ψῦχος ἦν that immediately
follows the mention of the fire. That is, it may very well be based on
first-hand experience. Even if it were to be understood as an obvious
implication derived from Mark,[55] it still contributes to the overall
function of v. 18 in a specific and purposeful way, for it adds to the
graphic picture being painted of a cold, dark spring night. A fire has
drawn servants and officers together to warm themselves while the

prisoner inside is being interrogated. Among these warming themselves is another suspect, Peter.

The last phrase of v. 18 explicitly states that Peter was among those around the fire. Special note may be made of the word μετ' αὐτῶν, in light of the special way these words are used earlier in ch. 18 to include Judas among those who arrested Jesus (cf. 18.5). If one were to extend the purposeful association employed in 18.5 to the similar construction pertaining to Peter here in v. 18, then one could conclude from the fact that Peter is described as being μετ' αὐτῶν (i.e. the servants and the officers) as signifying that Peter is no longer a true disciple, being among his accusers. However, this is not likely, because the Synoptics describe Peter in the same terms and the phrasing has a natural sense, whereas Judas has obviously been inserted for a reason in a place in which he is not logically necessary.

The stage has been set for the second and third denials, but before the reader can proceed the scene changes and vv. 19-24 recount Jesus' interrogation before Annas, where he is honest and candid in his responses to his questioner. The construction that situates Peter's denials around this interrogation of Jesus is very deliberate, for the contrast between the behaviour of Peter and that of Jesus is all the more stark. This construction alone should be enough of a clue to lead to the conclusion that the Beloved Disciple is not the primary counterpart of Peter in the narrative. Rather, Jesus and Peter make up the main contrast. The Beloved Disciple does indeed have a *secondary* role in the comparisons.

It was stated in the comparison with the Synoptics that only John declines to mention the passing of time between the individual denials. Moreover, the description of Peter standing and warming himself is explicitly reminiscent of v. 18.[56] Even the question put to Peter is a repeat of v. 17, except for the omission of τούτου. The impression left with the reader is that Peter's denials are happening in a concentrated period of time simultaneous with the interrogation of Jesus. This contrast is intended by the evangelist. Jesus stands up to his questioners and denies nothing. In fact, Jesus even states that those who know him will testify on his behalf (v. 21). Yet Peter fails to do so. At the same time, Peter does not stand up to his questioners and he denies everything.

One observation worthy of consideration is the difference in accusers between the first and second denials of John's account. In the first denial, the question is put to Peter by the servant-girl who kept the gate. In the second denial the accusers are among the servants and officers.[57] This difference in John may have been included in order to have a representative Roman group question Peter so that the 'world' in general may be seen to be involved in the events of the passion.

As was noted in the source-critical comparison with the Synoptics, only John offers the specific description of Peter's third accuser as εἷς ἐκ τῶν δούλων τοῦ ἀρχιερέως, συγγενὴς ὢν οὗ ἀπέκοψεν Πέτρος τὸ ὠτίον (Jn 18.26). John is alone in naming the man who was struck (18.10), and only he describe the familial relationship between Malchus and this servant who questions Peter. There are at least three possible explanations for the Johannine details.

First, they have been described as apocryphal embellishments. 'We must conclude either that behind the Johannine passion narrative there stands a first-hand source, or that John is himself elaborating in the manner of apocryphal gospels. The general lack of coherence in the narrative does not confirm the former alternative'.[58] Such embellishments were included for their dramatic effect or to create the illusion of realism.

The second possibility, which was dismissed so quickly in the commentary above, is that this specific description of the third accuser of Peter is evidence of a first-hand source. If this narrative is the account of an eyewitness, then one must conclude that the witness was familiar with many of the persons involved in the event. 'Some would explain this on the ground that the Beloved Disciple who is the source of the Gospel's tradition was the "another disciple" known to the high priest. If the name in v. 10 is fictional, the author has gone to pains to carry on the fiction'.[59] Furthermore, one is forced to conclude that the 'other disciple' in the narrative must be the Beloved Disciple, or else it is necessary to allow for *three* disciples to be present, which decreases the probability of the reconstruction.

While the present writer is inclined to accept that the Beloved Disciple is behind the first-hand source here, a third possible interpretation of the descriptive details commends itself. This third approach would assign theological import to the details, independent of questions of historicity.[60] The specific description of the accuser serves as a reminder of the scene at the garden. The reference to the relative of Malchus allows for the question, 'Didn't I *see* you in the garden?' In fact, the reference to the ear (ὠτίον) and the garden (κῆπω) relate v. 26 (and consequently the third denial of Peter) back to the narrative of 18.1-12 more than the Synoptic traditions do.[61] To put the comparison to the Synoptics in another way, Peter's action in the garden and not his dialect serves as the basis of the recognition of Peter here. 'According to Mark, Matthew and Luke, Peter was recognized because he was Galilean. Here is it quite different. He is recognized because he was seen at Gethsemane'.[62]

The persistent evocation of the garden may be intended to have the force of reminding the reader of Peter's valour now when he is most open to criticism. On the other hand, the reminder of events back in the garden now during his final denial may serve to double the condemnation of his behaviour. Note how Jn 18.11 records a rebuke of Peter for his violence[63] and now, in vv. 26-27, he is denying any association with Jesus. Indeed, he is actually denying that he was in the garden. In all of Peter's denials in the Gospel of John he denies any connection with his actions in the garden. In light of this, it could be that Peter's reticence in entering the courtyard is not so much a refusal to be identified with Jesus as it is a fear of retribution for cutting off the ear of the guard. As Neirynck comments

> In the other gospels, the assailant, who at the arrest of Jesus cut off the servant's ear, was 'one of those who stood by' (Mk. 14, 47), 'one of those with Jesus' (Mt 26, 51), 'one of them' (Lk. 22, 50). In John he is identified as Simon Peter and so Peter's presence in the courtyard is more dangerous for him than it is in the Synoptic account.[64]

In reference to Peter following ἀπὸ μακρόθεν, Neirynck goes on to say, 'Is it not to suggest that Peter is afraid of being recognized and that the entry in the courtyard implies personal danger for the disciple?'[65] This leaves us with two possible interpretations of the evangelist's deliberate pairing of the events in the garden with Peter's denials. Either he is bringing together two events that have the cumulative effect of highlighting aspects of Peter's behaviour that are inconsistent with true faithfulness and understanding with respect to the mission of Jesus or conversely he is seeking to point out why Peter, of all disciples, would have the most to worry about in this situation. His denials are denials of his violence in the garden more than they are denials of association with Christ.

No words are given to Peter's last denial in v. 27, whereas in the Synoptics his third denial is noticeably the most elaborate and lengthy. How does one account for this difference in presentation? It may be that on a literary level the Johannine account is the most primitive (although of course, Peter must have made some sort of oral response). On the other hand, it may be that John is being purposely anti-climatic by down-playing the denial, in order to soften criticism of Peter.

John is also the most sober of the evangelists in describing Peter's reaction to the cockcrow. 'It is difficult then to justify the contention that the Johannine account is consistently secondary'.[66] The simplicity of the response may be due to its relative primitiveness in the development of the tradition, but Maynard thinks that it is a deliberate omission. The 'absence of reference to his remorse' is 'clearly unfavourable to Peter'.[67] The difficulty with Maynard's reconstruction is that it goes against the direction one would expect the tradition to develop, i.e. from the shorter to the longer and from the more difficult to the easier. After all, one would expect the earlier, and not the later, form of the story to have some explanatory words in this final denial.

The abruptness of the ending in the narrative of Peter's denials has the dramatic effect of removing Peter from the gospel narrative. Fenton has made the interpretive observation here that, in light of Jn 13.36[68] Peter can no longer follow Jesus as he completes his work. 'Peter cannot follow Jesus through the passion, death, resurrection and return to the Father; Jesus must go first to prepare the way; then, afterward, Peter can and will follow'.[69]

Peter, having dramatically disappeared from the scene, does not reappear until ch. 20 at the empty tomb with the Beloved Disciple. Perhaps more pertinent to the narrative of his three-fold denial is his three-fold commissioning as recorded in 21.15-17, which may be intended as a parallel correspondence that serves to 're-instate' Peter.

> The Johannine tradition represented by John 21 found still another theological motif in the denials of Peter, namely that these denials could be atoned for only by a triple confession of Peter's love for Jesus (21.15-17)—a theological nicety not found in the Synoptic gospels.[70]

Both the re-appearance of Peter in the Gospel narrative (ch. 20.2-10) and his commissioning in ch. 21 will be examined in the following chapters, but at the present time it is necessary to continue our examination of events surrounding the arrest and crucifixion themselves. Peter may have left the scene, but the Beloved Disciple is still present. It is significant that from the point of the interrogations through to the crucifixion the Beloved Disciple remains with Jesus. It is possible to outline the broad chiastic structure of the main characters involved in these two chapters; the Beloved Disciple and Peter are paired in 18.15-16 (i.e. A & B); Peter is then juxtaposed to Jesus in 18.18-27 (i.e. B & C); and the Beloved Disciple returns as Peter drops out in ch. 19 (i.e. C & A). Note that John 19.26 describes him as 'standing by' (παρεστῶτα) at the foot of the cross.

C. *Jn 19.25-27*

Since the Beloved Disciple appears here at what must be considered a very significant point in the passion narrative, we must make at least a few comments regarding the evangelist's portrayal of his role and relationship to another central figure in the Gospel tradition— Mary, the mother of Jesus. The fact that Peter is not present may be noteworthy. Peter has been taken by some as conspicuous by his absence here, so that this passage has been taken as an indirect slighting of the figure. Agourides seems to imply this as he writes,

> After his denial, Peter vanished from the story. The beloved disciple, however, follows Jesus up to the end; he alone. Jesus from his cross entrusts his mother to John. He was next to the cross of the Master when he died, consoling his mother.[71]

If we were to follow Bultmann's interpretive scheme, we would be able to state that Peter's role as the representative of Jewish Christianity continues in this scene through the person of Mary

> The mother of Jesus, who tarries by the cross, represents Jewish Christianity that overcomes the offence of the cross. The beloved disciple represents Gentile Christianity, which is charged to honour the former as its mother from whom it has come, even as Jewish Christianity is charged to recognize itself as 'at home' within Gentile Christianity, i.e. included in the membership of the one great fellowship of the Church.[72]

Methodologically there is a problem with Bultmann's hermeneutic. If every person the Beloved Disciple is paired with is taken to be a representative of Jewish Christianity, as Bultmann and some others tend to conclude, then we may suspect that a rather rigid exegesis is governing the interpretation of the texts in which the Beloved Disciple occurs. Why must the Beloved Disciple invariably represent Gentile Christianity in all narratives? In turn, why must the different people he is paired with, in different situations, then be understood as representatives of Jewish Christianity? Are not the differences between the narratives significant and are not characters and contexts to be allowed to speak for themselves? If we first let the context and the particular dynamics of each individual narrative lead us to its own conclusions, then we are in a better position to evaluate the overall symbolism inherent in figures such as the Beloved Disciple, Peter, or, in this case, Mary.

Once more, as in our examination of other texts, it is wise to compare John's account of events at the foot of the cross with the Synoptic counterparts in order to isolate what may be particular Johannine emphases. In comparing this section of 19.25-27 with the Synoptics, we find some substantial differences. In the Synoptics the women are not mentioned until the end of the crucifixion scene, after the death of Jesus, whereas in its present setting, the women are mentioned before his death. Both Bultmann and Dauer, however, suggest that originally, even in the Gospel of John, this section was found later in the narrative.[73]

Dauer suggests that the traditional order of the account of the women at the cross was deliberately changed. Such a move has the effect of infusing the women's presence at the foot of the cross with deeper significance. The women no longer function *merely* as witnesses to the crucifixion, but they become definite counterparts to the unbelieving soldiers.

> So wird man mit großer Wahrscheinlichkeit annehmen können, daß erst Joh—und zwar bewußt—die Notiz von der Anwesenheit der Frauen hierherstellte, die er in seinem überlieferten Bericht (vielleicht entsprechend den Syn) an anderer Stelle vorstand. Ferner wird dann auch V. 24C vom Evangelisten gebildet sein; der Versteil ist an sich überflüssig, und dient lediglich zur Verdeutlichung der Kontrastierung Soldaten—Frauen, die sonst wegen des dazwischenstehenden Schriftzitates nicht so kräftig zum Ausdruck käme.[74]

There is some question as to the actual number of women present. The Synoptics state that there were πολλοί γυναῖκες (Mk 15.40; Mt. 27.55; Lk. 23.49—πάντες οἱ γνωστοί... καὶ γυναῖκες), with three explicitly named.[75] On the other hand, John could be read as referring to two, three or four,[76] although he probably intended this verse to be read as referring to four women, as a fitting counterpart to the four soldiers at hand who were involved in the crucifixion. 'They will stand by Jesus, quite in the Johannine manner'.[77] The μὲν. . . δὲ construction of vv. 24 and 25 which links the women with the soldiers substantiates this conclusion.[78] The confusion that arises when one tries to harmonize the Synoptics with John in the listing of the women at the cross should caution us against positing any literary dependence upon the Synoptics on the part of John. 'Our very difficulty in deciding whether the women mentioned in John are the same as the women mentioned by the Synoptics is eloquent argument against the thesis that John's list of the women was borrowed from the Synoptic lists'.[79]

In Matthew and Mark, the women are described as 'looking from afar' (ἀπὸ μακρόθεν θεωροῦσαι), in Lk. 23.49 they are 'standing at a distance' (εἰστήκεισαν... ἀπὸ μακρόθεν) while John states that they were 'standing by' (εἰστήκεισαν δὲ παρὰ) the cross.[80] R.E. Brown states

> Luke 23, 49, 'They stood at a distance', is almost a direct contradiction of John. (The Synoptic writers do not explain how the words of Jesus on the cross were heard and preserved). One can harmonize by claiming that during the crucifixion the women had stood close to the cross (John), but as death approached they were forced to move away (Synoptics).[81]

Bultmann reasons that John has to alter his source, which is contained in the Synoptic account in order to facilitate the interchange in vv. 26-27. Referring to v. 25, he writes,

> It serves as a transition to the episode in vv. 26f., which without doubt is the Evangelist's own composition. To make possible what is related in vv. 26f., the women have to stand immediately by the cross (v. 25), and for that reason the Evangelist has perhaps altered an ἀπὸ μακρόθεν of the source, such as is found in the Synoptics (Mk 15.40).[82]

Barrett holds that the Synoptic description is the most plausible, arguing that the women would not be allowed so near to the cross. Referring to Stauffer's work showing that sometimes friends would be allowd to come near the crucified,[83] he goes on to say that such precedents 'do not outweigh the military requirements of the execution of a rebel king'.[84]

> Josephus (*Vita*, 420f.) records that with special permission he was able to release three friends from their crosses; one survived. This shows both that there was a real danger of continued rebellious action, and that permission would be needed to approach the crosses.[85]

To balance Barrett's statements we must bear in mind that Jesus' crucifixion did not share the same level of intensity and security as the 'military execution of a rebel king'. The presence of *women* at the cross would probably not have aroused the suspicion and defensiveness of the guards in order to avoid insurgence.

While one may attempt to harmonize the Johannine and Synoptic accounts, or go the route of others and posit Johannine free handling of a tradition underlying the Synoptics, as Bultmann does, the discernment of theological motifs is perhaps the most illuminating method of accounting for an understanding the particularities of the different descriptions. Taking this approach, perhaps it is best to see the fulfilment of Old Testament prophecy in the Synoptic description. It may be that Lk. 23.49 represents a confirmation or fulfilment of Ps. 38.11, which reads 'My friends and companions stand aloof from my plague, my kinsmen stand afar off (ἀπὸ μακρόθεν ἔστησαν)'. In other words, John may reflect the actual situation more accuately than the Synoptics, which may be the product of a prophetic interpretation of Ps. 38.

To suggest that in this one detail John may be more accurate than the Synoptics is not to say that the Fourth Gospel does not reflect some degree of literary development of its own nor does this mean that John is not being creative in his own descriptions. Whatever material may be historically accurate in this narrative, John has taken it and worked it into his thematic and theological framework.

Mary the mother of Jesus and the Beloved Disciple are the central characters (again along with Jesus) for this section. The other characters are not important, relatively speaking. 'Clearly the names of the women have frequently oscillated in the tradition. On the other hand, the Evangelist is not interested in them as witnesses of the crucifixion; his interest centres on only one of them, the mother of Jesus'.[86] To Bultmann's observation we might add that Mary shares the evangelist's interest in the Beloved Disciple. How are we to understand the dynamics of the two and their relationship to one another and to Jesus in this narrative?

Not a few scholars have interpreted the significance of this passage on a purely literal level, i.e., that it shows Jesus' concern as a son for his mother to see that she is cared for after his death.[87] The usual reason offered as to why the Beloved Disciple was chosen, rather than one of Jesus' brothers, is well summed up by Sanders and Mastin:

... if they were the sons of Joseph by a former wife it is unlikely that they would be kindly disposed to his mother after he had been crucified. Jesus therefore makes provision for the care of his mother after his death.[88]

This interpretation has the advantages of simplicity and antiquity, but it is not without its shortcomings. If the scene is to be rooted in an actual event, filial care would have doubtless been its primary import, but as one author puts it:

The words spoken to Mary and the Disciple do more than express a concern for his mother after his death. Since he began his ministry, Jesus had left his home and family behind and so the use of the word 'son' has more theological significance than filial concern'.[89]

Even the context forces the reader to search for the deeper meaning. 'A non-theological interpretation would make this episode a misfit amid the highly symbolic episodes that surround it in the crucifixion narrative'.[90] On a more mundane level, Barrett raises a practical question concerning this situation that further causes us to look beyond the literal to the symbolic:

It is however, surprising that the brothers should be overlooked, for their lack of faith in Jesus (7.5) could not annul their legal claim, and indeed Mark suggests (3.31-35) that their unbelief was shared by the mother also.[91]

The unusual bonding carried out here, in a context that is pregnant with theological consequence which the evangelist has carefully constructed, leads to the conclusion that symbolism permeates the process of Mary and the Beloved Disciple being linked to one another by the pronouncement of Jesus. Its very setting at the foot of the cross gives it theological significance. R.E. Brown comments:

... The sonship and motherhood proclaimed from the cross are of value for God's plan and are related to what is being accomplished in the elevation of Jesus on the cross. A deeper meaning is also suggested by the verse that follows this episode in John: 'After this, [Jesus was] aware that all was now finished'. The action of Jesus in relation to his mother and the Beloved Disciple completes the work that the Father has given Jesus and fulfils the Scripture (see NOTE on 'in order to' in 19.28).[92]

If we were to judge the nature of the symbolism of this passage by the preponderance of material written on it, we would have to say that Mary is the primary character in this scene and that she represents, in one way or another, the Church. Volumes have been written from this perspective, focusing on Mary and what she symbolizes and it cannot be within the scope of this thesis to even attempt to deal with them, except to refer to some basic references.[93] Among more recent commentators who focus on the symbolism inherent in Mary, the majority tend to see her as somehow embodying 'Judaism',[94] 'Messianic Israel',[95] 'Israel (as over against the Benjamite Christians)',[96] 'Lady Zion',[97] or 'Eve'.[98]

However, it would be a mistake to focus on Mary as the sole, or even the prime symbolic figure here. It is certain that the Beloved Disciple is invested with as much symbolic character and import in this narrative as Mary. This becomes even more apparent if we accept R.E. Brown's literary reconstruction which leads us to conclude that the evangelist deliberately added the Beloved Disciple to a tradition that already contained the figure of Mary.[99] Snyder represents an approach that is most pertinent to our considerations:

> Whether Mary represents a certain branch of Christianity or Judaism or by the words of Jesus becomes the mother of all faithful or simply stands for herself, cannot be ascertained. But our approach does throw the scene into another frame of reference. . . I would say the figure of Mary serves to say more about the Beloved Disciple than about herself.[100]

Focusing upon the two in relationship and in particular upon the Beloved Disciple (as is the purpose of this study), we find a number of possible headings. Beginning with the natural sense of filial concern, Lindars has displayed a sound and moderate handling of the text, 'The piece takes the obviously appropriate theme of filial piety, and uses it creatively to suggest that the death of Jesus is not so much the end of his work as a new beginning'.[101] He resists what he calls a 'false path of exegesis' that attempts to assign a specific group to Mary's inherent symbolic character, stating that the pericope is concerned with the church only to the extent that 'it is concerned with the future'.[102] Further,

> A great depth of meaning is indicated by means of a very few words, composed with the utmost restraint. . . . What is actually said is that they should be in a new relationship. His mother loses her Son, but she gains a new son, one who most fully knows the mind of the Son whom she has lost. . . From this point of view the mother/son relationship of Mary and the Beloved Disciple has the

quality which could not have existed if Jesus had not been crucified. . . the point is the new life which results from the death of Jesus, a quality of life which transcends physical barriers.[103]

With Jesus' words 'γύναι, ἴδε ὁ υἱός σου' and (to the Beloved Disciple) 'ἴδε ἡ μήτηρ σου' the Beloved Disciple is shown to assume a special relationship to Mary akin to that which Jesus had with her. This has the effect of heightening the stature of the Beloved Disciple to that of 'brother' to Jesus. In fact, one author has suggested that the Beloved Disciple is 'closely identified with Jesus so as to be, in effect, his "alter ego"'.[104] Dauer has argued that this move to increase the importance of the Beloved Disciple by identification with Jesus was the primary motive behind this narrative. He offers two observations in support of this conclusion:

> a) Obwohl vom Jünger—im Gegensatz zur Mutter Jesu—noch gar nicht die Rede war, wird er plötzlich als anwesend gedacht und von Jesus angesprochen. Der Evangelist führt ihn also neu ein und zeigt damit sein Interesse an ihm.
> b) Entscheidend aber ist, daß in allen Stücken des Ev, in denen 'der Jünger, den Jesus liebte', auftritt, das Augenmerk jeweils in erster Linie auf ihn gelenkt werden soll. Um ihn geht es dem Evangelisten, und über ihn will er in immer neuer Weise eine wichtige Aussage machen.[105]

Snyder maintains that the Beloved Disciple is now to act in Jesus' place, emphasizing that 'this passing of authority occurred before the resurrection' in reaction to the post-resurrection claims to Petrine (i.e. apostolic) authority.[106] Goguel is another who sees in this passage a resistance to the claims of the apostolic tradition, particularly with respect to James, the brother of Jesus.

Actually, Goguel prefers to see this passage not so much as 'anti-apostolic' as 'anti-dynastic'.[107] Referring to James in particular, and the eventual belief of the brothers of Jesus, Goguel comments,

> At first sight it is natural to suppose that the Twelve made up his [i.e. Jesus'] spiritual family. But when the brothers of the Lord rallied to him, the idea occurred to some that those who were members of the natural family of Jesus because they were connected to him by ties of blood ought to take his place provisionally. . . We can justifiably maintain that a dynastic Christianity supplanted apostolic Christianity at Jerusalem in 44.[108]

Proceeding from this perspective, Goguel then interprets the passage
we are concerned with as an anti-dynastic response to the claims of
James for control over the church:

> ... The Fourth Gospel contains the incident of Jesus entrusting his
> mother to the beloved disciple (xix. 26-27) which we cannot help
> but consider to be an antidynastic point;. . . it remains true that the
> author of this incident did not know or did not wish to recall the
> presence of the brothers of Jesus in the church and disocciated his
> mother from them.[109]

Arguing from silence and pointing out the fact that Peter is not
connected with this narrative, except by his absence, those who
consistently find Peter and the Beloved Disciple contrasted throughout
the Fourth Gospel find in this narrative another strike against Peter.
'Difficult as are the details of the symbolism, it seems to say clearly
that the Beloved Disciple is the earthly successor to Jesus. This
would rule out Peter, and if Goguel is right, James as well, as having
unique authority in the church!'.[110] The problem with this assumption
is that, aside from the fact that Peter is not even remotely alluded to
in the text, the pronouncements made by Jesus cannot be taken with
any degree of certainty to affect the handing down of any ecclesial
authority. The case is stronger that these can be linked to 'adoption'
formulas[111] or the typical Johannine 'revelatory' formula[112] which
introduces to the insightful mind a revelation of salvific importance
that must be accepted on faith.[113]

Although Peter is consistently regarded as the chief historical
witness to the events of the death and resurrection of Jesus, in this
scene it does indeed appear as if the Beloved Disciple has assumed
the role that Peter carries out in other crucial areas, such as at the
empty tomb in ch. 20 and on the lake shore in ch. 21. Minear
highlights the special qualifications the Beloved Disciple would have
to testify to the certainty of Jesus' death

> Not only was this disciple a witness to the Supper, the betrayal and
> denial and trial; he was also the only male disciple placed by any
> Evangelist at the crucifixion (19.25-27). This surely bespeaks his
> courage in being present as the soldiers were carrying out their
> grim duty. It also qualifies him to verify the fact that Jesus had in
> fact died on the cross, whenever the rumour that he had not
> actually died should appear.[114]

If we are accurate in discerning this function as a witness with
respect to the Beloved Disciple here in 19.25-27, and we couple this

understanding with the reference to the witness of 19.35,[115] then we perceive a concern for actual witnesses to the events of the passion akin to the concerns reflected in ch. 21. As will be seen, this is an important observation as we consider the continuity between chs. 1–20 and 21 with respect to the function of the Beloved Disciple and the felt need in the community for empirical evidences for faith in Christ.

So to summarize the points gleaned from Jn 19.25-27 that are relevant to this study, it can be said that the Evangelist has creatively used traditional material concerning the witnesses at the cross. Tracing the movement of events, characters and themes, we find that Peter has disappeared from the scene, but the Beloved Disciple remains with Jesus right to the end. In this particular passage, which is at least intended to show that with Jesus' death a new life with new relationships is begun in the church, the main characters are now Jesus, the Beloved Disciple and Mary. It is overly speculative to attach too much specific symbolism to the figures of Mary and the Beloved Disciple here. It may be sufficient to maintain that the Beloved Disciple functions, at least for the Johannine community, as a witness to the actual death of Jesus. He also serves as a witness to the words of Jesus on the cross. There is not enough basis to say either that the Beloved Disciple is set up as a replacement for Jesus and his authority *or* as a challenge to Peter's authority in the church. At most, he serves as a channel of the revelation of Jesus in this particular context and as a substitute historical witness in place of Peter, who could not be present at this crucial scene due to the dynamics of the previous events in the courtyard.

D. *Conclusions*

This chapter has compared in some detail the Johannine account of Peter's denials with those contained in the Synoptic gospels, concluding that there is insufficient evidence to postulate literary dependency in a consistent direction. It appears that all the gospels based their work on a common tradition that must have been fairly well-known.

The particular Johannine treatment of this tradition reveals certain theological concerns. The fourth evangelist constructed his narrative in such a way as to convey the sense that Peter's denials of association with Jesus were simultaneous with Jesus' uncompromising defence of himself and his disciples before Annas. A dramatic contrast is created wherein Jesus denies nothing and Peter denies everything. This is a hermeneutical key to unlock the thrust of the passage. 'Peter as a representative disciple proves incapable of handling a situation in which Jesus has proved himself'.[116] Peter, like all the other disciples, is not able to follow in Jesus' footsteps to the end.[117]

Furthermore, by his composition, the author of the Gospel of John is able to bring to the fore the events in the garden at the climax of the denials. This graphic flashback has the effect of connecting the behaviour of Peter in the garden with his denials in the courtyard. It is suggested that this tactic is meant to present the reason behind and nature of Peter's denials, thereby softening the criticism to which Peter, the individual, becomes exposed. On another level, the pairing of these two events doubly serves to show Peter, and the disciples he represents, as lacking in faithfulness and understanding. Thus Snyder

> The naming of Peter (v. 10) as the disciple who cut off the ear of the high priest's servant simply stresses the importance of Jesus' real intent (v. 11), a stylistic *Dummheit* shared by all the disciples, and epitomized by Peter.[118]

In light of the picture painted of the all-too-human Peter, the mention of 'another disciple' in this narrative has been taken as a veiled reference to the Beloved Disciple in which the contrast between the two figures is then evident. 'The refusal of Peter to acknowledge his discipleship in the same surroundings in which John, the other disciple, stood, renders Peter's denial even worse'.[119] In the narrative the Beloved Disciple serves the peripheral function of gaining Peter access to the courtyard of the high priest—the scene of the denials. This action has been taken as another example of the mediatorial role the Beloved Disciple plays with respect to Peter and the disciples. 'Once more the conclusions from this narrative are that the Beloved Disciple stands on the side of Jesus and mediates to the disciples, represented by Peter'.[120] Again, in response to this postulation, one must ask the question, 'Was the Beloved Disciple actually serving as a mediator between Peter and Jesus?' In this case, it is even less clear that this is so than it was in ch. 13—after all, Jesus is not even involved in the narrative. It would be more accurate, and less helpful, to say that the Beloved Disciple served as a mediator between Peter and the doorkeeper. On another interpretive level it can be understood that the Beloved Disciple acts as a faithful, if not understanding, disciple who goes beyond Peter in following Jesus unhesitatingly to the foot of the cross. The Beloved Disciple is shown here to be intimately related to Jesus. By means of Mary and the Beloved Disciple Jesus reveals to the gospel readers that his crucifixion marks not the end, but the beginning of new relationships in the church. Because Peter is necessarily absent, the Beloved Disciple assumes certain testimonial functions alone. Peter and the Beloved Disciple are not directly compared and contrasted in either narrative examined in this chapter. Both are put in dynamic relationship with Jesus in order to illustrate very different theological themes.

Chapter 5

PETER AND THE BELOVED DISCIPLE
AT THE EMPTY TOMB

A. *Introduction*

The 'race' to the tomb by Peter and the Beloved Disciple in Jn 20.1-
10 is perhaps the one passage we are to examine in this work which
most obviously suggests to many readers a competitive relationship
between these two figures. Gunther represents the tenor of interpretations of this narrative along these lines:

> The fact that the beloved disciple ran quicker than Peter and
> reached the tomb first (πρῶτος) (20.4) could be explained by his
> youth; he was the last of the important disciples to die (21.22-23).
> But the Evangelist meant to emphasize not his vigour, endurance
> or age, but rather his primacy and Peter's following him (20.6) in
> love, devotion, expectant faith or at least in hope.[1]

However, in light of the more tacit findings of the previous
chapters and given the special history of the tradition involved in this
pericope, as well as the specific functions both characters will be seen
to play here, one must reserve judgment on this question until all the
evidence is balanced in perspective. We will discover that John's
account extends beyond his Synoptic counterparts in making the
empty tomb story a call to faith in the resurrection of Jesus. Both
Peter and the Beloved Disciple have vital roles to play in John's
reworking of the tradition.

The empty tomb stories as we have read them in John have their
parallels in all three Synoptics and research has ranged far and wide
in attempting to establish the relationships these accounts have to
one another. It is not possible to interpret Jn 20.1-10 apart from its
relationship to the Synoptics. As Neirynck concludes

> ... the Synoptics, the Synoptic tradition, the sources of the
> Synoptics, the Synoptic Gospels intervene constantly in the
> interpretation of Jn 20.1-18, and a Johannine scholar who would

prefer to neglect the Synoptic parallels will have to work in isolation from the current research on Jn 20. For each part of the text a synoptic parallel is to be considered: the woman at the tomb and the angelophany in Mk 16 and parallels, the visit of Peter to the tomb in Lk. 24.12, and the christophany in Mt. 28.9-10.[2]

Not only does a thorough comparison with the Synoptics enable us to evaluate the nature of the sources behind the four Gospels, but it also allows us to isolate the apologetic and theological concerns that are specific to John. Since John is alone in explicitly including the Beloved Disciple in this event, we must venture beyond source and redaction critical approaches, working with what we have isolated to be the Johannine emphases, in order to find *their* context and interpret their significance in light of that particular context.

In other words, source criticism will be foundational to our approach in this chapter, but while it is imperative, it does not answer the pertinent questions of this enquiry.[3] Our main task is to aim at a more exact definition of the concerns, understanding and intentions of the Fourth Evangelist, especially with regard to the roles and functions of the two who ran to the empty tomb—Peter and the Beloved Disciple.

With these comments in mind, let us turn now to an examination of the passage, beginning with a source-critical analysis and then moving beyond to John's message to his own readers.

B. *Jn 20.1-10*

The resurrection narratives of the discovery of the empty tomb all refer to Mary Magdalene as the first, or among the first, to see the empty tomb. Even though she is the only one named in all four Gospels, all accounts suggest that she was not the only one present.[4] Furthermore, in Matthew, Luke and John the initial discovery was then reported to the disciples (in the case of John only Peter and the Beloved Disciple receive the report).[5] It is only Luke and John which make reference to a visit by any disciple to the tomb. Luke 24.12, which is omitted by a minority of generally inferior texts,[6] reads, Ὁ δὲ Πέτρος ἀναστὰς ἔδραμεν ἐπὶ τὸ μνημεῖον καὶ παρακύψας βλέπει τὰ ὀθόνια μόνα, καὶ ἀπῆλθεν πρὸς ἑαυτὸν θαυμάζων τὸ γεγονός This verse seems preparatory for the passing remark of Lk. 24.24, although there is even some 'internal' inconsistency between Lk. 24.12 and 24.24[7] and it is very similar to the tradition reflected in Jn 20.3, 5, 6, and 10.

Even an examination of the Johannine account in isolation from its synoptic parallels produces some inconsistencies *within* the narrative itself. R.E. Brown has noted a number of these inconsistencies that reflect the combination and organization of disparate material:

(i) Magdalene comes to the tomb alone in v. 1, but she speaks as 'we' in 2.

(ii) She concludes that the body has been stolen, but apparently does not look into the tomb until 11.

(iii) There is duplication in the description of Peter and the Beloved Disciple:
—two 'to' phrases in 2;
—literally 'Peter went out. . . and they were coming' in 3;
—the repetition in what was seen in 5 and 6;
—the contrast between 'he saw and believed' in 8 and 'they did not understand' in 9.[8]

These and other discrepancies have posed problems for those who have tried to reconstruct the history of the composition of Jn 20.1-10. Did the Synoptics serve as the sources for what we find in John? Or, does the Fourth Gospel reflect an independent tradition? What was the form of the original tradition that John has built upon? How do(es) the original tradition(s) relate to the Synoptic account? Which descriptions are closest to the original? None of these questions have a ready answer, but perhaps the most strategic approach to take in isolating the process of composition of the resurrection narratives is to compare the two most similar accounts, that is, Lk. 24.12 (and 24) and Jn 20.1-10.

Before we can compare the Johannine with the Lucan account, however, we must note the differences between the two accounts of the visit to the tomb by the disciples which are found within this one chapter of Luke. Verse 12 describes Peter running to the tomb alone, seeing the grave clothes and going away in wonder. In comparison to this, v. 24 is a recounting of what happened at the tomb as told by the disciples on the Emmaus road. In this account, which is much less graphic, there are *at least* two disciples who went to the tomb. Note the plural in the text of Lk. 24.24; καὶ ἀπῆλθόν τινες τῶν σὺν ἡμῖν ἐπὶ τὸ μνημεῖον καὶ εὗρον οὕτως καθὼς καὶ αἱ γυναῖκες εἶπον, αὐτὸν δὲ οὐκ εἶδον. The apparent contrast between these two verses led Westcott and Hort, followed by a host of more contemporary scholars, to judge v. 12 to be a 'Western Non-Interpolation'.[9]

Schnackenburg notes that 'it is disputed from textual criticism whether this verse is original' and goes on to comment, 'In the context the verse fits badly. On account of this uncertainty, it is better not to reply on this verse from the view point of the history of tradition'.[10] Mahoney is even more direct in his understanding of the secondary nature of Lk. 24.12, calling it a 'late verse',[11] dependent upon Jn 20.1-10.[12] He concludes that 'internal criticism gives such support to the Western manuscripts at this point that we should prefer their reading to that of the normally superior Alexandrian text'.[13]

It is difficult to understand the reluctance of some scholars to recognize the obvious strength of the manuscript support given to Lk. 24.12.[14] Not only does it have the very early (i.e. 3rd century) support of the Bodmer papyrus (p^{75}), but it has a wide geographical and family range of support including Alexandrian (X, B, L, X, Δ, Ψ, 33, 1241), Caesarean (Θ, f¹, f¹³, 565, 700, 1071, Eusebius, Cyril), Western (W), and Byzantine (A, K, Π) manuscripts.

The difference between Lk. 24.12 and 24 can be explained in one of two ways. It is possible to see the development from the singular to the plural; i.e. originally the tradition had Peter going alone, but it later developed to include others in the visit to the tomb. Citing the support of Jeremias, Neirynck calls this a 'generalizing plural'[15] with the redactional purpose of minimizing the importance of the visit to the empty tomb as a basis for faith[16]

> 'Cleopas and his companion have to minimize the importance of the visits to the tomb, which are not grounds for hope. They do this by reducing the women to anonymity, γυναῖκές τινες, and the same vague plural is used of the second visit, even though Peter went alone...[17]

The other alternative is to regard the direction of development as moving from an original plural to mention of Peter alone. If this is the case, then it may be that Luke is indeed aware of a tradition involving others than Peter visiting the tomb,[18] but he chooses to narrow his emphasis to Peter in v. 12 in order to bring the account of Luke 24.1-12 to an appropriate climax. It has been noted

> By employing the plural in v. 24, Luke demonstrates his awareness of the more complex tradition. His focus on Peter in v. 12 is a stylistic ploy, designed to draw attention to this concluding verse of the empty tomb narrative.[19]

Richard Dillon has isolated a Lucan tendency to concentrate on Peter in scenes where parallels clearly involve others with him. In the calling of the first disciples and the miraculous catch of fish,[20] for instance, the Lucan account concentrates on Peter, to the point that the reader is mindful of no one else, yet we know that others are active participants. He concludes,

> The pattern is clear: reminiscence of sources in which a plurality of disciples were involved, but concentration on Peter... The plurality is the tradition's 'given', and it is Lk. who creates the impression of Peter's acting alone,—based, perhaps, on his having already obtained a position of leading exponent in the traditional story.[21]

If this is a genuine tendency of Luke, then we are justified in favouring the hypothesis that the original tradition was that Peter was not alone in visiting the empty tomb, and Luke prefers to focus on him in v. 12, *while being mindful of the plurality of disciples.*

The mention of the Lord's *appearance* (ὤφθη) to Simon in Lk. 24.34 may have been considered one more contradiction to v. 12 (in addition to the contrast created between 12 and 24) that prompted scribes to omit v. 12 in some of the manuscripts. It is relatively certain, on the basis of both textual criticism and the actual internal dynamics of ch. 24, that Lk. 24.12 does belong to the original Lucan text.[22] As many authors have noted, v. 12 serves as a natural, if not necessary, antecedent to v. 24.[23] Referring to Luke 24.24, Leaney has put it clearly: 'This refers to nothing in the previous narrative if we omit v. 12'.[24]

Even after we arrive at a satisfactory conclusion as to the originality of Lk. 24.12 on the basis of the text and 'internal' considerations, we are still confronted with the rather striking verbal similarities this verse shares with Jn 20.1-10, and so we have a further aspect to consider in our attempt to reconstruct the development of the tradition of the visit to the tomb. Note the similarities Luke and John share:

Luke 24.12	*John 20*
ὁ δὲ Πέτρος	ὁ Πέτρος (vv. 3, 4)
ἔδραμεν	ἔτρεχον
	προέδραμεν (v. 4)
τὸ μνημεῖον	τὸ μνημεῖον (vv. 3, 4, 6, 8)
παρακύψας βλέπει	παρακύψας βλέπει (v. 6)
τὰ ὀθόνια	τὰ ὀθόνια (v. 6)
	τῶν ὀθονίων (v. 7)

ἀπῆλθεν   ἀπῆλθον (v. 10)
πρὸς ἑαυτόν   πρὸς αὐτούς²⁵ (v. 10)

It has been suggested by some scholars that these phrases as they appear in Luke are to be understood as 'Johannisms' and as such are evidence of Lucan dependence upon John. Referring to the same terms listed in the above table, Schnackenburg argues 'their occurrence only once in Luke does speak for dependence on John (or his source)'.²⁶ This perspective is clearly a minority view on this point, basically because the evidence is so inconclusive. While on the one hand 'Johannine' vocabulary is discerned in Luke, on the other hand Luke's style is also evident in this one short sentence.²⁷ These factors have led both Lindars and Neirynck to suggest that Jn 20.1-10 is dependent upon Luke. Lindars is referring to Jn 20.1-10 when he states that 'it thus becomes possible to regard the episode as a fabrication based on the kind of hint given in Luke 24.24'.²⁸ Neirynck postulates that Lk. 24.12 is Luke's own composition, based on a free development of Mark 16:

> 'In sum, the possible connections with Mk. 16 (which is, I think, the only source used by Luke for his empty tomb story), the characteristically Lukan traits and the function of v. 12 in the composition of chapter 24 are, in my view, the indications for the Lukan origin of this little story.²⁹

He goes on to state that John depended to a relatively large extent upon this Synoptic source for his account in ch. 20

> The Synoptic influence, I think, surpasses the limits of so-called interpolations of 20.1-10 (Thyen, et al.), or 20.11b-14a (Boismard, et al.). It may have been determinative for the whole composition of Jn 20.1-18. The Johannine writer who depends on the Synoptics is not a secondary redactor but none other than the Fourth Evangelist.³⁰

In trying to establish the nature of the relationship between Lk. 24.12 and Jn 20.1-10 on the basis of shared vocabulary, one must realize the nature of the event that is being described. To some extent, the uniqueness of the event in its context limits the vocabulary that the evangelists could use. Jeremias goes so far as to say, 'The use of these words is required by the nature of the material and there can be no question of a specifically Johannine idiom'.³¹ Nevertheless, the verbal similarities between John and Luke are striking, especially the use of the historic present tense (βλέπει) with παρακύψας and Luke's use of ὀθόνια instead of σινδόνι as found in Lk. 23.53.

If we bear in mind that throughout the passion narrative, especially, Luke and John share some common details apart from Mark and Matthew, then this particular pericope becomes one more factor in support of the idea that Luke and John both borrowed from a common source independent of the greater Synoptic tradition.[32] 'It is important to recognize that the same source which we supposed for the passion and burial can and probably also does form the basis for this section too'.[33] In fact, the scholarly consensus has recently been favouring the 'common source' hypothesis for Lk. 24.12/Jn 20.1-10.[34] A reconstruction of the original source may run along these lines:

ὁ δὲ Πέτρος ἀναστὰς ἔδραμεν ἐπὶ τὸ μνημεῖον, καὶ παρακύψας βλέπει τὰ ὀθόνια κείμενα μόνα· καὶ ἀπῆλθεν πρὸς ἑαυτὸν θαυμάζων τὸ γεγονός, οὐδέπω γὰρ ᾔδει τὴν γραφήν, ὅτι δεῖ αὐτὸν ἐκ νεκρῶν ἀναστῆναι[35]

As previously discussed, the use of such a source does *not* preclude the knowledge, on the part of the evangelists, of the presence of *more* than one disciple at the tomb. In their original casting, the resurrection narratives of the empty tomb may have developed as apologetic traditions substantiating the reality of the resurrection. Peter's connection to them was valued as he was definitely to be regarded in the early church as the primary historical witness to the resurrection, as our oldest tradition on the subject makes explicit.[36] The specific witness of Peter at the empty tomb was probably to counter the argument that the body of Jesus was stolen, as Lindars defines:

> The motive for the tradition of Peter's visit to the tomb is to establish the fact that, though it was empty, the body of Jesus could not have been stolen, because the grave clothes were still there.[37]

It should be noted that the traditions of the visits to the tomb, both by the women and by the disciples, do not seem directed at interpreting the significance of the resurrection narratives or even eliciting faith in the resurrection. The women fled in fear and Peter went away puzzled.

> If we are correct in positing the existence of two Christian stories about visits to the tomb, one by women and one by disciples, it

would seem that in its earliest form neither story claimed that a visit to the tomb produced faith in the risen Jesus.[38]

On the other hand, Jn 20.1-10 reflects the editorial activity that has taken these traditions, and combined them along with particularly Johannine emphases, the most obvious being the highlighting of the Beloved Disciple.[39] The result is a theological statement that goes beyond that of the Synoptic scenes of the empty tomb. A comparison of the Synoptic accounts serves to isolate some particularly Johannine material, such as the words of Mary Magdalene to Peter, in 20.2, and the role of the Beloved Disciple in accompanying Peter, seeing the burial clothes, and believing in vv. 3-10. The evangelist/editor is incorporating some independent material and adding theological insights of his own. The question arises as to the stage at which the person of the Beloved Disciple was added to the narrative in the composition of the Gospel of John. Did the evangelist or a later editor incorporate this figure and his 'race' with Peter? Because of the typical way in which the Beloved Disciple is incorporated and the thoroughness of the reworking, in order to present a Johannine theological theme,[40] the hand of the evangelist himself seems evident. Thus Schnackenburg:

> ... the question must be seen and considered together with the other passages in which that disciple plays a part. For 13.23-26, it proved difficult to break out of the gospel's structure the scene with the uncovering of the traitor. Likewise, the striking out of 19.26f. is not convincing: how the editors actually worked can be recognized in 19.35... if we grant, the evangelist himself an interest in that disciple, his introduction into the visit to the tomb, that is the reworking of the narrative already there by the evangelist, becomes completely understandable.[41]

In highlighting the Beloved Disciple, John is transposing the narrative from a witness to the reality of the resurrection to an interpretation of the significance of the resurrection and as a model for the response of faith.

Such a theological reworking is not highly developed, as we shall see, but it nevertheless displays a definite development. Like Schnackenburg, Lindars compares this process with the one he has discerned in John 13 and the account of the Last Supper:

> So John uses more the homiletic technique which was so effective in his account of the Last Supper. Various traditions are retold in

such a way as to present one theme to the reader. In ch. 13 it was the theme of discipleship. In this chapter it is the act of faith.[42]

The observation that the Beloved Disciple and his act of faith are introduced here to accompany Peter to the tomb is enough of a clue to point in the direction the evangelist intended to go with this narrative. However, in order to arrive at a conclusion that accurately reflects the message of the narrative, it is now necessary to examine the pertinent details of the description of the relationship between the Beloved Disciple and Peter.

Jn 20.1 sets the stage by telling us that on the first day of the week, *while it was still dark*, Mary comes to the tomb to discover that it had been opened. The reference to the darkness (σκοτίας ἔτι οὔσης) has been taken as being theologically significant, especially given the reference to the sunrise in the Synoptics.[43] John is perhaps stressing the 'lack of understanding or spiritual blindness'[44] on behalf of Jesus' followers. Upon her discovery of the open tomb Mary Magdalene ran to report the news to Peter and the Beloved Disciple. It should be noted that the anonymous disciple is not described here in the same terms as in chs. 13 or 18. Here he is τὸν ἄλλον μαθητὴν ὅν ἐφίλει ὁ Ἰησοῦς (20.2) while in 13.23 he is ὅ ἠγάπα ὁ Ἰησοῦς and ἄλλος μαθητής in 18.15. If we were to make a distinction between φιλεῖν and ἀγαπᾶν it would be possible to argue that the Beloved Disciple of ch. 13 is to be distinguished from ἄλλον μαθητὴν ὅν ἐφίλει ὁ Ἰησοῦς here in ch. 20. Bernard has examined the use of φιλεῖν and ἀγαπᾶν in Greek literature in order to see if such a distinction can be made

> Of these two words it may be said that φιλεῖν is the more comprehensive, and includes every degree and kind of love or liking, while ἀγαπᾶν is the more dignified and restrained. But even so vague a description cannot be pressed very far... An analysis of the passages in which φιλεῖν and ἀγαπᾶν occur in Jn. shows that they are practically synonyms in the fourth Gospel.[45]

While we might like to qualify Bernard's characterization of ἀγαπᾶν as 'more restrained' most interpreters tend to agree with the conclusion that the two verbs are used synonymously in the Gospel of John. Both verbs are used to designate God's love for people, the Father's love for the Son, Jesus' love for people, the love of people for other people and the love of people for Jesus.[46] In light of this, and in light of the character of the Beloved Disciple reflected here, it is highly unlikely that this is a reference to a second 'beloved disciple'. Therefore the discussion will proceed on the assumption that the same person, the Beloved Disciple, is depicted as present in all three scenes and is the central hero of the Johannine community.

Even though Mary Magdalene reports that the body of her Lord is no longer in the tomb, the evangelist is careful to suggest that she did not actually go into the tomb to see that it was empty until after the two disciples had seen it (cf. 20.11. Her words οὐκ οἴδαμεν ποῦ ἔθηκαν αὐτόν have been read by Minear as a reflection of the Johannine community's mindset, the unexpressed subject of the verb ἔθηκαν being the Jews and the first person plural of οἴδαμεν being the 'we' of the Johannine community.

> It is strange that commentators who detect in other Johannine uses of *we* the voice of the Christian community (1.14; 3.11; 4.22; 9.31) do not allow Mary to be that voice in this instance. Such an identification here would strengthen the connections to the *we's* that are so prominent in First John. In this case we would have in 20.2 further evidence of the tension between church (we) and synagogue (they) in John's authorship.[47]

Minear's bewilderment at the hesitation of commentators to allow Mary to be the voice of the Johannine community here is in itself strange, for such reservation on the part of interpreters is no doubt based on a straightforward and sensible reading of the text. If the evangelist wished to form a contrast between the community and the synagogue, one would expect that pronouns would have been employed.[48]

That Mary is described as going first to Peter indicates that Peter was to be regarded as the leader of the disciples. On this point, then, the Fourth Gospel concurs with the Synoptics. Again Peter is mentioned first in the next verse (v. 3). It is difficult to ascertain too much from this, for the only reason for the primacy of Peter may be his place in the original stories before they were incorporated into the Gospel of John. 'Peter is mentioned first, as he is the subject of the underlying tradition'.[49]

If we try to keep a perspective on the context of the events leading up to this particular event, then Peter's proximity may be the reason why he would have been the first to hear the news. 'It must be remembered that he did not flee with the others and is recorded as being near at hand during Jesus' interrogation by the Jewish authorities (Jn 28.27)'.[50] Indeed, this may be a factor, but it does not explain why Peter would hear the report before the Beloved Disciple, for he was recorded as being present throughout the interrogation and crucifixion as well (cf. 18.15-16) and 19.26-27). Of course, even if both heard it at the same time, someone had to be listed first. The fact that Peter was the first to be listed is probably due to his position in the original tradition. If this is the case, then we need to note that it was not contrary to the evangelist's purpose to have him remain in that position. His importance in the scene is not disputed.

The Run to the Tomb
The two are pictured as running off toward the tomb together. They start off together, but halfway through this verse the evangelist separates the two and the Beloved Disciple reaches the tomb first. That they are running should not be regarded as any more significant than Mary's previous haste in making her way back from the tomb to report to them. That is, the sense of urgency and excitement would be enough to account for the two disciples taking off toward the tomb at a run, without any implication that the two were competing with one another in a race. Surely it is understandable that their attention would be focused on Jesus and the tomb rather than on each other.

Nevertheless, twice the Gospel makes it clear that the Beloved Disciple arrived at the tomb ahead of Peter. The point must be taken with the same emphasis it is given. To regard v. 4 as a pleonasm[51] which has no rhetorical purpose or comparative stress does not account for v. 8, which *again* reminds the reader that it was the Beloved Disciple who reached the tomb first. The problem, however, is one of interpretation.

What is the reader supposed to gather from the fact that the Beloved Disciple arrived at the tomb ahead of Peter? It must be more than a reflection of the youthful vigour of the Beloved Disciple.[52] Likewise, natural explanations such as the suggestion that 'the Beloved Disciple was more familiar with the way than Peter and took a short-cut to the tomb'[53] border on the naive. 'Ishodad of Merv traces John's greater speed to the fact that he was unmarried!'[54]

Since the evangelist stresses the Beloved Disciple's arrival at the tomb, a symbolic interpretation commends itself. Lindars interprets this as 'a hint of his being the first to believe in the resurrection'.[55] Indeed, others have seen in this verse a literary device of foreshadowing and suspense leading up to the climax of the pericope—i.e. the coming to faith of the Beloved Disciple.[56]

It is not strange to find in the Fourth Gospel the Beloved Disciple running the fastest to the tomb of his Lord and coming to belief first. After all, this Gospel was written to a community that emphasized his love and sought to emulate his discipleship. 'Naturally the Beloved Disciple outdistances Peter—he loves Jesus more'.[57] But does this suggest, then, that there was a *bona fide* race between Peter and Beloved Disciple, intended to depict a rivalry? This is not demanded by the narrative. Once more R.E. Brown offers a careful evaluation of the question of the two figures in relationship. Even though he is inclined to see a deliberate comparison of the Beloved Disciple and Peter throughout the Gospel, he does not interpret this particular scene as a slight against Peter. 'We see no basis for all the polemic and symbolic interpretations; the writer is simply telling us that the disciple who was bound closest to Jesus in love was the quickest to look for him'.[58] One could only infer that Peter is slighted here by accepting symbolic interpretations built entirely upon innuendo.

> The text permits too many different symbolic interpretations; if the evangelist had wanted his text to be understood symbolically, he would have at least given his reader more definite help: at the very least, even unintentionally, through more consistent use of his symbols.[59]

The description of the Beloved Disciple arriving at the tomb ahead of Peter serves at most to highlight the ideal love the Beloved Disciple had for Jesus. Mahoney suggests that even this was not intended. Rather v. 4 was a device to bring the two disciples separately on to the same scene for related but independent assignments'.[60] That they had to arrive separately is reasoned out in convincing detail by him. Beginning with the postulation that the Beloved Disciple and Peter had *different* but related assignments in a story that had the single climax of one disciple coming to faith, he outlines the different disadvantages of having Peter arriving first and carrying out his assignment, followed by the Beloved Disciple's arrival and coming to faith. Basically, the story lacks integration this way. Having the two arrive together to carry out separate assignments is similarly inadequate in terms of integration, graphic description and intensity.

> The present arrangement, whereby the other disciple arrives, glimpses into the tomb's interior, then Peter arrives, enters and

fulfils his assignment, followed by the other disciple, whose faith forms the climax to the story has the following clear advantages: 1) the story is better woven together, so that the disciples' two assignments are two aspects of the same story and not two stories; 2) the burial cloths in the tomb's interior are brought more clearly to our attention; and 3) the general dramatic effect is much greater, delivering the other disciple's faith as a more convincing climax.[61]

As sensible and attractive as Mahoney's interpretation is, we need to add to it and suggest that it was not merely good literary style, that dictated that the Beloved Disciple should arrive first and yet 'act' last. To consider stylistic factors alone is to ignore the sentiments of the Johannine writer and his readers. At the same time, if Peter was to be snubbed by losing a so-called 'race' to the tomb, it is difficult to see the motives behind the complimentary protrayal of him in the next few verses (5-8).

Peter's Entrance into the Tomb

Even though the Beloved Disciple reached the tomb first, v. 5 describes him as stopping short of actually entering the tomb. He is described only as 'stooping to peer' (παρακύψας βλέπει) into it from the outside. Mention has already been made of the fact that John shares this use of the historic present with Luke. The actual meaning of the phrase is 'to peer in'.[62] We need only to note, at the present time, that this is the first of four phrases conveying the idea of 'seeing' (i.e. βλέπω, ὁράω and θεωρέω) found in this pericope.[63] He waited for Peter to arrive, and after Peter went in (v. 6), he followed.

Needless to say, interpretations vary as to why the Beloved Disciple is made to stop and allow Peter to enter first. Morris attributes this action to the personality of the Beloved Disciple.

> Apparently the Beloved Disciple was a somewhat diffident or hesitant man. He had not begun this race to the tomb, but he had waited until Peter took the initiative. Now arrived at his destination, he hesitated to go into the tomb. He contented himself with standing outside and looking in.[64]

This may simply be a continuing of the climactic dynamics employed by the writer, as was previously suggested. Lindars adopts such an interpretation, stating, 'This feature is part of John's delaying tactics, so as to build the narrative to a climax'.[65] Hoskyns explains it further by suggesting 'his entrance is delayed in order that his faith may form the climax of the narrative'.[66]

If the figures in this passage are to be understood symbolically, difficulties in a straightforward interpretation are encountered, for 'the narrative is constructed in such a way that each can claim precedence over the other'.[67] However, the symbolism may not be so straightforward in favouring one figure over the other. Kremer has discerned purposefulness in such ambiguity. Because the Beloved Disciple had won the 'race' against Peter in v. 4, he suggests that some of Peter's honour is returned to him in this sixth verse:

> Dabei lief der Lieblingsjünger schneller und gelangte vor Petrus zum Grab. . . Er beugte sich vor und sah die Linnentücher liegen. Auffallenderweise ging er aber nicht als erster in das Grab hinein. Er überließ Simon den Vorrang. Dieser ging zuerst in das Grab. . .[68]

Schnackenburg maintains that both figures are depicted positively, primarily for the benefit of the Beloved Disciple. The prestige of Peter serves to strengthen that of the Beloved Disciple. 'In no place is Peter criticized or devalued. Perhaps, the "other disciple" is meant, in a certain sense, to be "up-valued" even, by way of Peter's authority'.[69]

Agourides has proposed the interesting hypothesis that serves to highlight the Beloved Disciple *in spite* of the fact that Jesus did not appear to him (as he did later to the Twelve),[70] because he did not *need* to see Jesus.

> If we look a little further, we can say that there is no tradition in the Church about a private appearance of Jesus to His beloved disciple. Verses 1-9 in Chapter 20 would suggest, I think, that this was unnecessary, because it was John who first, among Jesus's disciples and followers, believed in Christ's resurrection on the basis of the empty tomb.[71]

If we take into account the earlier tradition upon which the Johannine account is built, we may arrive at the most accurate interpretation of the two disciples in relationship. The older tradition apparently held that Peter was the only one to enter the tomb, and some suggest that in light of this the writer of the Fourth Gospel was compelled to accommodate himself to this.[72] However, it could very well be that the evangelist himself may not have resisted the pressure to conform to this tradition; he may have welcomed it. This all depends on whether or not he wanted to highlight the particular role of Peter for his own purposes. In any case,

Peter was in the original form of the story; and so, while the introduction of the Beloved Disciple inevitably created a contrast, to an extent that contrast is accidental and scarcely a major aspect of Johannine polemic. Moreover, to be precise, the Beloved Disciple is placed in Peter's company and is not set over against him.[73]

In short, then, the hesitancy of the Beloved Disciple is best seen as an accommodation of the inclusion of the Beloved Disciple into the original tradition. It has the effect of building to the climax of v. 8 and, further, it may be designed to highlight the function or roles of both characters in the story.

That Peter follows the Beloved Disciple to the tomb, yet enters it first has also been interpreted variously. Some, such as Barrett and Maynard, suggest that the description of Peter following the Beloved Disciple (ἀκολουθῶν αὐτῷ) has more than merely descriptive, literal significance. 'Since the term "to follow" is a technical term for becoming a disciple in the Fourth Gospel, it is probable that it is here used to subordinate Peter to the Beloved Disciple'.[74] This conclusion rests entirely upon a specialized interpretation of a word that has a more basic meaning, even in the Fourth Gospel.[75] Furthermore, in John it would be most inappropriate for the evangelist to suggest that Peter, or any other of Christ's disciples, was a 'follower' of someone other than Jesus.[76]

Peter's immediate entrance into the tomb has been contrasted with the Beloved Disciple's hesitancy in terms of reverence on the part of the Beloved Disciple, as compared to the characteristic impetuosity of Peter. Thus Lightfoot:

> We are perhaps to understand that a natural reverence and reserve
> at first prevent the beloved disciple from entering the tomb; only
> where his companion, who is of a different temperament, has
> entered does he follow.[77]

It would not be out of character for Peter to behave in this way, but the very observation that *twice* the Beloved Disciple is described as arriving there first and yet waiting for Peter to enter the tomb first suggests that the evangelist may have wished to highlight the fact that Peter was first to go in. To emphasize the order of events merely to affirm a characteristic trait of Peter's personality seems superfluous. There must have been more to the description than that.

Mahoney has made a discerning observation that may validate this consideration. He notes that the full name of 'Simon Peter' is uncharacteristically used here. As discussed earlier in this work,[78] it is the normal practice in the Gospel of John to use the full name for the first time Peter is named in a pericope. The full name is used in the midst of a pericope in John 13.9; 20.6 and 21.3, 7, 11. Given the context of these passages, this variation does seem to be significant. The evangelist is fully aware of Peter's important role in the scenes. This 'swelling of emphasis' or 'unexpected formality'[79] may betray the intended significance Peter had in mind of the evangelist at the particular moment in the narrative.

Peter—Witness to the Empty Tomb
For what reason should the reader take note of Peter's presence here? The passage describes him as entering the tomb and seeing the linen clothes lying there separate from the napkin which was around Jesus' head. The Johannine description seems to stress the way in which the grave-clothes were arranged (cf. 20.5, 6, 7). Some scholars have interpreted this to mean that the clothes remained in a bodily form like an empty shell lying in position where the crucified body of Jesus had lain before his resurrection.[80] Commenting on the word ὀθόνια, as found in both John and Luke, Fitzmyer counters this postulation.

> The word, however, says nothing of the shape of the cloth. Bands such as those used on Egyptian mummies are unknown for corpses in Palestine; hence it is out of the question here.[81]

A more considered suggestion is that the clothes are actually described as folded in a tidy arrangement.[82] While both possibilities concerning the condition of the grave clothes would suggest that Christ had come back to life, the former situation is less likely to be the case for a number of reasons, not the least of which is, as R.E. Brown has noted:

> Such a theory demands that Peter also should have come to believe; for if the position of the clothes miraculously preserved the image or location of the body, Peter could scarcely have missed the import. Yet Luke 24.12 reports that Peter 'saw the cloth wrappings lying there, and he went home wondering what happened'.[83]

That the Gospel of John reports only the belief of the Beloved Disciple is not insignificant to this observation, and it merits discussion later. The details of the condition of the grave clothes are emphasized to suggest that Jesus' body was not stolen. That Peter was there first to see it indicates that he serves to verify this claim. Peter serves as an observer of the actual conditions of the empty tomb and thereby verifies the conditions of the empty tomb for the early church, as is evidenced by Luke and John.[84] His function is to verify the resurrection by serving as the best-known witness to the earliest evidences of the resurrection. It is the 'evangelist's own concern to anchor each stage of Jesus' going to the Father in tangible, earthly reality. Peter's assignment at the tomb is to carry this emphasis'.[85]

Contrary to what might be expected, the capacity in which Peter performs is actually heightened by *not* being linked to any response of faith on the part of Peter pertaining to the significance of what he saw. Peter did not immediately understand the significance of what he saw, therefore his witness can be regarded as an objective report of the actual physical situation. There was no anticipation or incipient faith to cloud his vision.

The Beloved Disciple—The Response of Faith

In contrast the Beloved Disciple performs an entirely different function in this narrative. Verse 8 reads τότε οὖν εἰσῆλθεν καὶ ὁ ἄλλος μαθητὴς ὁ ἐλθὼν πρῶτος εἰς τὸ μνηεῖον καὶ εἶδεν καὶ ἐπίστευεν. Juxtaposed to Peter's assignment in this pericope is that of the Beloved Disciple. 'The assignment of the other disciple is having seen what Peter saw, then to believe'.[86] The Beloved Disciple, the hero and example for the Johannine community, 'drew the only possible conclusion from the facts'.[87] Picking up on the use of three separate words for 'seeing (i.e. βλέπω, ὁράω and θεωρέω) in this passage, Maynard finds a distinction being made here between the discernment of Peter and that of the Beloved Disciple.

> These three words for seeing have been used with strict respect for their variant shades of meaning. Before he enters the tomb the other disciple 'sees' in a general sense, Peter when he enters only 'observes' the physical scene, but the Beloved Disciple upon entering 'sees with spiritual insight' and the result is faith. Thus the evangelist has recognized the tradition that Peter was the first to observe the empty tomb, but by choice of words as well as by outright statement he has suggested that Peter came following another, that his observance did not lead to faith, and the first to hold the resurrection faith is the Beloved Disciple. Peter does not fare well in this story.[88]

It does not say that the Beloved Disciple believed, and perhaps one is to understand from v. 9 that his faith was not yet fully formulated. Some have followed the lead of Augustine in suggesting that the Beloved Disciple did not believe that the resurrection had taken place, but rather he merely believed the words of Mary Magdalene when she reported the body was missing.[89] 'They now believed Mary's report and thus joined in her confession of ignorance, "we don't know where"'.[90] In support of this conclusion, Minear offers three arguments:

1. Verse 9 (i.e. '. . . as yet they did not know the Scripture') makes no sense 'at all' if at this time the beloved disciple saw and believed in the Resurrection.
2. Verse 10 (i.e. 'they went back to their homes') 'excludes' the possibility that this verse refers to the resurrection.
3. John proceeds in chapter 20 as if the later narratives are the first instances of appearances and attendant resurrection faith.[91]

Besides the fact that vv. 9 and 10 do not rule out a prior belief in the resurrection (as Minear would try to argue),[92] a simplistic interpretation such as this hardly seems adequate for the thrust of the passage, in light of the portrayal of the Beloved Disciple throughout the Gospel. As R.E. Brown comments, '. . . The evangelist certainly did not introduce the Beloved Disciple into the scene only to have him reach such a trite conclusion'.[93] Bultmann suggests that the faith of the Beloved Disciple was a full-fledged faith in the resurrection of Jesus.

> In this context the faith that is meant can only be faith in the resurrection of Jesus; it can be signified by the abs. πιστεύειν, because this means faith in Jesus in the full sense, and so includes the resurrection faith.[94]

Consequently, Bultmann concurs with Benoit and Hartmann in interpreting v. 9 (i.e. οὐδέπω γὰρ ᾔδεισαν τὴν γραφὴν ὅτι δεῖ αὐτὸν ἐκ νεκρῶν ἀναστῆναι) as an ecclesiastical redaction reflecting the thought of the community.[95] On the other hand, it is legitimate to consider this reference to be part of John's source, as we see similarities in Lk. 24.4-6 and 24.46. The community theology interested in the prediction of the resurrection[96] is no doubt present here but it is most difficult to ascertain the stage at which such community theology was incorporated into the Gospel. For example,

John 12.14-16 reflects a similar perspective, yet Bultmann takes this passage to be original, whether it be from the evangelist or his source.[97]

Haenchen perceptively explains how v. 9 functions to clarify how the Beloved Disciple came to a point of belief that Jesus was resurrected while Peter still remained in the dark. It has the advantage of neatly placing v. 9 into the narrative as an integral part of the whole, rather than a paranthetical addition.

> Verse 9 gives the reason it was necessary for the disciples to see the empty tomb, the bandages and the like in order to come to faith: they did not yet know the scripture foretold the resurrection of Jesus... There is thus no reason to omit this verse as a later addition, or to think that Peter also became a believer. The lack of knowledge of the scripture makes both points comprehensible: one disciple becomes a believer, the other doesn't.[98]

Furthermore, the tradition that Peter and his companion(s) left the site wondering what happened, as evidenced by Lk. 24.12, may have been behind v. 9, which would explain, in part, the change from the third person singular in v. 8 to the plural in v. 9. If the evangelist actually intended v. 9 to refer to both Peter and the Beloved Disciple, then it would be necessary to interpret this verse to mean that the faith of the Beloved Disciple was not yet fully developed. That is, the Beloved Disciple had faith that Jesus had in fact risen, yet the significance and ramifications of that fact had not yet been fully realized. 'The Beloved Disciple has understood it correctly, and so come through to faith, but the substance of his faith has still not been formulated'.[99]

The Complementary Significance of the Partners

Nothing is said of the faith, or lack thereof, of Peter. Bultmann maintains that Peter did believe

> Clearly it is presupposed that Peter before him [*i.e. the Beloved Disciple*] was likewise brought to faith through the sight of the empty grave; for if the writer had meant otherwise, and if the two disciples were set over each other with respect to their πιστεῦσαι, it would have had to be expressedly stated that Peter did not believe.[100]

In order for Bultmann and others to presuppose that Peter was brought to faith at the sight of the empty tomb, it must at least be presupposed that it was the author's intention to set the two disciples over each other with respect to their faith response. Such a presupposition causes problems, for as we have noted in other passages, we cannot start with the assumption that the two disciples are set over each other in a direct contrast. If it was *not* the evangelist's intention to portray the two in a rivalry corresponding to their capacity for faith, then one would not expect to have a reference to Peter's response regarding belief juxtaposed to that of the Beloved Disciple's.

Hoskyns,[101] Barrett,[102] R.E. Brown,[103] Haenchen[104] and Lorenzen,[105] among many others, all suggest that Peter did not believe until later, which seems most likely. Nevertheless, it is pushing our interpretation into the realm of imagination to state, 'Presumably the beloved disciple explained to him the meaning of the empty tomb while they were returning home'.[106] On the basis of this passage alone the question of Peter's faith must remain open. It is the Beloved Disciple's act of faith without seeing the resurrected Lord that is highlighted. It is not within the evangelist's purpose to reveal whether Peter came to faith or not, although one might assume that if Peter did come to faith, there would be no reason even to introduce the Beloved Disciple into the story.[107]

No contrast is intended between the faith of the Beloved Disciple and apparent lack of faith on Peter's part. Rather, the faith of the Beloved Disciple is emphasized for the purpose of encouraging the readers to respond in a similar act of faith. 'John is not interested in such polemical questions. He is concerned that the reader should believe, and sets the Beloved Disciple before him as the first example for him to follow'.[108]

As an example of the ideal response of faith, the Beloved Disciple epitomizes the highest form of faith as a personal encounter with Jesus independent of a resurrection appearance. Osborne has proposed that throughout Jn 20–21 we have a deliberate outline of the types or levels of faith at which Jesus encounters his followers

> John moves beyond Luke in this emphasis, presenting his evidence in a kind of descending spiral form from the highest type of faith to the lowest or most meagre kind of faith. He thus presents the 'beloved disciple' who comes to faith apart from empirical proof (or from 'understanding', v. 9) on the basis of love, to the lowest type, or cynical Thomas who demands physical proof. Somewhere between these extremes is Mary who did not recognize the truth without the 'call' of the Good Shepherd (cp. 10.34), and the

Twelve, who needed to see the Risen Lord to overcome their fear. The Gospel of John emphasizes that Christ encounters each person at the level of his faith, since faith, whether great or small, is still valid for belief.[109]

From this scheme we can see that Osborne correlates Peter and the Beloved Disciple, giving them identical roles to assume (i.e. models of 'faith responses'). Indeed he does state that he theorizes 'a positive role for both [i.e. the Beloved Disciple and Peter] as paradigms for discipleship'.[110] He also sees the Beloved Disciple as 'the apostolic authority behind the resurrection claims (witness)' in the same way he regards Peter.[111] In light of our analysis of this passage and of earlier sections, we may question whether or not Peter is upheld in the Gospel of John as a paradigm for discipleship. It appears he does not serve as the perfect model that the Beloved Disciple does.

If the evangelist constructed this particular narrative to bring his readers to faith in the resurrection of Jesus on the basis of Peter's objective historical witness to the empty tomb, it is not difficult to understand why he would hesitate to say 'Peter believed' or 'Peter did not believe'.

> We must assume that if pressed to answer the evangelist would have said, 'No, Peter did not believe'. But even this explicit negative statement would be unwelcome as a negative example of what he wants to demonstrate with the facts so carefully assembled: the impulse to faith.[112]

Conversely, we should be asking ourselves the question of whether or not the Beloved Disciple is highlighted as a witness to the empty tomb in the same way Peter's role as witness is emphasized. Certainly the Beloved Disciple was not considered *the* apostolic authority behind the resurrection claims in the greater Christian tradition—Peter was associated with this authority. Note that the exact condition inside the tomb, with the particular arrangement of the grave-clothes is explicitly linked to what *Peter* saw (v. 7) whereas the nature or content of what the Beloved Disciple saw is put in much more vague terms (cf. vv. 4, 8). Perhaps the Beloved Disciple is not to be regarded primarily as a witness to the resurrection proofs in the same way Peter is and likewise Peter is not to be compared to the Beloved Disciple in his response of faith to those conditions he verifies.

With the two disciples walking away to their homes in v. 10 their individual roles have been fulfilled and the evangelist has made his point. The scene returns to Mary Magdalene until the narrative of Jesus' appearance to the disciples in 20.19-23. Before we proceed to our conclusions we must make reference to this event as recorded in the Gospel of John.

C. *The Commissioning of the Disciples*

Even though Peter and the Beloved Disciple are not mentioned in the rest of this chapter, Jesus' appearance to the disciples (20.19-23) has been interpreted by Maynard as 'anti-Petrine'. Verses 22-23 in particular, where Jesus bestows the Spirit upon and commissions the disciples are compared to Mt. 16.18-19 and 18.18, where Peter is given the authority 'to loose and to bind'. Maynard contends,

> Unless we assume that the Fourth Evangelist did not know Matthew, an assumption which seems unlikely, this passage must be regarded as anti-Petrine, for it bestows upon all the disciples the authority which Matthew bestows alternately on Peter and the Church. Even if the Fourth Evangelist did not know Matthew, he clearly sees apostolic authority invested upon all of the disciples.[113]

We must note another distinction between the Matthean account and John's beside the lack of an explicit reference to Peter. John relates this commissioning to the giving of the Holy Spirit, signifying that Jesus had indeed been glorified (cf. Jn 7.39).[114] In other words, this account may be intended more as a christological statement than as an ecclesiological statement.

Furthermore, we must maintain that because Matthew *alone* relates his bestowal of ecclesiastical authority to Peter, whether or not John is aware of it, does *not* mean John' failure to do so makes him 'anti-Petrine'. It does no more than signify a particular Petrine interest on the part of Matthew.

D. *Conclusions*

To summarize, it is possible to see in Jn 20.1-10 reflections of some earlier traditions of visits to the empty tomb. These originally portrayed at least Mary Magdalene, Peter and someone else as witnesses to the unexpected phenomena of the empty tomb and abandoned grave clothes. Although these accounts may have been used as refutations of the charge that the body of Jesus was stolen, they did not have as their main purpose the elicitation of faith in the resurrection of Jesus or contribution to an understanding of the significance of such an event.

On the other hand, Jn 20.1-10 in its final form seems to be directed to this call for 'faith without seeking'. With the addition of the Beloved Disciple into the tradition the new dimension of faith is added. The pericope then becomes an appeal to follow the lead of the Beloved Disciple and respond to the evidence of the empty tomb.

An analysis of the passage betrays the author's attempts to combine the traditions of the visits with some unique Johannine material. This process explains some of the duplication in the description of Peter and the Beloved Disciple, and perhaps it lies behind the separate arrivals of the two disciples although they set off toward the tomb together.

Certain distinct features, such as the description of the Beloved Disciple arriving first, yet waiting for Peter to enter the tomb first, may be due to deliberate literary devices of delay and foreshadowing that built up to the climax of the Beloved Disciple's act of faith.

Certainly it should not be surprising that the Beloved Disciple is depicted as arriving on the scene first. After all, he is being described to the community that identifies itself with him. He exemplifies true discipleship and a close, loving relationship with Jesus. It would only be natural for him to run as fast as humanly possible to the grave of the one who loved him. However, to go further in interpreting the run to the tomb as a *race* between Peter and Beloved Disciple in which Peter loses does no justice to the spirit of passage.

The function of the Beloved Disciple is to provide the example of a true disciple of Jesus. In this situation to be a true disciple is to come to a point of belief. However, belief is precipitated by an historical witness to the evidences of the resurrection, embodied in the character and function of Peter.

Thus the two are put into a complementary relationship for the purposes of eliciting faith in the resurrection of Jesus based upon the empirical evidence testified to by the best-known of the Twelve. One might ask, 'Why is Peter related in this way to the community of readers?' Would not the Beloved Disciple have served as their testimony to the conditions of the empty tomb? Besides the fact that this narrative is obviously built upon traditional sources that focus upon Peter, one might respond to the question by pointing out, as we have in earlier chapters, that the need was arising for the Johannine community to hold fast to the anchor of their faith, and the traditions surrounding Peter embodied that anchor. One could expect that as the Johannine community matured, the Beloved Disciple's identity as a witness paled while his exemplary discipleship continued as his legacy. For his legacy to continue unabated and uncorrupted, the Johannine community had to embrace the more secure Apostolic traditions.

The need of the Johannine Christians to join themselves to the Apostolic stream becomes more obvious in John 21. Specific concerns pertaining to both the Beloved Disciple and Peter are addressed and Christ's provision for the continuance of his own are highlighted in John 21. We will now turn our attention to this appendix to the Gospel.

Chapter 6

PETER AND THE BELOVED DISCIPLE IN JOHN 21

A. *Introduction*

The final section of the Gospel of John which brings Peter and the Beloved Disciple together also has the most to say about the roles, functions and relationships of these two. In fact, the structural development of ch. 21 itself reveals a certain chiastic order that focuses upon the Beloved Disciple and Peter.[1] Yet, it is not certain how best to correlate what is said about our two figures in John 21 with what is said about them in the rest of the Gospel. It is the consensus that ch. 21 of John is a distinct chapter reflecting unique concerns on the part of at least some Johannine Christians. Because of its distinctive provenance, this chapter of the Gospel may provide some insight into the history of the Johannine community as it matured. Inasmuch as John 21 reflects the perspectives of the writer and his community, this final chapter of the Gospel can serve to elucidate our interpretation of the Johannine portrayal of Peter and the Beloved Disciple.

In order to pursue the concerns of this enquiry, we will examine ch. 21 of the Gospel of John by first discussing its origin, background and relationship to the rest of the Gospel. Then we will try to summarize the basic purpose and thrusts inherent in the Gospel. Finally, in light of these findings we will seek to discern and relate the roles and relationship of Peter and the Beloved Disciple as presented in John 21. The question of how the portrayal of Peter in this chapter is to be related to his depiction in chs. 1–20 will be addressed in our conclusions.

The Provenance of Chapter 21
Even a cursory reading of chs. 20 and 21 of the Gospel of John will lead the reader to recognize the disjunction between the two chapters. The final statements of ch. 20 bring the chapter—and the entire Gospel—to a fitting close. Chapter 21 then appears anti-

climactic. Further, the internal unity of the last chapter seems somewhat strained and anachronistic, for the narrative appears to be composed of several elements that would more naturally belong to an earlier period, perhaps among the earliest of the resurrection appearances. These earlier scenes are combined with information that could only have come from a later period of development in the Christian communities.[2] In light of these impressions many students of the Fourth Gospel have come to regard the twenty-first chapter as an editorial epilogue or appendix added after the evangelist had completed the original Gospel.

The very fact that even the earliest manuscripts include ch. 21 as part of the Fourth Gospel makes some scholars understandably hesitant in regarding this chapter as a later addition.[3] To be sure, a few have made the case that this chapter is original to the Gospel as an integral part of the author's intended message.[4] If the Gospel proper were to end at 20.31 as the general consensus holds, then it would be the important 'commissioning' that characterizes a true Gospel, according to Hoskyns:

> A Christian gospel ends properly, not with the appearance of the risen Lord to his disciples, and their belief in Him, but with a confident statement that this mission to the world, undertaken at His command and under His authority, will be the means by which many are saved.[5]

Related to this argument is the observation that the apparent conclusions of Jn 20.30, 31 are strikingly similar to another Johannine statement in 1 Jn 5.13 which also stands before the actual conclusion of the writing.[6] On the other hand, Lagrange has suggested that the narrative run uninterrupted from 20.29 on to 21.1, placing 20.29, 30 at the end of the Gospel.

> μετὰ ταῦτα est une tradition familière à Jo. (5.1; 6.11 7.1). La suite avec 20.29 serait très naturelle, si une conclusion de l'évangile n'avait été interposée (20.30).[7]

John Marsh interprets John 21 as an original attempt to proclaim the ongoing force of the Gospel. He describes the evangelist's attempt to break out of the context of the Passover feast:

> Ch. 20 is a record of what took place within the octave of the Passover during which the true Paschal lamb, Jesus Christ, died. However miraculous the resurrection appearances there recorded were, they occurred only during that Passover, and offer no sort of

guarantee that they have any validity or even promise outside the feast. Is it possible that the evangelist was aware of this, and that ch. 21 affords, at least for him the link between that Passover and the subsequent life of all Christian men?[8]

Most recently Smalley has suggested that although the Fourth Gospel in its present form was the product of the Johannine school after the death of John the Apostle (whose tradition formed the basis of the Gospel) this final chapter came from the same hand(s) as the first twenty.[9] It forms an integral part of the 'signs' schema, and he traces the order of composition of the Gospel as follows: 'the main body of the Gospel, the epilogue, and last of all (once the writer knew what had been said), the prologue'.[10]

Minear has argued, on the other hand, that ch. 21 is an integral and necessary part of the Gospel and 'the Evangelist planned from the beginning to include the material of chapter 21'.[11] The final chapter is necessary, he reasons, because of the conspicuous roles of two important figures in the Gospel narrative, Peter and the Beloved Disciple, who have a very anticlimactic and indecisive exit from the Gospel story if ch. 20 is the Gospel's last chapter. The evangelist 'intended from the outset to balance the triple denial, predicted in 13.38 and narrated in 18.15-17, with the triple pledge of love in 21.15-17'.[12] As for the Beloved Disciple, Minear reasons,

> It is hardly credible that the same Evangelist who so enlarged the role of this disciple should end his story with the journey to his home in 20.10. Rather the picture in chapter 21 provides the only fitting conclusion to his story.[13]

As reasonable as Minear's argument appears, we must realize that the Beloved Disciple is described as going home *after* he comes to believe in 20.8, and coming to belief is his primary function as a true disciple throughout the Gospel. One can legitimately say that his 'job' is done. He has fulfilled the role of being an example of loving, discerning belief in Jesus. Furthermore, ch. 20 does fittingly end with not one, but *two* appearances of Jesus to his disciples where belief is expressed, confessions are made and blessings and commissions are given by Jesus to his disciples.

R.E. Brown comes to terms with Hoskyn's argument that the Gospel requires the commissioning contained in ch. 21. While he does recognize the valid place a commission has in the Gospel, he discerns one in ch. 20.21 and 29. Referring to Hoskyns, he states,

... his argument for the inclusion of 21 is weakened by the fact that there is a reference to mission in 20.21: 'As the Father has sent me, so do I send you'. The universality of the mission is not explicit in 20, but its wide success is postulated by the beatitude concerning those who have not seen but have believed (20.29). If ch. 21 had never been composed, we may safely guess that Hoskyns would not have judged as inadequate the closing of the Gospel in ch. 20.[14]

Likewise Barrett notes the commission to evangelize in 20.21ff. It is his contention that the nature of the commissioning is foreign to the basic message of the first 20 chapters:

To demonstrate their [*i.e. the apostles*'] success as fishers of men, even under the threat of death, does not in the same way fit into John's framework, though it is readily understandable as a supplement, especially when it is coupled with a comment on the importance of and the relations between, Peter and the beloved disciple.[15]

Scholars have noted other peculiarities in the twenty-first chapter that suggest, even apart from questions of authorship, that this chapter was not originally part of the Gospel of John.[16] Dodd concedes that there are certain Johannine traits in this chapter, but on the basis of the 'non-Johannine' eschatology and the ecclesiastical claims of this chapter he regards it as an appendix with motives 'more akin to those of the Synoptics':[17]

The naive conception of Christ's second Advent in 21.22 is unlike anything else in the Fourth Gospel. For the rest, it may be that those critics are right who surmise in the background some adjustments in the claims of Rome (for Peter) and Ephesus (for the Beloved Disciple).[18]

Bultmann focuses on the eschatological distinctiveness of this final chapter, stating that the Gospel maintains a polemic against the 'realistic eschatology' which is found in ch. 21.[19] Whereas Bultmann posits a purely figurative representation of the Beloved Disciple in the first 20 chapters, he detects an historical understanding of the disciple in ch. 21. Furthermore, he detects what he considers to be a non-Johannine use of allegory in the 153 fish in 21.11.

In this passage [*ch. 21*] the beloved disciple is not representative of Gentile Christianity, but a definite historical person. It is also symptomatic that whereas allegory is foreign to the Gospel, it appears in v. 11 even if the precise meaning of the number is not to be unravelled.[20]

Shaw has compared the use of symbolism in John 21 to that found in the rest of the Gospel, suggesting that two distinct genres are evident.

> In chs. 1-20 the imagery, more allusive than definite in the early chapters, is personal in character and centred upon Jesus... By contrast, the symbolism of ch. 21 is not in this way personal or direct. The imagery here may be described as more mechanical in character, more disposed to use an allegorical, even an arithmetical, form, and less Christ-centred.[21]

Lindars, who maintains that 1-20 and 21 have a common author, explains the difference between the two sections as due to a change of intended audience, so that the concluding chapter of the Gospel was added by the evangelist soon after the first twenty chapters were written, at the time of 'publication' in order to make it more relative to a wider audience than just the Johannine circle.[22]

On the basis of the factors examined, the weight of the evidence seems to favour the later addition of ch. 21 to the already existing Gospel comprised of chs. 1-20. The conclusion of 20.30-31 and the distinct concerns of ch. 21 combine to suggest such a conclusion. This is not to say that there is no connnection in the authorship of the two; it only suggests that ch. 21 was added to the Gospel as an afterthought, or in response to new concerns among the readership.

If the first twenty chapters of John are to be attributed to the pen of one man, rather than to the co-operative effort of the Johannine community, then the postulation of a common authorship for chs. 1-20 and ch. 21 becomes problematic. Nevertheless, a number of scholars have sought to present exactly this—the same individual who was responsible for John 1-20 was also the author of John 21.[23]

Dods, who finds no inconsistency in attributing 21.1-23 to the Apostle John, is faced with the witness of vv. 24 and 25, which, on a simple reading, seem to come from someone other than the Beloved Disciple

> It is by no means certain that ver. 25 is Johannine. It seems an inflated version of xx 30. The twenty-fourth verse is also rejected by several critics on the grounds of οἴδαμεν. This may be valid as an objection, but it is in the manner of the Apostle to testify to his own truthfulness, xix 35; and the use of the plural instead of the singular is not decisive.[24]

Sanders and Mastin postulate that the same individual (be it the author or consequent editor of the whole Gospel) was responsible for both 1–20 and 21 and the differences between the two writings are to be explained by the urgency with which ch. 21 was written.

> However, if it [*i.e. ch. 21*] was composed subsequently to i-xx to meet specific urgent needs, it may be that the author (or editor) of the FG had not meditated on these needs as fully as on those contained in the original draft, which was intended to be complete and that this accounts for the lack of polish here.[25]

These comments of various authors pertaining to the authorship of John 21 have failed to take sufficiently into account the differences in style, symbolism and perspective throughout this chapter while they have quite properly recognized the Johannine character of much of this material. When the differences with John 1–20 are taken into account, together with the witness of 21.24, 25 and the indication that the traditional source of the Gospel (i.e. the Beloved Disciple) is dead or approaching death (cf. 21.23), then one is forced to find another explanation that allows for the obviously Johannine aspects of the chapter.

Mahoney has theorized that the material in John 21 is not original to the evangelist but has been added on to the Gospel by a later editor, motivated by a desire to preserve these early traditions.

> Only a different editor would have such respect for an existing text as to leave the work of a predecessor intact, and opt rather for the form of a clear postscript, while settling for the weaker ending of 21.24ff.[26]

It is noted by many commentators that the vocabulary of John 21 is distinctive, containing 28 words that are not used elsewhere in John.[27] This has led Boismard to adopt the questionable opinion that the redactor of ch. 21 was the redactor of the Gospel of Luke.[28] Yet, for the most part, the linguistic differences are not convincing to many scholars, even those who ultimately reject a common authorship. This is due, in part, to the explanation that differences in subject matter necessitate differences in vocabulary. Broomfield has made the case that every chapter in the Gospel of John has a distinct vocabulary and ch. 21 has rather less than the average.[29] A recent study employing the mathematical method of factor analysis confirms this, concluding that on the basis of certain word frequencies, John 21 belongs with other narrative chapters in John such as 2, 4, 9, 11 and chs. 18–20.[30]

Thus, the linguistic evidence is not decisive in determining either an identity or a differentiation in the authorship of 1–20 and 21. On the basis of all the evidence examined, a relationship between the two writings must be recognized, yet it needs to be held in tension with obvious differences. Although solidly in the Johannine tradition and definitely a member of the ongoing Johannine community, the editor/redactor has not left his mark merely in terms of style, but also in terms of content. His theological perspective and his concern for the continuing life of the Johannine Christian community are evident not only in this twenty-first chapter, but perhaps even in the letter of 1 John.[31]

A probable solution is that this final chapter of the Gospel of John is as much a part of the Johannine school as is the rest of the Gospel. It reworks the Johannine tradition while by applying it to new situations faced by the community which centred around the Beloved Disciple. The Johannine Christian(s) responsible for this final form of ch. 21 must be differentiated from the original author while at the same time being regarded as trying to represent the original traditions and message behind the Gospel which are associated with the Beloved Disciple and his community. Perhaps R.E. Brown's profile of the writer of John 21 is most accurate, for he describes him as 'a Johannine disciple who shared the same general world of thought as the evangelist and who desired more to complete the Gospel than to change its impact'.[32]

In terms of structure, ch. 21 can be divided up into two main sections (vv. 1-14 and vv. 15-23) plus the concluding remarks of vv. 24 and 25. Verses 1-14 narrate an appearance of Jesus while the disciples were fishing in Galilee. Verses 15-23 relate more directly to the persons of Peter and the Beloved Disciple.

Turning specifically to 21.1-14, it is noteworthy that the fishing scene bears resemblance to the one recorded in Lk. 5.1-11. Furthermore, the first Galilean resurrection appearance of Jesus to the disciples at a meal of bread and fish may be related to the resurrection appearance in Lk. 24 where a meal of bread and fish is also described (Lk. 24.30, 31, 35, 42, 43).

> This part of the chapter may consist of a combination of the story of the first appearance to Peter in a fishing scene and the story of the first Galilean appearance of Jesus to the Twelve at a meal of bread and fish. Although added to the Gospel at its last stage, John xxi apparently draws on very old material from the Galilean tradition of post-resurrectional narratives.[33]

It is the general consensus[34] of present scholarship that the narrative in John is indeed a combination of the two traditional narratives.[35] However, opinion is divided on the question of whether these two narratives were combined prior to their inclusion in John 21 or the author of this chapter combined them himself.[36] To decide whether the author of ch. 21.1-14 was dependent upon Luke, or vice versa is another open question. One scholar who postulates Lucan dependence upon John is Johnson,[37] but due to the distinctiveness of both the Lucan and Johannine narratives most scholars concur with Smalley's evaluation.

> The dissimilarities in the two accounts are as noteworthy as the similarities, and it could be that we have here two incidents belonging to an independent cycle of Peter stories.[38]

Even though there are dissimilarities between vv. 1-14 and 15-23,[39] it is apparent that whatever the original setting of the narratives, this chapter must be taken in its present form to perceive its intended message. It would appear that vv. 15ff. are necessary for an explanation of the role of Peter in the church, for without this expository section Peter's actions as described in 1-14 remain enigmatic, and questions pertaining to his role in relation to the community remain unresolved.

Just as evidence suggests a purposeful combination and adaptation of particular traditions in ch. 21, the addition of material is also evident. The conclusion of 21.24-25 and the reference to the Beloved Disciple in v. 7 appear to have been added. The section in 21.18-23 has also been understood as material original to the redactor responsible for ch. 21. R.E. Brown comments:

> The redactor who added the narrative to the Gospel may have been responsible for introducing the figure of the Beloved Disciple into vs. 7 (and also appending the words of Jesus pertinent to the fates of Peter and the Beloved Disciple in vss. 18-23).[40]

Finally then, it is possible to conclude that the writer of John 21 has apparently drawn from ancient traditions concerning a Galilean post-resurrectional appearance of Jesus and traditions associated with Peter which were also reflected in the Synoptic accounts. With this frame has been included material that has a distinctly Johannine emphasis. The writer has purposely synthesized it all to produce the entire chapter. Although it is a composite work, the chapter must be read as it stands in order to perceive the intended message of the complete literary unit.

If we are correct in discerning the purposes in the collection, arrangement and supplementation that give rise to ch. 21, then it behoves us to isolate the basic concerns inherent in the author's purpose. A careful examination of the emphases does reveal an ecclesial concern on the part of the writer and, for the purposes of this work, this ecclesial concern is of paramount importance for interpreting the relationship between Peter and the Beloved Disciple.

B. *The Basic Concerns of the Chapter*

It has been suggested that the primary motive behind the composition of John 21 was the preservation of some of the traditions ascribed to the Beloved Disciple which were left out of chs. 1–20 for one reason or another. Mahoney regards these traditions as added by 'an editor who wished to preserve the material now in chapter 21'.[41] Likewise, N.E. Johnson suggests that the followers of the Beloved Disciple, after his death, discovered some of the Beloved Disciple's material

> When this group of disciples, whom we must call the 'final editors', saw their own Beloved Disciple, in his own work, playing such an important part in the narrative, they probably felt compelled to add the chapter to the rest of the Gospel.[42]

However, there must be more to the formation of this chapter than *just* the motive of preservation, for very purposeful selection, composition and arrangement is involved. We must also account for the theological motives for the inclusion and treatment of these particular narratives. Worthy of note is the final statement of Jn 21.25; Ἔστιν δὲ καὶ ἄλλα πολλὰ ἃ ἐποίησεν ὁ Ἰησοῦς, ἅτινα ἐὰν γράφηται καθ᾽ ἕν, οὐδὲ αὐτὸν οἶμαι τὸν κόσμον χωρῆσαι τὰ γραφόμενα βιβλία.

Numerous motivations underlying the composition of this chapter have been isolated so that one is able to discern the desire to present: (1) the revelation of the person and work of Christ, (2) the illustration of the nature of true discipleship, (3) the commission to evangelize all people (4) the witness to the restoration and authorization of Peter as a pastoral authority, and finally, (5) the correction of eschatological error. It may be that each of these emphases are united by a comprehensive ecclesiastical concern that gave rise to the publication of John 21. As R.E. Brown observes,

> The themes of Peter's rehabilitation, his role as shepherd of the sheep, his death as a martyr, the role of the Beloved Disciple, his

death, its relation to the second coming—these are questions that
affected the relation of the Johannine community to the Church at
large.[43]

Basic to this chapter is the function the narrative of 21.1-14 has in
bearing witness to the resurrection of Jesus. Verses 1, 7, 12 and 14 all
manifest the concern that through this narrative Jesus is revealed.

The verb φανεροῦν is used nine times in the Gospel, three of those
uses being in 21.1-14.[44] In these verses it serves as a bridge or
transition between chs. 20 and 21, since this *recognition theme* is
evident in Jn 20.11-18.[45] That it is the Beloved Disciple who
identifies Jesus is not without significance. That he, rather than
Peter, is the first to recognize the risen Lord has been cited as a
'deliberate re-exegesis of the early tradition as found in 1 Cor. 15'.[46]
We will have to forego our evaluation of this interpretation until our
basic overview of the chapter is complete. The beloved Disciple's
function as a witness to the revelation of Jesus for the Johannine
Christians is integral to a proper understanding of the Fourth
Gospel. O'Grady has made the case that the Beloved Disciple, even
after his death, had an important function in the Church as a witness
to the revelation of Jesus, and ch. 21, which was prompted by his
death, ensures that this remains understood.[47]

Verses 15-17 have also been interpreted from a christological
perspective, 'showing how it was that *Jesus* took these measures to
provide for the care of his sheep, that *Jesus* was the one responsible
for the factual role that Peter obviously played'.[48] Interpreted from
an ecclesiological perspective, the message becomes that the church
is to be centred around the revelation of Jesus, the Lord, and faith in
his resurrection. Does this suggest that the author of John 21 was
trying to draw attention back to Jesus and away from Peter in a time
when Peter may have become the focus of the church, or does it
suggest that the continuation of the community of believers has been
provided for by the instructions of Jesus to Peter? This is a question
of emphasis, and nuances are hard to discern for the reader.
Nevertheless, these are questions that we must grapple with in the
coming discourse.

Rather than taking the manifestation of Christ as the main
emphasis of this chapter, a number of scholars have suggested that
the major purpose of this chapter in its present form is to explain and
illustrate the nature of true Christian discipleship. 'It [*ch. 21*] is a
quite independent, fundamental and universal exposition of the

nature of Christian discipleship'.[49] That discipleship is to be based on following the example of Christ in self-giving love. As R.E. Brown illustrates,

> The category of discipleship based on love makes any other distinction in the Johannine community relatively unimportant, so that even the well-known Petrine and presbyterial image of the shepherd is not introduced without the conditioning question, 'Do you love me?'[50]

By implication, then, this chapter is said to focus on the theme of discipleship, teaching that the church is to consist of those who have decided, out of their love for him, to follow Jesus. This particularly applies to those who are in positions of authority in the church.

Inextricably linked to the concept of discipleship is that of the mission of all disciples, as illustrated in John 21. The fishing scene of Jn 21.1-14 is symbolic of the mandate the Christian community has to become 'fishers of men'. The lack of success on the part of the disciples has been understood by some interpreters to suggest the necessity of Christ's presence and enabling in evangelistic efforts. 'It is notable that never in the Gospels do the disciples catch a fish without Jesus' help'.[51] The description of the disciples fishing at night may be little more than a reflection of the custom of nocturnal fishing prevalent in Galilee. Cognizant of this, Lindars ventures to suggest that one might well attach symbolic value to νυκτί in v. 3. 'The detail could be symbolical representing the fruitlessness of working on mission without the light of the Master's presence, but such an interpretation is not required by the text'.[52]

Most commentators recognize that the mention of exactly 153 fish in v. 11 is symbolic, and they all outline the various zoological, mathematical, allegorical, geometrical and gematriacal solutions that have been proposed.[53] On the other hand, probably in reaction to the speculative nature of many of these analyses, a simple solution has been suggested, that the exact number was preserved because of its magnitude and its 'authentic eyewitness character'.[54] Morris evaluates the symbolic interpretations:

> Such explanations of the number may carry conviction to some, but I must confess to remaining completely unimpressed. . . If John meant us to see such meanings he has given us no guidance. It is much simpler to see a fisherman's record of a fact.[55]

The variety of interpretations of this number should not prompt us to retreat and discard *all* attempts to understand the symbolism, for that would be denying the Fourth Gospel an integral aspect of its character, that is, its symbolism. Rather, we should strive to apply tight control in our approach to John's symbolism when we do not have clear guidance within the text for an interpretation. Even with the variety of views concerning this tantalizing detail of 153 fish, most ultimately conclude that it is the universality or completeness of the catch that is being highlighted.

> The difficulty, if not impossibility, of ever narrowing down the possible interpretations of the figure has led many today to say generally that in some way the universal character and promised results of the church's mission are depicted.[56]

Hence Jn 21.11 teaches that the commission is to go out and evangelize all men, everywhere. 'The figure must represent totality in some way, because the catch prefigures the ultimate universal salvation through the church's mission (cf. 11.52)'.[57] One question we might ask ourselves is this: if the commission to evangelize is already present in 20.20-23, then what is the significance of a repeated commission in ch. 21? The universal nature of the call and the call to unity within the greater Christian community may be what is being highlighted.

The observation that the net did not break gives a further clue to the 'ecclesiastical' nature of this passage. This becomes particularly apparent when we compare John's use of the concessive participial phrase (καὶ τοσούτων ὄντων—Jn 21.11) and the statement that the net did not break (οὐκ ἐσχίσθη τὸ δίκτυον—Jn 21.11), with Luke's description in the imperfect tense that the nets were breaking (διερρήσσετο δὲ τὰ δίκτυα αὐτῶν—Lk. 5.6). Lindars comments:

> Moreover, the net was not torn. As John has altered the symbolism to apply to the internal pastoral ministry of the Church it is natural to see in this a reference to John's vital interest in the maintenance of unity of the Church. Commentators are generally agreed about this.[58]

As Schnackenburg points out, the net symbolizes more for John than it does for Luke; it symbolizes 'the universal Church which has come about as the fruit of Jesus' ministry'.[59] That the net is not rent symbolizes the same desire for unity of the believers that is found in Christ's prayer in John 17. Another support for this interpretation is the use of the term σχίζειν in Jn 21.11. As one author notes, this word 'is employed in 19.24 of the soldiers dividing Jesus' robe (a symbol of unity?) and is related to σχίσμα, used in Jn (7.43, 9.16, 10.19) of the division of people over Jesus' significance'.[60] It may be that the author of John 21 is calling the Johannine Christians to unity with other Christian communities. If this desire for unity does indeed lie behind the composition of John 21, then what is said about Peter in vv. 15-19 has an appropriate context.

Building upon a christological function, the author of John 21 was able to relate the concepts of discipleship and mission to the unity of the Christian church. In addition to these general theological motivations, this chapter provided the opportunity to address specific and urgent concerns of the Johannine community pertaining to the status of Peter and the Beloved Disciple.

> The opportunity is taken to answer two questions which were causing perplexity to that generation for which the Gospel was originally written. The first of these concerned the position in the church occupied by Peter from the earliest days after the ascension (Acts i, 15 etc.). The other concerned the apparent probability that the Lord's coming would not take place until the last of the Apostolic band was already dead, though He Himself has said, 'There be some here of them that stand by, which shall in no wise taste of death, till they see the kingdom of God come with power'. (St. Mark ix.1).[61]

C. *Peter in John 21*

The picture of Peter we have in the last chapter of the Gospel of John has been seen by most scholars as quite positive compared to how he fares in the rest of the Gospel. Indeed, as was noted in the introductory chapter of this work,[62] some who have seen a depreciation of Peter in the first twenty chapters of the Gospel now detect a reversal of attitude in John 21. Maynard is one of these:

> When we turn to the Appendix the situation is very different. We find two instances there in which Peter seems to be depreciated after the manner of the body of the Gospel. He leads the disciples back to their old way of life as fishermen in denial of the resurrection, and he fails to understand the meaning of Jesus' probing about his love. But this apparent harmony with the body of the Gospel is reversed in the total impact of these two incidents. They both lead to the restoration of Peter's authority in the Church. Just as the evangelist picked up the Synoptic picture of

Peter, apparently recognized it but reversed it; so the Redactor has picked up the Evangelist's picture of Peter, apparently recognized it, but reversed it so that it is now back to the Synoptic view![63]

On the other hand, other interpreters discern the same 'anti-Petrine' sentiments in this chapter as they did in the rest of the Gospel.[64] Agourides, for example, suggests that the picture of Peter in John 21 'coincides with the whole trend in the Fourth Gospel which tends to stress gently, but unmistakeably, the weak points in Peter's relation to Jesus'.[65] He sees in Peter's actions in this chapter 'unreasoned vigour' and a 'failure to stand firm'.[66]

It may be, as we have discovered in our examinations of other Johannine depictions of Peter, that here in ch. 21 we do not have a clear anti-Petrine or condescending sentiment and consequently there exists no inconsistency between the attitude towards Peter contained in chs. 1–20 and that of ch. 21.

That the restoration of Peter and his personal commissioning were included in ch. 21 reveals the perspective and concerns of a Christian community beginning its second generation.

> How Peter came to be restored to his apostolic office would not seem to the first generation of Christians to be of sufficient importance for inclusion in a Gospel, but when the second generation began to look back it was recognized as of peculiar interest.[67]

The Apostolic Christian church sought to solidify and preserve its traditions to compensate for the loss of first-hand, living witnesses.

Chapter 21 begins by stating that Jesus revealed himself to the disciples, and in v. 2 it may be noted that, as in the Synoptics, Simon Peter is listed first among the disciples. The next verse (3) illustrates that Simon Peter assumes the leadership of the disciples as he initiates a fishing expedition. It is noteworthy that verse 3 repeats the full name Σίμων Πέτρος as it is found in the list in the previous verse. The use of the full name certainly is a Johannine stylistic characteristic.[68] However, the immediate repetition of the full name is distinctive. 'To repeat the full name of Σίμων Πέτρος is not in accordance with John's habit'.[69] This may be significant as another example of the 'swelling of emphasis'[70] with reference to Peter.

To classify this decision to go fishing as a return 'to their old way of life as fishermen in denial of the resurrection'[71] seems more than a bit harsh and reads much into the text. Building upon the use of the infinitive (ἁλιεύειν) with a verb in the present tense (ὑπάγω) to express Peter's intention, it has been argued that Peter is announcing a permanent return to his earlier way of life. 'The story presupposes that the disciples have returned to their trade, after the shattering events in Jerusalem'.[72] McDowell is the most definite in his assertions to this effect. He stresses the concept that the present tense expresses 'linear or continuous action'.[73] From this he goes on to argue,

> Peter meant that he was going back to his old business and that he was to continue at it. The fact that Peter carried with him four, and perhaps six, of the Apostles, all evidently bent on resuming their old occupation, precipitated what was a crisis indeed.[74]

It is, then, only through his encounter with Jesus that Peter is drawn to change his mind.

Most commentators are justifiably hesitant of giving much credence to this interpretation. What else are the disciples to be expected to do in this situation? 'There is no need to be surprised that the disciples went fishing. They had after all to earn their living somehow or other; there is as yet no full-time paid ministry'.[75] In any case, speculation as to motives and attitudes behind this fishing trip is unfounded. As Morris has noted, 'Whatever Peter's ultimate intentions it is pressing the meaning of the present tense too hard to see in it a proposal to resume his former life as a fisherman'.[76]

We are on more solid ground if we stay with the function of the words in the context of the narrative itself. In other words, as Schnackenburg has maintained,

> Staying with the text, it is to be said about v. 3 that, to begin with, it is the introduction to the miracle catch of fish, as the closing sentence, which cannot be detached, shows: 'But that night they caught nothing'.[77]

Since it is a Johannine characteristic to employ the device of 'double meaning' in the narratives and dialogues[78] it may be that Peter's proposal to go fishing is to be taken as a reference to 'the apostolic mission of "catching men"'.[79] Barrett, who proposes this interpretation, admits that this certainly is not the face value of Peter's words, but he does illustrate how this fits in well with the evangelistic task as it is commissioned and enabled by Jesus in the following paragraph of the narrative.[80] In any case, it is sufficient to conclude that Peter continues in his function as the leader of the disciples in this post-resurrection appearance context.

As Jesus stands on the shore and speaks to the men in the boat, *none* of the disciples recognizes him. Under his direction they are able to net a large quantity of fish, and as they are hauling it aboard, the Beloved Disciple realizes who has helped them and tells Peter ὁ κύριός ἐστιν. The fact that the Beloved Disciple first identifies Jesus is in itself important for our inquiry, and it will be discussed shortly, but it is also significant that he specifically tells *Peter* (λέγει. . . τῷ Πέτρῳ) who it is.

This observation can be read in two ways which are not mutually exclusive. Firstly, as we have already noted, in what has been described a a 'deliberate re-exegesis of the early tradition as found in 1 Cor. 15',[81] this account can be understood as depriving Peter of the honour of being the first to recognize Jesus. 'The author allows Peter to be the first to see the empty tomb, but not the first to recognize the risen Lord'.[82] The problem with this interpretation is that the Gospel of John assumes the early traditions surrounding Peter rather than denying them. The second interpretation emphasizes the fact that, as soon as the Beloved Disciple recognizes Jesus, he tells *Peter*. It is interesting to note that the narrative is so constructed that it is only Peter who is told and no one else.

Verse 7, then, can be interpreted to suggest that Peter is dependent upon the mediation of the Beloved Disciple for his understanding of the identity of Jesus,[83] but at the same time, one may read in it the Beloved Disciple's recognition of Peter's leadership position, since only Peter needs to be told this important information.

As we will discover when we speak about the Beloved Disciple's role, his recognition of Jesus seems to depend more on theological insight than on physical recognition. Peter reacted upon *hearing* (ἀκούσας) that the figure on the shore was Jesus, that is, Jesus was not yet physically recognizable on the distant shore. One may assume that the Beloved Disciple discerned Jesus' identity by the *sign* of the full net.

Peter's physical situation and ensuing reaction has been interpreted symbolically. The reference to his nakedness is compared to Rev. 3.17-18, 16.15 and 17.16 where 'spiritual nakedness and loss of virtue is presented'.[84] That Peter is said to clothe himself before jumping into the water is taken to indicate his conversion by one writer,[85] and repentance by another,[86] but there is some question as to the extent of his 'nakedness' and his action of 'putting on' clothes that must be answered before such speculation on the symbolism can even be entertained. The passage in question reads:... τὸν ἐπενδύτην διεζώσατο, ἦν γὰρ γυμνός, καὶ ἔβαλεν ἑαυτὸν εἰς τὴν θάλασσαν. The word ἐπενδύτην refers to an outer garment[87] which is put on over underwear. By extension, 'the word can be used to describe a working man's overalls, and in this case it was probably a fisherman's smock'.[88] It could either be that Peter was working completely naked, or what he was working with *just* his ἐπενδύτην on. Apparently, if he was working in his ἐπενδύτην he could still be described as (otherwise) naked.[89] 'Total nudity would offend Jewish sensibilities and would not fit the picture of his working throughout the cool night'.[90] The verb διεζώατο can mean simply 'to tie (clothes) around' or to 'put on', so it is possible that we have a picture of Peter here tucking up his smock and tying it, giving him the freedom to swim. Lagrange comments:

> —διεζώσατο au moyen avec l'accusatif ne peut signifier qu'une chose: il serra son vêtement à la ceinture; cf. Lucien, somn. (sa vie) 6: διεζωσμένη τὴν ἐσθῆτα. Il faut donc que dans ce cas Jo. ait entendu ἐπενδύτης d'une sorte de sarrau tel que les gens du peuple en portent pour préserver leurs habits, mais que Pierre avait mis *cette fois* sur la peau pour travailler, car il était nu, n'avait pas autre chose. Avant de se lancer à la nage, il le noue solidement à sa ceinture.[91]

Barrett has cited Mishnaic sources that teach that to offer greetings to someone, which was essentially a religious act, one had to be clothed.[92] Therefore, he reasons, since Peter planned on greeting Jesus, he needed to clothe himself. Thus, he suggests that the passage should be read to mean that Peter was naked and, before jumping into the water, he puts on his loosest garment.[93] It is difficult to imagine Peter reasoning in this manner prior to jumping into the water, especially when it involves putting on clothes rather than taking them off in order to swim. The explanation offered by Lagrange is the simplest solution to all our difficulties.

Peter's jump into the water may be a sign of his characteristic impetuosity.[94] 'The love of Peter is full of unreasoning vigour, and therefore it suffers trial'.[95] One might wonder why his hurried swim to get to Jesus would not be regarded as indicative of his eagerness and the depth of his attachment to Jesus, rather than as a sign of rashness or impulsiveness.[96] The distance of 200 cubits which Peter had to swim had been taken, on the basis of Philo,[97] to be a reference to his repentance and purification.[98] One problem with such an interpretation is that the distance is given in relation to the boat (v. 8), so that the distance that Peter swam can only be inferred. The idea of repentance and purification is indeed closely tied to water, even within the Gospel of John,[99] but Jesus' comments to Peter in Jn 13.11 would seem to preclude his need for purification.

The best interpretation of Peter's action of 'tucking in' his smock and jumping into the water is that of Hartman. It suggests a symbolic significance that is directly tied to the context of ch. 21 itself. Hartman sees Peter's 'tucking in' his clothes as a foreshadowing of Jesus' words to him in vv. 18 and 19 of this chapter, i.e., it foreshadows his arrest and martyrdom

> [the action of Peter]. . . may be a point of departure for the foretelling of the girding of martyrdom of the elderly Peter in v. 18. One could even imagine an interpretation according to which the jumping in the water prefigures the death of Peter.[100]

A few scholars minimize the significance of the threefold questioning and commissioning of Peter,[101] holding that this is *not* to be understood as a scene of rehabilitation corresponding to the three-fold denial of Peter. Regarding 21.15-17, Bultmann asserts,

> If the section is taken by itself, it provides no hint of a relation to the account of the denial. Surely the denial and the repentance of Peter ought to have found mention! And nothing like an absolution is expressed in the statement of Jesus.[102]

Bultmann's reference to 'absolution' is anachronistic; one cannot presume what would be a proper rehabilitation of Peter. The three-fold questioning in John 21 is so reminiscent of the three-fold questioning in ch. 18 that the reader is drawn to connect the two events. As R.E. Brown notes,

> Most commentators have found in Jesus' thrice-repeated question 'Do you love me?' and in Peter's threefold 'You know that I love you' a symbolic undoing of Peter's threefold denial of Jesus. Consequently they have seen in 15-17 Peter's rehabilitation to discipleship after his fall.[103]

Verse 9 supports this connection, for in this descriptive sentence we read of a charcoal fire which Jesus presumably had prepared. The word used to describe the fire (i.e. ἀνθρακιάν) is the same word that is found in the description of the scene in the High Priest's courtyard when Peter denied that he was a disciple of Jesus (Jn 18.18, 25). Only in these two places in the New Testament is the word found. The effect created in the mind of the reader is to bring this scene in John 21 together with the scene of Peter's denials.

Another scene that becomes linked to Jn 18.18, 25 and Jn 21.15-19 is the prediction of Peter's denials (Jn 13.36-38) that we have examined in Chapter 3 above.[104] In ch. 13, Peter insists that he will follow Jesus, and Jesus tells him that he will not be able to follow now (νῦν) but he will 'afterward' (ὕστερον). Then, in ch. 18 we see highlighted Peter's inability to follow as exemplified by his triple denial of discipleship. Now, in ch. 21, after a corresponding three-fold 'interrogation', this time by Jesus, Peter is again given the chance, and indeed the command, to follow (cf. ἀκολούθει μοι—Jn 21.19, 22).

Before we look at the dialogue between Peter and Jesus after their breakfast, we should make note of Peter's actions in v. 11. At the direction of Jesus, Peter hauled (εἵλκυσεν) the net ashore, full of the 153 large fish.[105] If, as we concluded, the catch of 153 fish in an unbroken net symbolizes the universal character of a unified church,[106] then we may further maintain that Peter, acting upon Jesus' instruction, is responsible for maintaining the unity of the church in its mission.[107] The use of the term εἵλκυσεν may itself be symbolically significant, recalling the words of Jesus in Jn 12.32[108]— ἐὰν ὑψωθῶ ἐκ τῆς γῆς, πάντας ἑλκύσω πρὸς ἐμαυτόν. The verb had already occurred in v. 6 of this chapter, so its repetition may be deliberate. 'The fact that ἑλκύειν is repeated in verse 11 may provide more than merely historical interest, especially if the catch of fish does have some theological import'.[109] Again, let it be said that this focus on Peter's role is for the benefit of the Johannine readership, and so it must have some intended applicability to them in particular.

In vv. 15-17 Jesus asks Peter three times whether or not Peter loves him. Three times Peter responds affirmatively. Jesus' first question is worded Σίμων Ἰωάννου, ἀγαπᾷς με πλέον τούτων; the gender of πλέον τούτων can be taken to be either neuter or masculine. If it is understood to be neuter, Jesus is asking Peter 'Do you love me more than (you love) these *things*?' Some argue that 'the phrase would read μᾶλλον ἤ if it [τούτων] were neuter (cf. 3.19, 12.43) and. . . the verb would be repeated in such a construction'.[110] If the phrase is indeed masculine, it could have one of two meanings. Either Jesus is comparing Peter's love for his Lord with the love the other disciples have for Jesus (i.e. 'Simon Peter, do you love me more than these others love me?')[111] or he is asking Peter if he loves Jesus more than Peter loves these other people (i.e. 'Simon Peter, do you love me more than you love these others?'). It is interesting to note that in connection with the prediction of his denials, it is Matthew and Mark who have Peter maintain that although others fall away, he will never do so,[112] while John (and Luke) do not hint at this comparison made by Peter. Rather than setting up a rivalry of love between the apostles, which as Osborne notes, 'has no place in the resurrection narratives',[113] Peter's attachment to either his livelihood (or whatever else is implied in the neuter noun) or to other people is preferred as the thrust of Jesus' first question to Peter.[114]

The second question Jesus posed was similar to the first in that it uses the same term for love (i.e. Σίμων Ιωάννου, ἀγαπᾷς με;). In his final question, Jesus changes the word for love to ask Σίμων Ιωάννου, φιλεῖς με. In each response Peter uses φιλῶ σε in his confessions, rather than the word ἀγαπῶ, which would correspond with Jesus' confession. The variation in the verbs has been understood as deflating the quality of love Peter confesses in comparison to that which Jesus desires, as Maynard concludes,

> ...Jesus is challenging Peter to the kind of love which finds expression in full devotion and obedience while Peter asserts only a feeling of personal devotion; until Jesus is forced to challenge that, also, and to force him to face that fact that even his personal love has failed.[115]

It appears that most modern scholars who do differentiate between ἀγαπᾶν and φιλεῖν build upon the work of Spicq for support.[116] He has sought to illustrate that ἀγαπᾶν is to be distinguished from φιλεῖν:

> Dès lors ἀγαπᾶν ne signifie pas un amour plus rationnel et volontaire que φιλεῖν, mais a son sens technique des Septante: *attachement religieux, consécration à Dieu* qui se traduit au plan moral par une *totale fidélité et l'obéissance*, finalement en *service exclusif au Seigneur, toutes nuances ignorées de la* φιλία et qui sont à coup sûr celles que Jésus veut évoquer au renégat.[117]

In short, proponents of this interpretation maintain that the religious devotion or 'spiritual love'[118] that is connected with ἀγαπᾶν[119] is what Jesus is asking of Peter, and all Peter can do is respond by affirming his 'affection humaine',[120] 'friendship love'[121] or 'manly attachment'.[122]

In his final question to Peter, Jesus is seen either to accommodate himself to Peter,[123] or else to challenge even that aspect of Peter's love.[124] Spicq makes the case that Jesus was in fact touched by Peter's double insistence of his affection towards Jesus and thus uses Peter's own description of his feelings.[125]

Only recently has an excellent study been published which traces the use of the two terms for love throughout Greek literature with particular application to Jn 21.15-17.[126] While in classical Greek ἀγαπᾶν and φιλεῖν are virtual synonyms, in some passages they are juxtaposed, revealing a literary convention that is probably also operative here in Jn 21.15-17.

> In such passages, of course, the writers are following a common enough practice, that of contrasting synonyms in a way which arbitrarily allocates a distinction between them, the force of which is to be deduced from the context.[127]

Nevertheless, McKay does note (along with Spicq) that the preference of ἀγαπᾶν in the Septuagint no doubt influenced the prevalence of the term in the New Testament, although it still overlapped with φιλεῖν in meaning. John appears to have preferred ἀγαπᾶν in most references to God's love, 'so if a need arose to distinguish between them it was likely that ἀγαπάω would be chosen for the higher meaning'.[128] Generally in John, the two words are repeated in clusters (14.21-24, 16.27). Speaking with particular reference to how the Beloved Disciple is described, McKay suggests a pattern,

> The fact is that if the writer saw them as approximately synonymous and both appropriate for the description, he is likely to have chosen afresh each time. There appears to be no pattern in the sequence or the circumstances of the contexts, so the probability is that each choice was a random one, possibly influenced by a subjective reaction to the general sound and rhythm of the sentence.[129]

Another problem in maintaining that the two verbs are to be contrasted in 21.15-17 is that 'it is difficult to explain how the terminological switch would be meaningful if Peter were assenting to Jesus' question while at the same time giving that question a different definition'.[130] Of course, such an evaluation is somewhat weakened by the observation that we are reading the Greek of the writer, and not the actual language of the dialogue, but that only transposes the difficulty.[131] A solution to the difficulty may lie in noting that a lack of obvious significance in the variation should be taken as a sign that any intended distinctions are to be subordinated to the general thrust of the dialogue and the more significant exhortation which follows (i.e. ἀκολούθει μοι—21.19, 22).[132] It may be that the use of two verbs is intended to suggest the 'universal aspect' of 'love in its totality'.[133] We should probably look elsewhere for the primary significance of vv. 15-17. R.E. Brown, concurring with Gaechter,[134] suggests that the 'real stress is not on the use of *philein* but on *to triton*: 'Still a third time Jesus asked'—a translation that implies the synonymous character of the questions'.[135]

The three-fold commission given to Peter by Jesus has been understood by Gaechter in the context of the Near Eastern ceremonial and legal custom of repeating something three times before witnesses, thereby establishing a legal disposition.

> Er [*i.e. Jesus*] folgte dabei dem von uns aufgezeigten Rechtsbrauch, der in besonderer Weise für feierliche Rechtshandlungen Verwendung fand und noch findet. Damit sind alle Elemente der Feierlichkeit der Stelle erklärt und ist zugleich deutlich gemacht, wieso der dreifache Auftrag das alles Beherrschende des ganzen Dialogs war.[136]

Although it may be problematic to push the conclusion that we have a legal formula intentionally corresponding to the forensic conventions of the time to the extent that Gaechter does, it is necessary to recognize Jesus' charge as being solemn and authoritative. 'A three-fold repetition automatically has an air of solemnity without the suggestion of such a legal parallel'.[137]

On the three-fold emphasis in this final chapter of the Gospel, Agourides notes, with respect to v. 14,[138] 'In the first and second appearance, no restoration takes place. Only in the third is Peter restored'.[139] The reference to this *third* appearance of the resurrected Lord may be taken primarily to confirm the reality of the resurrection and not the certainty of Peter's restoration and/or commission.

That Peter is invested with authority is not only conveyed in the authoritative force of a three-fold commissioning but also by the nature of the charges. Jesus varies his charge to Peter in the three instances; (1) βόσκε τὰ ἀρνία μου, (2) ποίμαινε τὰ πρόβατά μου, (3) βόσκε τὰ πρόβατά μου. Generally speaking, the concept of shepherding conveys a certain sense of authority, especially as it is conveyed through the Old Testament traditions. 'The figure [*of the shepherd*] is used in situations which emphasize that Israel's leaders share in divine authority and act as God's delegates in the use of that authority'.[140]

The observation that the parallel exhortations alternate and that no verb–direct object combination is repeated presents one more opportunity to consider whether or not the writer is saying more in the three constructions than he can say in one. Osborne notes that 'the two words for "feed" translate the same Aramaic original (רעה)'[141] and he goes on to suggest that

> . . . John wished to signify to his readers the complete activity of pastoral care, in this case feeding and tending. This variation, then, refers to every aspect of pastoral activity by paralleling the 'shepherd' analogy (chapter 10) with a similar variation in the 'flock' terminology. . . it accentuates the all-inclusive nature of the 'flock'.[142]

The two words for 'sheep' or 'flock' are probably best understood as virtual synonyms[143] and at most contribute to the effect of conveying the sense of a well-rounded pastoral role over diverse Christian communities.

Whether the authority of Peter lies in the area of pastoral guidance among those within the church[144] or includes also the area of missions to those outside the church[145] is a question that is answered by combining the symbolism of vv. 15-17 with that contained in vv. 1-14. Peter has a role to play in both the growth and the maintenance of the Church. Because of the shared imagery between ch. 10 of John and this final chapter, Gunther has even proceeded to link Peter's commission to include responsibility for protection from heresy. 'The good shepherd protects his sheep from the wolf . . (10.11ff.). This could be symbolic for protecting them from heresy (Acts 20.28-30; cf. Mt 7.15)'.[146] This connection is unacceptable (as helpful as it may be for our particular thesis), for in the context of ch. 10 the good shepherd is the one who lays down his life for the sheep. One can only tie the shepherd motif in John to protection from heresy by importing a Lucan or Matthean symbolism.

Earlier in this chapter, we noted how the dialogues between Jesus and Peter are connected to Jesus' prediction in Jn 13.36-38 and

Peter's denials in ch. 18. Integral to the connection is the Johannine stress on 'following' Jesus, indicative of true discipleship. Peter is again given the opportunity and indeed the command, to follow (cf. ἀκολούθει μοι—Jn 21.19, 22). It has been argued that this repeated command of Jesus to Peter to follow is in fact the primary exhortation, in comparison to the ones to tend the flock.[147] Peter, enjoined to follow Jesus, is, in effect, being called afresh to become a disciple and assume his pastoral role. But more than that, he is being invited to follow Jesus in death. This is made clear by the words of Jesus which immediately precede the command to follow, in which Peter's own arrest and martyrdom is related, and it is supported by Jn 13.36-38. 'The present imperative, then, must include both Peter's present pastoral role (vv. 15-17) and its future culmination in his martyrdom as "following Jesus"'.[148]

While the rehabilitation and comissioning of Peter may have been perceived as necessary in order to re-instate Peter as a disciple and invest his pastoral role with some authority, it has also been suggested that this whole process was a pre-condition for Peter's martyrdom. 'After Peter is so reconstituted, then his martyrdom is a possibility'.[149] The reference to Peter's commissioning and death seems complimentary to this leader of the Twelve, although not all interpreters agree. For instance, according to Agourides, John 21 puts Peter's martyrdom in a context which tends to deflate it. Peter's martyrdom is

> . . . the end of a man who denied his Lord and for whom it was necessary to finish his life by a public ὁμολογία (witness) of Jesus,. . . the martyrdom of Peter is in close relation to his denial of Christ and his restoration to the apostolic office.[150]

Such an evaluation fails to take into account the fact that Peter's death is said to 'glorify God' (v. 19).

In summary, we can conclude that Peter is portrayed in a positive light in ch. 21. Furthermore, this attitude does not contrast with the general picture of Peter we encountered in the earlier chapters. It certainly cannot be regarded as a 'reversal'. The full name 'Simon Peter' is used here, perhaps to draw attention to his stature or importance in the narrative. He appears on both the literal and symbolic level as the leader of the disciples, and this is supported by the actions of the Beloved Disciple in the boat. Peter confesses his love to Jesus, as required of a true disciple in the Johannine scheme. He is given another chance to make good his promise to follow Jesus even to death (Jn 13.37). Peter is invested with authority in the church. He received a pastoral office with responsibilities over a united church and its mission. His arrest and death are foreshadowed in the first half of the chapter, and vv. 18 and 19 his martyrdom is seen as glorifying God.

What we see here in John is not the creation of a new ministry for Peter, but rather an interpretation of an already existing ministry with particular applicability to the Johannine community.

> The editor responsible for the final chapter of John would not seek to establish the legitimacy of the ministry of Peter since this was already well-accepted in the early church. The purpose of this inclusion was to give an interpretation to this existing ministry.
> The additional element that is also included in the conferral of office is the conviction that this office does find its foundation in Jesus himself... There is no polemic against the authority of Peter but rather an historical remembrance of the conditions upon which this ministry is to be based.[151]

O'Grady asserts that the conditions for office or authority in the church, according to John 21, are 'love of Jesus and willingness to die for him'.[152] Although ch. 21 may be taken as a caution to those within the Apostolic stream of Christianity, it is probably better to understand it as a confirmation to Johannine readers that Peter and the tradition he represents meet these conditions.

If Peter is highlighted and commended to the Johannine readers in the manner we have discerned, then we must compare this to the picture we find of the Beloved Disciple in this same chapter. How is the Beloved Disciple portrayed and how does this relate to what we see of Peter?

D. *The Beloved Disciple in John 21*

Chapter 21 focuses on the Beloved Disciple to an extent unequalled in the earlier chapters of the Gospel. This has led some scholars to discern a shift in the portrayal of the Beloved Disciple.

> In ch. 21 the beloved disciple's recognition of Jesus after the miraculous catch of fish *is* communicated to Peter and Peter responds. No longer is the beloved disciple present and absent; he is really present and affects the behaviour of Peter.[153]

Such a distinction is difficult to maintain, for in ch. 13 the Beloved

Disciple speaks to Jesus in response to Peter, and in ch. 18 he is reported to have spoken to the maid at the door. What he does definitely affects the behaviour of Peter. Although ch. 21 seems to focus on the person of the Beloved Disciple to a greater extent, he is not any more active than in the rest of the Gospel. However, by referring to the death of the Beloved Disciple, John 21 makes clear that he was indeed a historical person.

While the disciples are fishing in the boat and begin to haul in the full net, the Beloved Disciple recognizes the sign inherent in the full net—that is, that the person on the shore actually is the Lord. It is apparent that his recognition of Jesus is dependent upon theological insight and not physical recognition of the figure on the shore. This observation fits well with the role the Beloved Disciple has played in other narratives. The hero of the Johannine community has an insight and a theological discernment that are unparalleled by Peter and the other disciples.[154] This is the first time, however, that we read of the Beloved Disciple communicating his insight to Peter. Can we conclude that the Beloved Disciple is the 'revelational source'[155] for all other disciples? It is pushing the simple phrase ὁ κύριός ἐστιν much too far to state, as de Jonge does, that 'the dependence of the whole "Church" on the beloved disciple is indicated by the dependence of Peter on this disciple's insight and witness in v. 7'.[156]

As noted several times previously the Johannine use of ἀκολουθεῖν is intimately joined to the concept of discipleship. Therefore, when the Beloved Disciple follows (ἀκολουθοῦντα) both Jesus and Peter in 21.20, he functions as the 'ideal follower, the epitome of what it means to be a believer'.[157] The post-resurrection context of this particular depiction of discipleship may be significant.

> The redactor who added chapter 21 to the Johannine Gospel reminds us that the Beloved Disciple was a disciple who followed after Jesus (and Peter). In this way he dramatized the notion that the Beloved Disciple continued to be a disciple of Jesus even after the Resurrection. By so doing, he continues and reinforces the earlier Johannine tradition which was consistent in describing the Beloved Disciple as *mathetes* (disciple).[158]

Given the ecclesial concerns that underlie the compilation of ch. 21, it should not be surprising to find an ecclesial function ascribed to the Beloved Disciple that goes beyond a simple depiction of theological insight and faithful discipleship. As O'Grady reasons,

If he [the Beloved Disciple] is placed on the side of Peter in a
chapter that has clear ecclesial overtones can we deduce that the
Beloved Disciple exercised a function that was important for the
Church?[159]

Verse 24 provides us with another function of the Beloved Disciple
that has a definite ecclesial context: οὗτός ἐστιν ὁ μαθητὴς ὁ
μαρτυρῶν περὶ τούτων καὶ ὁ γράψας ταῦτα, καὶ οἴδαμεν ὅτι ἀληθὴς
αὐτοῦ ἡ μαρτυρία ἐστίν. While there may be considerable variance
in the interpretations of the role the Beloved Disciple played in the
actual authorship of this chapter[160] (and the Gospel as a whole),
there can be little doubt that he played an important function as a
witness to Jesus' teachings for his community.[161] It is an open
question whether the Beloved Disciple's function as witness extended
into the greater Christian community beyond the Johannine circle at
the time of writing, but if the Gospel was written *primarily* for the
Johannine community itself, then in this chapter the editor is giving
the Beloved Disciple's testimony to the community concerning
Peter.

From 21.20-23 we can gather that the Johannine community was
confronted with the unexpected death of the Beloved Disciple and
the accompanying threat to their communal faith and identity. Some
scholars argue that the Beloved Disciple has not yet died, basing
their positions on the 'ambiguous wording'[162] of vv. 22-24, especially
the present participle μαρτυρῶν in v. 24, as contrasted with the
aorist participle γράψας. The effect of the combination of these two
participles doubtless 'is intended to say that he continues to witness
but has completed his writing'.[163] However, to maintain that the
witness of the Beloved Disciple continues is not necessarily to
maintain that his physical life continues. 'This disciple remains with
the believers, even after his death, as witness (ὁ μαρτυρῶν present!)
in what he has written (ὁ γράψας ταῦτα)'.[164] Indeed, the emphasis
on the 'remaining' of the Beloved Disciple in this chapter may point
to a figurative understanding couched in physical descriptions.

Pamment has re-interpreted the references to the death of the
Beloved Disciple to mean references to the death of Gentile
Christianity. It will be remembered that she follows Bultmann's
scheme of seeing the Beloved Disciple as the representative of
Gentile Christianity while Peter is the embodiment of Jewish
Christianity.[165] Citing the words of Jesus in Jn 21.22 about the
Beloved Disciple remaining 'until I come', she states,

The saying would naturally give rise to the belief that gentile
Christianity or gentile Christians would not die before the final
transformation of the world. . the saying in Jn 21.23 tries to obviate
these difficulties. . . in other words, the saying is open ended. The
fate of gentile Christianity is uncertain.[166]

It is questionable whether Pamment's demythologization was in the
minds of the first generation readers of this chapter, so that every
time they read 'Beloved Disciple' they thought 'gentile Christianity'.

These verses show not only that the Beloved Disciple was a
historical person[167] known to the Johannine community, but also
that 'the Johannine tradition did not escape the apocalyptic
enthusiasm which ran through the early church'.[168] This is probably
to be regarded as a vestige of the early eschatological expectations of
Christians (as seen in Paul's early letters and in Mk 13) rather than
as a heightening expectation that started to develop as the Johannine
community and the Beloved Disciple aged. 'The enigmatical promise
(Mk. 9 and parallels) that there were some among the disciples who
would not die until "the kingdom of God came with power" must
have made a profound impression'.[169]

In light of the general eschatological tenor of the times it is
reasonable to conclude that the message in ch. 21 is intended to
dispel such apocalyptic urgency and misapprehensions concerning
the second coming of Christ. This correction is entirely in keeping
with the eschatological perspective of the rest of the Fourth Gospel.
The belief that the Beloved Disciple would not die before Christ
came was a minority view that was not taught by the Beloved
Disciple himself.

The solution to the eschatological drama that the writer offers (i.e.
οὐκ εἶπεν δὲ αὐτῷ ὁ ᾿Ιησοῦς ὅτι οὐκ ἀποθνῄσκει ἀλλὰ ἐὰν αὐτὸν
θέλω μένειν ἕως ἔρχομαι, τί πρὸς σέ;) has been interpreted to mean
that Jesus pronounced *not* an actual prophecy but merely a
conditional or 'hypothetical'[170] statement.

Another view, somewhat more complex, but in complete accordance
with the concern of John 21 to provide for the continuance of the
Johannine community within the Church, is presented by Schnackenburg.
Beginning with the grammatical principle that ἐάν with the
subjunctive can have the same force of probability as εἰ with the
indicative verb in a primary tense,[171] he emphasizes not the
conditional quality of the sentence, but the verb μένειν. In other
words, the author of John 21 is calling for the continuance of the

traditions and community of the Beloved Disciple even after his death.

> Jesus desires that his disciple 'remains' yet not in an outward sense of 'remaining alive' but in another figurative way. That can then be understood as the continuing effect in the circle of his disciples and his Church, or as the continuance of his words, his Spirit-borne proclamation (as it is found in the gospel). Perhaps the writer who only wanted to defend against false interpretation, did not want to commit himself precisely. But this spiritual 'remaining' and continuing effect of the disciple is in line with what is also recognizable in v. 24.[172]

The continuation of the Johannine community ensures the 'remaining' of the Beloved Disciple and his witness. Conversely, the only way the Johannine community is to continue is by remaining faithful to the teaching of the Beloved Disciple, whose authority comes from being a witness to Jesus. Part of his witness, according to the author of John 21, is to the commissioning of Peter as pastor.

To summarize, the Beloved Disciple in John 21 has the insight to recognize the full net as a sign revealing Christ. Furthermore, the Beloved Disciple remains a faithful follower of Jesus right to the end of the Gospel account. He serves as a witness to words of Jesus that were important for the maturing church. The eschatological misunderstanding that prompted much of what was said about the Beloved Disciple in this chapter is utilized by the author to address the issue of the continuance of the Johannine community. The Beloved Disciple will 'remain' because this is Jesus' wish (v. 21). All of the Beloved Disciple's functions in this chapter are related to Peter in one way or another.

E. *Peter and the Beloved Disciple*

In John 21 Peter and the Beloved Disciple *do not* have identical roles in the believing community. Peter leads, the Beloved Disciple follows. The Beloved Disciple shares his spiritual discernment with Peter, who then acts upon it. The Beloved Disciple is a witness to Peter's pastoral role. Even the deaths of the two figures are contrasted, although not in order to commend one above the other.

Peter's actions have been understood to reflect an unstable or irrational impetuosity. This is contrasted with the faithful serenity of the Beloved Disciple, 'The love of Peter is full of unreasoning vigour, and therefore suffers trial. The beloved disciple loves calmly, securely, without doubt or vacillation'.[173] The quality of Peter's love is 'imperfect',[174] according to this perspective.

> The heavenly quality of ἀγάπη which the Son mediates is more characteristic of his relation to the disciple whom he ἠγάπα (13.23; 19.26; 21.7, 20; but cf. 20.2). Peter's friendship love was not as serene and consistent, or as based on understanding and truth.[175]

In view of our discussion of ἀγαπᾶν and φιλεῖν, it is not wise to make such a distinction. Peter professes an intense love for Jesus by both his confessions and his actions. 'Peter's impetuosity is nevertheless conditioned by an obvious love for his Master'.[176] The Beloved Disciple may exemplify the intimate love that marks a faithful disciple of Jesus, but the stress is on love for the Beloved Disciple, and not the other way around. It was in the experience of Jesus' love for them that the Johannine Christians were to identify with their hero.

The testimony of the Beloved Disciple is presented in the context of a particular stream of the Christian church. Therefore, his positive witness to the role of Peter has special significance for his community. 'There is no rivalry between him [*i.e. Peter*] and the BD; on the contrary the pronouncements of v. 15-17 belong to the *tauta* (v. 24) 'written' by the trustworthy BD'.[177] In other words, the Beloved Disciple validates Peter's role for the Johannine community.

The theme of discipleship is basic to John's Gospel, and the primary criterion for discipleship is a relationship of love with Jesus. Since Peter's love for his Lord has been re-affirmed, he is indeed a true disciple.

The faithful discipleship of the hero of the Johannine community continued right to the end (21.20). Here the Beloved Disciple follows *Peter* as well as Jesus.[178] The writer, through the actions of the Beloved Disciple, may be directing the allegiance of the Johannine community to Peter. However, this is admittedly tenuous.

Lindars, who traces the concept of discipleship throughout the Gospel of John, merits consideration in this regard. He distinguishes between the discipleship epitomized by Peter and that epitomized by the Beloved Disciple. Each character illustrates a facet of being a disciple of Christ.

> The contrast between the two disciples in verses 15-23 is not a mirror of church polemics, but a way of teaching discipleship. The

key word is 'following' (verse 20, cf. 20.6). Peter is generally
regarded as the greatest of the Twelve, and he does indeed receive
the prime responsibility for the Church (verse 15-17). Moreover,
his loyal discipleship has gained him the most coveted prize, that of
imitating his Master in death as well as in life (for it is difficult to
resist the impression that verse 18 is a prophecy *ex eventu*). But
still, the Beloved Disciple is a better model, for he remains a loyal
follower, he seeks no place of authority (for none is mentioned),
and his end is in obscurity, without the glamour of a martyr's
crown.[179]

While these comments are helpful, Lindars' value judgment may
be questioned.

In sharp contrast to the martyrdom of Peter stands the apparently
natural death of the Beloved Disciple whose long life stands in
theological conflict with the martyr death of Peter.[180]

The positive evaluation given to Peter's martyrdom in 21.19
mitigates against Lindars' view that an obscure demise without the
'glamour of a martyr's crown' is a better model for a loyal follower of
Jesus than Peter's final witness.[181] Peter's martyrdom would probably
have been regarded as 'better' than the natural death of the Beloved
Disciple, even by the Johannine Christians. Schuyler Brown
comments:

The embarrassment of the Johannine community over the demise
of its leader, whose martyrdom is not mentioned and who appears
to have died of natural causes (vv. 22-23), is underlined by the
contrast with the death by which Peter had glorified God (v. 18-
19).[182]

But the overall effect of vv. 20-23 is to downplay any comparison
between the deaths of the two disciples. The author affirms that 'it
was the Master's will that the respective ends of the two apostles
should be such'.[183] The two lives are related insofar as the Beloved
Disciple (Johannine community) continues by identifying with the
Petrine pastoral tradition (Apostolic church).

F. *Conclusions*

Faced with an uncertain future, the Johannine community reads in
John 21 that Jesus has provided for their continuation after the death
of the Beloved Disciple. The reference to τοὺς ἀδελφούς (21.23)
indicates that the Johannine community is being addressed.

> In xx 17 we saw this term [*i.e. the brothers*] applied to the
> immediate disciples of Jesus, because they would be begotten as
> God's children, through the gift of the Spirit and thus become
> Jesus' brothers. Here [*i.e. 21.23*] it is applied to the Christians of
> the Johannine community (probably with the same theological
> understanding), a usage attested also in III John 5...[184]

If this chapter was aimed at a Johannine readership, then what it
has to say about *Peter* and the Beloved Disciple has a direct bearing
on the Johannine community. This chapter was not added by a
Johannine redactor to legitimize his community in the eyes of
'outside' readers.[185] On the contrary, the portrayal of Peter in this
chapter is directed to the Johannine community, in which he is to
play an important role.

Chapter 21 may be reflecting the historical situation of the
Johannine community as it began the second generation of its
existence. A number of scholars have sought to show that 'the
authority and breadth of apostleship was a major problem within the
church at the turn of the century'.[186] The Epistles of John reveal a
crisis of authority in at least two local Johannine communities. 1
John reflects a split in the Johannine community over pneumatic
leadership.[187] 3 John reveals tensions revolving around the exercise
of personal authority.[188] If ch. 21 of John is written with these
problems in mind, then O'Grady may well be right:

> By establishing the conditions of office in the church, love of Jesus
> and willingness to die for him, the editor is reminding the church of
> how authority is to be exercised.[189]

The emphasis on unity goes hand in hand with the concern for
authority in the Christian community. Minear discerns not only a
desire for unity among contemporary Christian communities at the
time of writing, but also a 'unity between the two generations'.[190]

In summary, this final chapter of the Gospel of John reveals a
desire to preserve some of the traditions which the Beloved Disciple
shared with his community, but which did not find a place in the
body of the Fourth Gospel. The editor uses these traditions to
illustrate how the church is to be centred upon the resurrected Jesus,
who has provided for the care of his sheep. The positions of
leadership in the church are to be filled by true disciples, i.e. Peter
and the Beloved Disciple, although they have different functions in
relation to the community. Under their influence the church is to
evangelize *all* men, while still maintaining its unity.

Chapter 7

CONCLUSION

A. *Introduction*

Even when Johannine scholarship at large reflects broad consensus
... a residual uncertainty remains... The nagging and not infrequent
uncertainty is due in large measure to a kaleidoscopic quality of the
Fourth Gospel; its parts and the whole are so closely interdependent
that a small shift in interpreting one element can cause all the
others to revolve ever so slightly into a new and likewise coherent
constellation.[1]

It has been the task of this work to seek an accurate understanding of
the roles and inter-relationship of Peter and the Beloved Disciple as
depicted by the Fourth Evangelist, a task that was prompted by the
'residual uncertainty' Mahoney so aptly describes. The narratives
have been examined individually and evaluations have been made.
What remains is to synthesize our findings and to show how the
historical context of the Johannine community influenced the
portrayal of Peter and the Beloved Disciple.

The two disciples are not merely 'supporting props' in narratives
concerned solely with the presentation of one central theological
theme.[2] The many-faceted symbolism of John, his 'signs schema',
which operates with different levels of perception among his readers,
his use of double-meanings and careful staging which draw the
reader into the drama—all these devices attest to the intricate
structure of John's Gospel. The two figures of Peter and the Beloved
Disciple are part of this structure. They are not simply 'rivals', with
Peter being consistently superseded by the Beloved Disciple.

Can our findings be correlated so as to produce an overall picture
of the two figures in relationship? If the intended readership of the
Gospel is the Johannine community, what is written about Peter and
the Beloved Disciple is an exhortation to the community rather than
a reflection of the community's attitude. Painter's distinction
between the theology of the Johannine school (with the evangelist)

and the greater Johannine community supports this approach to the text.[3] While some members of the Joahnnine community may have seen the Beloved Disciple as superior to Peter, the Gospel in its present form may reflect an attempt to correct such an attitude. We must read the portrayals of the two figures with this possibility in mind.

The Gospel of John falls into two main divisions,[4] with an epilogue.[5] Peter and the Beloved Disciple appear together in the 'Book of Glory' (chs. 13-20) and the epilogue (ch. 21). But the portrayal of Peter in John 1–12 is the basis for Peter's relationship to the Beloved Disciple in the subsequent sections of the Gospel.

In the first section, Peter is presented in much the same way as he is in the Synoptic tradition. He has a central place in the calling of the disciples and in the christological confession of Jn 6.60-71. But the Fourth Evangelist does not merely reproduce a Synoptic portrayal of Peter. He reworks the traditional material, infusing it with his own concerns.[6]

Chapters 1–12 illustrate how Peter is depicted by the Fourth Evangelist *independent* of any comparison with the Beloved Disciple. Even though Peter can be regarded in chs. 13–20 as a foil for the Beloved Disciple, the narratives do not present an obvious and consistent contrast.

In evaluating the depictions of Peter and the Beloved Disciple, we must bear in mind the purpose behind each narrative. In ch. 13, Peter and the Beloved Disciple are of secondary importance; the drama focuses upon Jesus and Judas. Peter and the Beloved Disciple are used to keep all the participants in ignorance of Jesus' actions and Judas' intentions, while these actions and intentions are communicated to the reader.

In chs. 18 and 19, the Beloved Disciple follows Jesus faithfully throughout his arrest and interrogation right to the foot of the cross. In ch. 19 he is part of the new family of God brought about by the work which Jesus culminated on the cross. In ch. 18, the disciples, represented by Peter, are unable to go where Jesus goes. They prove Jesus' words in Jn 13.36.[7] Peter and the Beloved Disciple have significance only in the context of Jesus' 'hour'.

The empty tomb stories underlying ch. 20 of John have been reworked to illustrate 'faith without seeing' (Jn 20.29), which is exemplified by the Beloved Disciple. The sign of the empty tomb is validated by the witness of Peter.

In ch. 21, the author's concern for the continuance of his community governs the collection, arrangement and interpretation of traditional materials. The editor, faced with a crisis in his community, puts Peter in a crucial role for the Johannine readers.

The portrayal of Peter in relation to the Beloved Disciple undergoes a development between John 13–20 and John 21. The second half of the Gospel presents a somewhat ambiguous picture of Peter in relation to the Beloved Disciple, while the appendix to the Gospel enhances the role of Peter. The editor responsible for ch. 21 of the Gospel of John must have thought that the relationship between Peter and the Beloved Disciple in 13–20 served his purposes. He, at least, did not view the comparisons between Peter and the Beloved Disciple in chapters 13–20 as reflecting badly on Peter.

Although we recognize the differences between the three sections of the Gospel, we must read the Gospel as a coherent whole. As Childs put it,

> To describe the various layers reflected within the Fourth Gospel may often have significance for understanding the final form of the book, but this approach is not to be simply identified with the canonical meaning of the Gospel. The pre-history of the Fourth Gospel stands in an indirect, dialectical relation to its final form and aids to the extent in which it illuminates the canonical intentionality.[8]

Furthermore, the relationship between Peter and the Beloved Disciple must also be subordinated to the overriding concerns and themes of the individual narratives. With this in mind, we turn to the portrayal of the Beloved Disciple in the Gospel.

B. *The Beloved Disciple*

The person of the Beloved Disciple is found throughout the second half of the Gospel, from ch. 13 until the final paragraph of ch. 21. In the final chapter, *after* the reference to Peter's martyrdom, the Beloved Disciple 'follows' Jesus (v. 20) and Jesus speaks of him 'remaining' (μένειν) (v. 22). While he does not have an active part or voice in the evangelist's narratives, it is evident from ch. 21 that he was regarded as an actual person. His peripheral function in the narratives may be the result of his having been inserted into traditions in which he was not originally present.

But because he is in a peripheral role as an anonymous 'observer', the Beloved Disciple becomes a symbolic and representative figure with which the readers are drawn to identify themselves, like the 'silent partner' in Gnostic writings.[9] The anonymity of this figure was purposeful and necessary.[10] But this literary device may have served to link these narratives to a well-known witness.

Perhaps the most basic characteristic of the Beloved Disciple is that of *follower*, or *disciple*. He follows Jesus into the courtyard of the High Priest during the interrogation and even to the foot of the cross. After the resurrection he follows both Jesus and Peter (Jn 21.20). He illustrates by his actions what it means to be loved by Jesus and to be a believer and a true disciple.

The Beloved Disciple also epitomizes the intimate and continuing relationship of a disciple to his Master. The Beloved Disciple abides (μένειν) with Jesus and is designated as the disciple whom Jesus loved. Chapter 13 describes the intimate relationship between the Beloved Disciple and Jesus in the same terms that are used to describe the Son's intimacy with the Father in Jn 1.18.[11] In ch. 19 the Beloved Disciple is 'adopted' into a new family. Jesus' charge to the Beloved Disciple and Mary in ch. 19 is not a bestowal of ecclesial office; rather, it is the beginning of a new order of relationships in the family of God inaugurated by Jesus' completed work on the cross.[12] The Beloved Disciple's presence shows the readers of the Gospel that Jesus' work enables the beginning of new relationships in the church. In Jn 21.20 we are again reminded that the Beloved Disciple had lain in the bosom of Jesus. This allusion to Jn 13.21-30 is followed by a reference o the Beloved Disciple as one who faithfully 'remains', i.e., he continues even after his death through the ongoing community.[13]

The result of the Beloved Disciple's intimate relationship with Jesus is spiritual sensitivity and insight into certain 'signs' and their significance for the person and work of Christ. For example, in Jn 20.2-10 the Beloved Disciple is able to come to a point of belief upon experiencing the empty tomb, independent of any other factors. In Jn 21.7 we see that he is able to recognize the presence of Christ at the 'sign' of the full net of fish.

While the insight of the Beloved Disciple serves as a source of revelation for the reader of the Gospel, the narratives are constructed in such a way as to preclude such a role with respect to others in the story. The Beloved Disciple is not a source of revelation for the other disciples. In 13.21-30 he is as ignorant as the rest of the disciples, he displays no special knowledge of Jesus and after asking the disciples' question, he appears to remain as ignorant as he was before. It could be argued that he serves as 'mediator' or 'facilitator' in 18.15, 16 when he helps Peter get into the courtyard at the time of Jesus' interrogation. In 20.8ff. we read nothing of the Beloved Disciple disclosing the significance of the empty tomb to Peter. However, in 21.7, upon realizing the identity of the figure on the shore through the sign of the full net, the Beloved Disciple does share his insight with Peter. This single, limited reference is the only place in the Gospel where the Beloved Disciple mediates a spiritual insight to someone else in a narrative. In light of this, Collins is inaccurate, when he says:

> The intimacy with Jesus which is so characteristic of the Beloved Disciple is that which enables him to give the testimony of and about Jesus to others. Within the tradition of the Johannine circle it is he to whom Peter addresses himself when he would have knowledge of the events leading to Jesus' glorification and it is to him that Jesus grants that knowledge.[14]

Rather, the Beloved Disciple serves as an interpreter for the benefit of the readers of the Gospel, that is, for the Johannine community itself.

It has been suggested that the Johannine community, with its emphasis on 'believing without seeing' (cf. Jn 20.29; 21.7), points to the stress the Johannine Christians put on spiritual insight and discernment and the relative unimportance of Apostolic testimony to the resurrection. Schuyler Brown comments:

> Such intuitive insight into the sign value of incidents connected with Jesus' life is characteristic of the faith of the Johannine community, which needs neither the Easter experience nor apostolic testimony to this experience, in order to believe.[15]

Although the Johannine tradition stressed the guidance of the Spirit (13.16) the Johannine community did not feel itself to be completely without the need for authoritative witness. Jn 21.24[16] expresses a concern for a validating testimony and in Jn 19.35 we see a similar interest.[17] From this we see that the Beloved Disciple was regarded as a witness to certain events important for the faith of his community. The two specific contexts in which the appeal to the witness of the Beloved Disciple is given are particularly relevant to this enquiry. First of all, the Beloved Disciple serves as a witness to the events at the foot of the cross, when Peter has disappeared from the scene. Second, the Beloved Disciple is a witness to the restoration and commissioning of Peter in ch. 21. The Beloved Disciple assumes a role as witness in the absence of Peter (ch. 19) and as witness *to* Peter (ch. 21).

The Beloved Disciple is an example of the true disciple's response of πίστις in its fullest sense; belief and faithfulness. In ch. 20.2-10 the original import of the story has been changed so as to present a call to faith as exemplified by the Beloved Disciple. He is the 'prototype of all others loved by Jesus Christ'.[18] He abides in an intimate relationship with Jesus, following him throughout his passion. He serves as a witness to some crucial aspects of the work and words of Jesus. His faithfulness is utilized by the author to address the problem regarding the continuance of the community: the Beloved Disciple remains through the community that continues to abide in Jesus and faithfully follows his direction.

C. *Peter*

Unlike the Beloved Disciple, Peter is referred to frequently in the Synoptic Gospels as well as in the Fourth Gospel. Peter was prominent in the traditions underlying the Gospels. Was the only reason he is mentioned in John's narratives because he was part of the original tradition with which John is working?[19] Detailed exegesis and careful comparison with the Synoptic parallels have shown that the Gospel of John presents the Petrine traditions in its own way. Furthermore, the Johannine Peter fares well in comparison with the Synoptics. This is particularly noticeable in ch. 6, at the Last Supper, in the denials, and in the epilogue.

The first reference to Peter we have in the Gospel of John is set in the context of the calling of the first disciples. Peter is not the first called; rather, his brother Andrew and another disciple of John the Baptist are the first to follow Jesus. The honour of the first messianic confession belongs to Andrew, and not Peter, who gives the first confession in the Synoptics.[20] In other words, Peter is not the first person to express belief in Jesus as the Christ.

However, Simon Peter was a well-known and respected figure, according to the Johannine account, from the very beginning of Jesus' ministry. His naming and commissioning signify his importance. Jesus also singles Peter out for a special charge in ch. 21, which builds upon the positive depiction of Peter in the earlier chapters.

In Jn 6.60-71, Peter represents those who remain faithful at a time when other disciples of Christ are falling away *en masse*, particularly in Galilee. Only in John's Gospel is Peter's confession juxtaposed to this falling away, which heightens its effect. In his three-part confession, Peter models the Johannine understanding of what it means to become a believer and a true disciple.[21] Peter is not identified with Satan here, as in Matthew and Mark.

When Jn 6.60-71 is coupled with Jn 1.35-42, we see that Peter is portrayed in a positive light. Both of these scenes with Peter in the first half of the Gospel are crucial. He is the spokesman for the disciples. His faith may not be ideal, but it is exemplary. He does not stand on a pedestal above the other disciples, but, at the same time, there are no aspersions cast on his character, faith or status. He is recognized by the Fourth Evangelist for the integral part he plays in the early Christian community.

Peter's leadership is also evident in John 13-21. His actions throughout Jesus' hour commend his allegiance and love. In the revelation of the betrayer, Peter acts as spokesman for the group at the Last Supper. In ch. 20 he is the one to whom Mary reports her discovery. Upon arrival at the tomb, the Beloved Disciple stops to let Peter enter first. In Jn 21.3 Peter acts as leader for the disciples. When the Beloved Disciple realizes who is on the shore, he reports it to Peter (21.7). Peter leads the way to the shore and, in a highly symbolic act, he hauls the full, unbroken net ashore (21.11). He is given a pastoral charge by Jesus to care for his sheep (21.15-17). All of these passages point to the leadership role Peter is given in the Gospel of John.

In the scene of the footwashing, Peter misunderstands the actions of Jesus, but even in his misunderstanding he reveals his attachment to Jesus (cf. 13.6-9). In 13.36-38, where Jesus predicts Peter's denials, we see another example of the eager but ignorant commitment of Peter (representing the Twelve?), who did not yet understand the significance of Jesus' hour of glorification. Peter impulsively acts out of loyalty in Jn 18.10 when he takes up his sword to defend Jesus. Then he proceeds to follow Jesus and his arresters into the courtyard.

Even Peter's denials in ch. 18.15-18, 25-27, can be understood in a less condemnatory way than the Synoptic counterparts. The three-fold repetition of the questions to Peter, and the mention of a coal fire (ἀνθρακιάν) link the denials with a restoration and commission in Jn

21.15-19. In John 18 Peter's answers to the questions put to him do not reflect as badly on him as in the Synoptics: they focus on his actions in the garden rather than on his allegiance to Jesus. Peter's denials seem to be linked to a fear of punishment for drawing the sword. John's account of Peter's third denial is less elaborate. 'There is no reference to the Synoptic "oaths and curses" at the denial, and Peter does not deny knowledge of Jesus. . .'[22] Although Jesus insists that Peter will *not* be able to follow him as he goes through his final hour (13.36), he calls Peter anew in Jn 21.19, 22. In ch. 18 Peter and Jesus are both interrogated, but Jesus *alone* is able to complete the work the Father has called him to do.

The certainty of Peter's love for Jesus is highlighted by his triple insistence in ch. 21. He maintains that he loves Jesus more than he loves his livelihood and his friends. The three-fold repetition implies the synonymity of the words for love, rather than a distinction of meaning between ἀγαπᾶν and φιλεῖν[23] The effect is to stress the genuineness of Peter's love and the authoritativeness of the accompanying pastoral charge.

Peter's discipleship extends to the point of death (Jn 21.18-19). His martyrdom is commended as a means of glorifying God. His arrest and death are an extension of his following Jesus. In other words, Peter is a true disciple in the Johannine tradition.

In Jn 20.1-10 Peter testifies to the conditions of the empty tomb. He is able to confirm from the arrangement of the grave-clothes that the body of Jesus was not stolen. Peter serves here as the best-known witness, as he does also in Lk. 24.12, 24, 34.[24]

In conclusion, Peter is commended to the Johannine reader as leader, spokesman, witness, disciple, and pastor. The appreciation of Peter in the epilogue is not incompatible with the picture we find in the first twenty chapters of the Gospel, and ch. 21 certainly does not reflect a *reversal* in the Johannine estimate of Peter.[25]

D. *The Two in Relationship*

In the introductory pages of the book it was argued that since Peter and the Beloved Disciple are paired in a number of strategic places in the Gospel of John, we should conclude that 'the evangelist wanted to convey a particular understanding of the relationship between Peter and the Beloved Disciple'.[26] This relationship between the two may not be *the* primary concern behind each of the narratives, but their structure and content suggest that Peter and the Beloved Disciple are important characters in the narratives. In chs. 1 and 21 Peter carries on a significant dialogue with Jesus, and in ch. 21 Jesus singles him out for a special charge.

In Jn 13.21-30 Peter and the Beloved Disciple share a limited relationship with one another in the narrative, and their relationship is not a primary concern in this narrative. The narrative focuses on Jesus and Judas and shows Jesus' full and conscious participation in the initiation of Jesus' final 'hour'. Nevertheless, both the Beloved Disciple and Peter have a role in this narrative which brings them into relationship with each other.

In chs. 18 and 19 the Beloved Disciple and Peter are central characters. The Beloved Disciple and Peter are paired in 18.15-17; Peter is then juxtaposed to Jesus in 18.18-27; and then the Beloved Disciple takes Peter's place alongside Jesus in ch. 19 (A & B—B & C—C & A). Jesus alone can complete the work he was sent to do, but the Beloved Disciple, at the foot of the cross with Mary, the mother of Jesus, marks the initiation of a new order of relationships in the family of God.

Jn 20.2-10 represents a transposition of traditional narratives from a witness to the conditions of the empty tomb to a call to faith in the resurrection of Jesus Christ.

Finally, we note the chiastic arrangement of ch. 21, as Osborne construes

> Here the AB:BA would centre upon the BD and Peter, with A=BD centred passages and B=Peter passages. The two BD passages (21.1-14, 20-23) centre upon his authority in recognizing the Lord and providing authentic witness. The two Peter passages (21.15-17, 18-19) centre upon pastoral responsibility. There is also a certain unity of development with the four as a whole, all exhibiting ecclesiological force'.[26]

The context again is christological: Jesus provides for the continuance of the Christian community when he will no longer be with them. The deaths of Peter and the Beloved Disciple are *not* to be compared, since both were in accord with the will of Jesus.

A few principles guide our interpretation of the relationship between Peter and the Beloved Disciple:

1. Peter and the Beloved Disciple are highlighted in the Johannine narratives and are thus significant characters.
2. They are to be interpreted in relationship to one another.

3.   The relationship between Peter and the Beloved Disciple is
     subservient to the christological thrust of each narrative.
4.   Peter and the Beloved Disciple have separate functions
     which vary from narrative to narrative.
5.   The representation of Peter develops from one section of the
     Gospel to another.

If Peter and the Beloved Disciple are understood as representatives
of their respective communities, then both communities share in the
Gospel heritage. Each community has its own understanding of the
person, work and words of Christ, and these varying perspectives can
peacefully co-exist. But the Johannine community appears to have a
condescending attitude toward the circle of Christians represented
by Peter. The Apostolic Christians do not have the intimacy with
Jesus and the accompanying spiritual insight which the Johannine
Christians experience. Nevertheless they too are disciples of Christ
although over dependent upon empirical evidence for their limited
insight and faith.

With the addition of the final chapter to the Gospel of John, a new
significance is infused into the relationship. The addition of ch. 21
has caused the Johannine kaleidoscope to revolve into a new
constellation, as it were. How does the Beloved Disciple serve the
interest of Peter, and how does Peter serve the interest of the Beloved
Disciple?

The Beloved Disciple serves as an 'instrument' or 'vehicle' for
Peter's access to Jesus. In ch. 13 Peter communicates his question to
Jesus through the Beloved Disciple. In ch. 18 he is allowed access
into the courtyard through the intervention of the Beloved Disciple.
In ch. 21, the Beloved Disciple informs Peter that Jesus is on the
shore. However, the Beloved Disciple does not serve as a source of
revelation or saving faith for Peter and those he represents.

Such episodes illustrate the perspective of the Johannine Christians:
they know Jesus and abide in him in a special way, and consequently
they have something to offer Peter and the Apostolic tradition.
Agourides argues that the depictions of the two in relationship are
designed to serve as a corrective to Petrine traditions:

> I think that such expressions describing the intimate relationship
> to Jesus may signify, in view of the disciple's comparison to Peter
> throughout the Gospel, that John is in a position to correct
> traditions founded on the authority of Peter, or rather false
> interpretations of the Marcan Gospel relating to events in the life

of Christ and also the personal authority of Peter among the other Apostles.[27]

However, we do not find any explicit correction of Petrine claims in the Gospel of John. Naturally the Johannine Christians would be proud of their distinctiveness. But the Gospel as a whole is not likely to enhance this attitude. The Johannine community's continuance is being threatened by internal divisions. The portrayal of the relationship between Peter and the Beloved Disciple emphasizes how Peter, i.e. Apostolic Christianity, serves the interests of the Johannine community as it enters into its second generation. Faith, intimacy with Jesus and spiritual insight are assumed, but the Gospel recognizes the community's need for other qualities which Peter represents.

Although the Beloved Disciple is close to the mind and heart of Jesus, he does not assume a role of leadership among the group of disciples in the narrative. Peter, on the other hand, is portrayed as the leader and spokesman for the disciples, and his leadership includes even the Beloved Disciple. In 13.24 Peter directs the Beloved Disciple to ask the question which is on the minds of all of the disciples, and the Beloved Disciple follows Peter's direction.

In 20.4-8 the Beloved Disciple arrives at the empty tomb first, but he stops and waits for Peter to enter the tomb before going in himself. Peter's leadership role may be a factor in the evangelist's construction of the narrative.

In ch. 21, Peter exercises leadership over the Beloved disciple both as fisherman and as a disciple of Jesus. When the Beloved Disciple discerns the identity of Jesus, he reports it to Peter. Jesus tells Peter to tend the flock and to follow him even to the point of death, and the Beloved Disciple follows both Jesus and Peter. Such is the leadership accorded Peter in the Gospel of John.

E. *The Historical Context*

The existence of a Johannine community, although hypothetical, is so strongly supported by the Johannine Gospel and Epistles it has become a working hypothesis for virtually all New Testament scholars.[28] R.E. Brown and J.P. Meier maintain that an adequate interpretation of any of our New Testament documents requires an effort to discover the interrelationships between the various traditions and communities centring around leading figures in the Christian church:

Peter, Paul, and James dealt with each other, keeping *koinonia* or communion, seemingly even when they disputed. A work written afterwards in the name and tradition of one sometimes mentions another (II Peter mentions Paul), or implicitly refers to the thought of the other (James rejects the Pauline slogan of faith and works), or deals with the same cast of characters (both Ignatius and I Clement mention Peter and Paul, both Pauline writings and I Peter mention Mark). In other words, the Christianity of the works we have discussed was interrelated, and an adequate interpretation of these works requires an effort to discover the interrelationship.[29]

The Johannine community was a distinct strain of the Christian tradition that had its own problems to contend with. The crisis of authority and the ensuing schism within the Johannine community[30] must be considered in our attempt to interpret the presentation of Peter and the Beloved Disciple. The schism within the Johannine community resulted in the absorption of the Johannine community into either the Apostolic churches or Gnosticism: O'Grady comments:

> Our evidence points to a use of the gospel by Gnostics and an eventual acceptance by the orthodox community represented by Irenaeus. It is quite possible and even likely that the use of the Gospel by Gnostics in the second century as well as its acceptance by Iranaeus points back to the dissolution of the Johannine community with some strains falling into Gnosticism and others becoming attached to the developing church at the end of the first century. If the documents of the Johannine community turn up in the Gnostic circles as well as orthodox circles someone had to preserve them and bring them into these communities. Because of the sectarian nature of the community, those who preserved the traditions must have been part of the original community.[31]

The situation of the Johannine community at the time that the Gospel was written is reflected in the description of the falling away of many of the disciples (Jn 6.60-71). The author's concern for the continuance of the community is joined to the question of the function and authority of apostleship. The continuance of the Johannine community is perceived by the Johannine editor to be dependent upon unity—a unity between the diverse Christian communities as well as a unity between the two generations *within* the Johannine community. Schuyler Brown comments on the move of the Johannine community towards the unity with other Christian communities:

> It [*the Johannine community*] does not appear to deny all fellowship with communities such as the one addressed in Matthew's gospel. It may, in fact, have had such believers in mind when Jesus refers to 'other sheep I have, that are not of this fold. I must bring them also, and they will heed my voice. So there will be one flock, one shepherd' (10.16; cf. 17.21). If so, the prayed-for unity with the 'other sheep' did finally come about.[32]

Peter, both in what he symbolizes and in his relationship to the Beloved Disciple, serves as the focal point of that 'intercommunity' and 'inter-generational' unity called for in the epilogue to the Gospel.

The death of the Beloved Disciple was obviously a crucial factor in this development.

> As long as the founder and guide of the community was alive, the Johannine community could feel secure in its authentic expression of the christian life as founded upon Jesus. But now they would have to re-examine their position vis-a-vis the rest of the developing communities.[33]

However, it would not only be the passing of the Beloved Disciple from the scene that would cause the Johannine community to consider its relationship to Peter and the other Christian communities. The nature of the Beloved Disciple's relationship to the community and his modelling of the ideal disciple in close, believing relationship with Jesus did not lend itself to the needs of the threatened community. The Johannine Christians were searching for an anchor for their faith, and that anchor was embodied in the traditions surrounding Peter.

As the Johannine community matured, the Beloved Disciple's function as a link to their first-century origins weakened, while the legacy of his exemplary discipleship and spiritual insight continued. But, for that legacy to continue, the Johannine community had to be connected with the more secure Apostolic traditions. Indeed, the anonymity of the Beloved Disciple may have created a need for a well-known historical figure like Peter, with whom the community could also identify itself as it entered a new era.

While most scholars understand the Johannine presentation of Peter as a caution aimed at those within the Apostolic stream of Christianity, it is better understood as directed toward Johannine readers. A positive attitude towards Peter is cultivated to the point that in the epilogue he is being explicitly commended to the

Johannine community. We need to remember the distinction between the author and his readers, and between the Johannine 'school' and the greater Johannine *community*. The Gospel does not necessarily represent the 'majority' view: rather, it confronts an exclusivist attitude within the Johannine community.

A move toward bringing the Apostolic and Johannine Christians together is discernible throughout the Gospel of John, and it finds its culmination in the final chapter of the Gospel. The passages which bring Peter and the Beloved Disciple together may reflect a later stage in the composition of the Gospel, but this is not to suggest that they are contrary to the Johannine tradition.[34] At least a part of the Johannine community eventually followed the lead of the Gospel and entered in to a 'partnership' with the Apostolic stream . This is indicated by the presence of the Johannine literature in the New Testament canon.[35]

The delicate relationship between the Johannine community and the communities which aligned themselves under the Petrine traditions is one of the many dynamic influences that shaped the Gospel of John.

NOTES

Notes to Chapter 1

1. Robert K. Mahoney, *Two Disciples at the Tomb* (Frankfurt: Peter Lang, 1975), pp. 6-8.

2. The Gospel of Philip portrays a special relationship of intimacy and insight between Jesus and Mary Magdalene which causes rivalry among the disciples that may be similar to the situation with the Beloved Disciple in the Gospel of John: '... the companion of the [Saviour is] Mary Magdalene. [But Christ loved: more than [all] the disciples [and used to] kiss her [often] on her [mouth]. The rest of [the disciples were offended] by it [and expressed disapproval]. They said to him, 'Why do you love her more than all of us?' The Saviour answered and said to them, 'Why do I not love you like her?' When a blind man and one who sees are both together in darkness, they are not different from one another. When the light comes, then he who sees will see the light and he who is blind will remain in darkness' (*The Gospel of Philip*, II, 3, 63-64); James M. Robinson, *The Nag Hammadi Library: In English* (New York: Harper and Row, 1977), p. 138.

3. It is not the purpose of this study to seek to answer the question of the identity of the disciple and the unavoidable exegetical corollary concerning authorship. While these issues are somewhat relevant to the discussion, they are neither central nor crucial to its development.

4. Graydon, F. Snyder, 'John 13.16 and the Anti-Petrinism of the Johannine Tradition', *Biblical Research* 16 (1971), p. 14.

5. In addition to the interpreters that will be cited in the following discussion, cf. also, Eric L. Titus, *The Message of the Fourth Gospel* (New York: Abingdon, 1957), p. 220; Snyder, 'Jn 13.16 and the Anti-Petrinism of the Johannine Tradition', pp. 5-15; Edwyn Clement Hoskyns and Francis N. Davey, *The Riddle of the New Testament* (London: Faber & Faber, 1958), p. 282.

6. B.W. Bacon, *The Fourth Gospel in Research and Debate* (New Haven: Yale University Press, 1918), pp. 303-304. Bacon postulates a 'marked subordination' of Peter to the Beloved Disciple, *ibid.*, pp. 198-98.

7. Rudolf Bultmann, *The Gospel of John: A Commentary* (Oxford: Basil Blackwell, 1971), p. 530.

8. Margaret Pamment, 'The Fourth Gospel's Beloved Disciple', *Expository Times* 94 (1983), p. 367.

9. S. Agourides, 'Peter and John in the Fourth Gospel', *Studia Evangelica*, vol. 4, ed. F.L. Cross (Berlin: Akadamie, 1968).

10. Francis Neirynck, 'The Other Disciple in Jn 18.15-16', *Ephemerides Theologicae Louvanienses* 51 (1981), p. 141.

11. David J. Hawkin, 'The Function of the Beloved Disciple Motif in the Johannine Redaction', *Laval Théologique Philosophique* 33 (1977), pp. 136, 149-50.

12. Paul S. Minear, 'The Beloved Disciple in the Gospel of John. Some Clues and Conjectures', *Novum Testamentum* 19 (1977), p. 116.

13. J.E. Bruns, 'Ananda: The fourth evangelist's model for "the disciple whom Jesus loved"?' *Studies in Religion/Sciences Religieuses* 3 (1973), pp. 236-43.

14. W.W. Watty, 'The Signficance of Anonymity in the Fourth Gospel', *Expository Times* 90 (1979), pp. 209-12.

15. J.J. Gunther, 'The Relation of the Beloved Disciple to the Twelve', *Theologische Zeitschrift* 37 (1981), pp. 129-48.

16. Watty, *op. cit.*, p. 211. N.B. also Gunther's comments, '. . . he [the Beloved Disciple] is vested with theological authority to cope with misuse of a tradition which made Peter proponent of objectionable teachings', *op. cit.* p. 137. Cf. also S. Agourides, 'Peter and John in the Fourth Gospel', p. 5.

17. J.J. Gunther, *op. cit.*, p. 135.

18. Schuyler Brown, 'Apostleship in the New Testament as an Historical and Theological Problem', *New Testament Studies*, 30 (1984), pp. 476, 490 n. 13. See also S. Brown *The Testament* (Oxford: Oxford University Press, 1984), pp. 116-17, 141-46.

19. R.F. Collins, 'The Representative Figures of the Fourth Gospel—II', *Downside Review* 94 (1976), pp. 126-27.

20. A.H. Maynard, 'The Role of Peter in the Fourth Gospel', *New Testament Studies* 30 (1984), p. 546.

21. Alv Kragerud, *Der Lieblingsjünger im Johannesevangelium: Ein exegetischer Versuch* (Hamburg: Grosshaus Wegner, 1959), pp. 65-67. See also Barnabas Lindars, *The Gospel of John* (Grand Rapids: Eerdmans, 1981), p. 602, who distinguishes between the 'prophetic ministry' of the Beloved Disciple and the local 'pastoral ministry' of Peter.

22. *Ibid.*, p. 82.

23. R.F. Collins, *op. cit.*, p. 131.

24. Raymond E. Brown, *The Community of the Beloved Disciple* (New York: Paulist Press, 1979), p. 191.

25. Rudolf Schnackenburg, 'Der Jünger, den Jesus liebte', *Evangelisch-Katholischer Kommentar zum Neuen Testament: Vorarbeiten*, vol. 2 (Zürich: Neukirchener Verlag, 1970), pp. 105-107.

26. F.M. Braun, *Jean le théologien et son évangile dans l'Eglise Ancienne* (Paris: Gabalda, 1959), pp. 302-303, 327.

27. Oscar Cullmann, *Peter: Disciple, Apostle, Martyr* (London: SCM, 1976), p. 27.

28. Robert K. Mahoney, *Two Disciples at the Tomb*, pp. 82-103, 237-77.

29. Minear, *The Beloved Disciple in the Gospel of John. Some Clues and Conjectures*, pp. 122-23.

30. Cf. e.g. R.E. Brown, Martyn, Richter, Cullmann, Boismard, Langbrandtner.

31. My preliminary study has produced the following hypothesis which needs, as yet, to be tested and no doubt revised by in-depth exegesis: the evangelist/editor may have been calling the attention of the Johannine readers to the role of Peter and his relevance to the community. In anticipation of (or in direct response to) the developing crisis of authority within the Johannine community he may have been attempting to establish an external basis of authority for faith by linking the Johannine community to the greater stream of the Christian church represented by Peter and the Twelve.

32. J. Louis Martyn, *The Gospel of John in Christian History* (New York: Paulist Press, 1978), p. 91. J. O'Grady asserts, 'No one would doubt the existence of this Johannine community', 'The Role of the Beloved Disciple', *Biblical Theology Bulletin* 9 (1979), p. 64.

33. Schuyler Brown, *The Origins of Christianity*, p. 108.

34. M.E. Boismard and A. Lamouille, *L'Evangile de Jean*, vol. 3 (Louvain: Desclée de Brouwer, 1958); Schnackenburg *The Gospel According to St. John*, vol. 1 (New York: Crossroads, 1980), pp. 59-74; R.E. Brown, *The Gospel According to John*, vol. 29, pp. xxxiv-xxxix; and Barnabas Lindars, *The Gospel of John*, pp. 46-54, all subscribe to one variation or another of this developmental approach to the composition of the Gospel which regards the final edition of the Gospel as a community product.

35. N.E. Johnson, 'The Beloved Disciple and the Fourth Gospel, *Church Quarterly Review*, 167 (1966), p. 285. Johnson maintains that the original author, John Zebedee, could not have written "the long theological discourses" (p. 283), but these were "invented by the apostle's disciple" who interspersed his editings with the Beloved Disciple's work.

36. Just how we are to interpret these strata is another matter. Cf. Martyn, *op. cit.*, p. 90; also R.E. Brown, *The Gospel According to John*, vol. 29, pp. xxiv-xxxi. J.S. King presents a caution that these 'stratified' approaches to discerning Johannine community history are not the only explanations of the evidence. The characteristic approach of Brown, Martyn and Painter, charges King, '"fossilizes" a living tradition by insisting upon a uniformity of presentation and interpretation at any given "level"'. It thus presupposes and demands a rigidity that is alien to John's apparent method; 'Is Johannine Archeology Really Necessary?' *The Evangelical Quarterly* 56 (1984), p. 204.

37. John Painter, 'The Farewell Discourses and the History of Johannine Christianity', *New Testament Studies* 27 (1981), p. 526.

38. *Ibid.*

39. O'Grady, *op. cit.*, p. 64.

40. Schuyler Brown, *The Origins of Christianity*, pp. 12, 95-96.

41. R.E. Brown, *The Community of the Beloved Disciple*, p. 139.

42. For example, Martyn, Pancaro, Kysar, Moody-Smith, Minear.

43. Severino Pancaro, *The Law in the Fourth Gospel: The Torah and the Gospel, Moses and Jesus, Judaism and Christianity According to John* (Leiden: E.J. Brill, 1975), p. 497.

44. Robert Kysar, 'Community and Gospel: Vectors in Fourth Gospel Criticism', *Interpretation* 31 (1977), p. 361.

45. Contra Bultmann, Pamment, etc. 'A reader of the XX century, who disposes of the tools of modern research, need not be steeped in the Jewish tradition to understand Jn, but what appeal would the Johannine presentation of Jewish unbelief have for a Gentile? The only Gentile mentioned in the Fourth Gospel is Pilate and the whole Jewish problematic behind the conflict between Jesus and the Jews remains foreign to him!'; Pancaro, *op. cit.*, p. 532.

46. Paul S. Minear, 'The Beloved Disciple in the Gospel of John: Some Clues and Conjectures', p. 107. See also, Martyn, *op. cit.*, pp. 91, 105, and Pancaro, *op. cit.*, p. 533, who writes, 'Jn is writing for Jews who already believe or who are, at least, "hidden believers"—only indirectly is he writing to win over non-believing Jews'.

47. Painter, *op. cit.*, p. 527; see also p. 531.

48. Maynard sees evidence for this crisis of authority in 3 John, as well. See 'The Role of Peter in the Fourth Gospel', *op. cit.*, pp. 545-46.

49. Schuyler Brown, 'Apostleship in the New Testament', p. 476.

50. J. Painter, *op. cit.*, p. 541.

51. Schuyler Brown, *The Origins of Christianity*, pp. 140-41.

52. R.E. Brown, *The Community of the Beloved Disciple*, p. 31.

53. 'Such a depiction would have been counterproductive if the Beloved Disciple were a purely imaginative symbol or if he had never been with Jesus, for the community's self-defence would surely have crumbled under such circumstances' (R.E. Brown, *The Community of the Beloved Disciple*, p. 32).

54. For further discussion on the significance of the anonymity of the Beloved Disciple see Chapter 1.E of this book.

55. Oscar Cullmann, *The Johannine Circle* (London: SCM Press, 1976), p. 77.

56. J.J. Gunther, 'The Relation of the Beloved Disciple to the Twelve', p. 135.

57. In the past, notable proponents of this position were R.E. Brown, *The Gospel According to John*, pp. xcvi-cii; and Schnackenburg, *The Gospel According to St. John*, vol. 1, pp. 75-104. Since these particular works were written, both Brown and Schnackenburg have re-evaluated and changed their positions—cf. Brown, *The Community of the Beloved Disciple*, p. 33-34.

This traditional position is still argued by Leon Morris, *The Gospel According to John (The New International Commentary on the New Testament)* (Grand Rapids: Eerdmans, 1971), pp. 8-30.

58. Cf. Thorwald Lorenzen, *Der Lieblingsjünger im Johannesevangelium: Eine redaktionsgeschichtliche Studie* (Stuttgart: Katholisches Bibelwerk, 1971), pp. 73-83; H. Thyen, *Tradition und Glaube: Festschrift für K.G. Kuhn* (Göttingen: Vandenhoeck & Ruprecht, 1971), p. 343, n. 2; Schuyler Brown, *The Origins of Christianity*, p. 137.

59. Schuyler Brown, *The Origins of Christianity*, p. 137.

60. Barnabas Lindars, *The Gospel of John*, p. 34.

61. Cf. Cullmann, *The Johannine Circle*, p. 78; R.E. Brown, *The Community of the Beloved Disciple*, p. 34; Schnackenburg, *The Gospel According to St. John*, vol. 3, pp. 383-87; Hawkin, etc.

62. Schnackenburg, *The Gospel According to St. John*, vol. 3, p. 385.

63. G.W. Broomfield, *John, Peter and the Fourth Gospel* (London: SPCK, 1934), p. 156.

64. R. Potter, 'The Disciple whom Jesus Loved', *Life of the Spirit* 16 (1962), p. 295.

65. W.W. Watty, *op. cit.*, p. 210.

66. Pamment, *op. cit.*, pp. 363-64.

67. Schuyler Brown, *The Origins of Christianity*, p. 133.

68. *Ibid.*, p. 136. See also Kurt Aland, 'The Problem of Anonymity and Pseudonymity in Christian Literature of the First Two Centuries', *The Authorship and Integrity of the New Testament* (London: SPCK, 1965), p. 5: 'Not only the four canonical ones, but also the other gospels of the earlier period were not thought of as the "gospel of *Mark*", the "gospel of *Matthew*", and so on, but, in their original home, as "*the* gospel". The more the individual gospels won common acknowledgement, and the more numerous they were in any one place, the more it proved necessary to differentiate between them. . . '

69. Aland, *op. cit.*, p. 8.

70. J.J. Gunther, 'The Relation of the Beloved Disciple to the Twelve', p. 141.

71. *Ibid.*

72. Watty, *op. cit.*, p. 211.

73. *Ibid.*, p. 212.

74. Hawkin, *op. cit.*, p. 141.

75. R.E. Brown, *The Gospel According to John*, vol. 29, p. xcv. Others who hold this position are: T. Lorenzen, *op. cit.*, p. 80; and Schnackenburg, *The Gospel According to St. John*, vol. 3, p. 387; M. Dibelius, *From Tradition to Gospel* (London: Ivor Nicolson and Watson, 1934), p. 216, n. 2.

76. R.F. Collins, *op. cit.*, pp. 26-46, 118-32.

77. Oscar Cullmann, *Peter: Disciple, Apostle, Martyr*, p. 26.

78. Leon Morris, *Studies in the Fourth Gospel* (Grand Rapids: Eerdmans, 1969), pp. 247-48.

79. I.e. Jn 6.67, 70, 71 and 20.24.

80. Compare the numerous references to the Twelve in the Synoptic tradition—10.1, 2, 5; 11.1; 19.28; 20.17; 26.14, 20, 47: 3.14; 4.10; 6.7; 9.35; 10.32; 14.10, 17, 20, 43: 6.13; 8.1; 9.1, 12; 18.31; 22.3, 47.

81. James D.G. Dunn, *Unity and Diversity in the New Testament* (London: SCM Press, 1977), p. 119.

82. J.J. Gunther, 'The Relation of the Beloved Disciple to the Twelve', p. 142.

83. M.H. Shepherd, 'The Twelve', *The Interpreter's Dictionary of the Bible*, vol. 4 (New York: Abingdon Press, 1962), p. 719.

84. Shepherd, *ibid.*

85. W. Bauder, 'Disciple', *The New International Dictionary of New Testament Theology*, vol. 1 (Colin Brown, ed.) (Grand Rapids: Zondervan, 1976), p. 487.

86. Gunther, 'The Relation of the Beloved Disciple to the Twelve', p. 147.

87. Such as 'Unbelievers', 'The World', 'The Jews', 'The Disciples of John the Baptist', 'Crypto-Christians', and 'Jewish Christians of Inadequate Faith'. See R.E. Brown for his discerning analysis of these types; *The Community of the Beloved Disciple*, pp. 55-91.

88. R.E. Brown, *The Community of the Beloved Disciple*, p. 82.

89. *Ibid.*, pp. 82-83.

90. *Ibid.*, p. 82 n. 156.

91. Shepherd, *loc. cit.*; cf. also Dunn, *op. cit.*, pp. 354-55; Colin Brown, *op. cit.*, vol. 1, p. 489; and Eduard Schweizer, *Church Order in the New Testament* (London: SCM, 1961), p. 28.

92. Schuyler Brown, *The Origins of Christianity*, p. 135; cf. also 'Apostleship in the New Testament as an Historical and Theological Problem', p. 478.

Notes to Chapter 2

1. E.g. Lindars, *The Gospel of John*, p. 112.

2. Cf. J.H. Bernard, *A Critical and Exegetical Commentary on the Gospel According to St. John*, vol. 1, p. 306; Morris, *The Gospel According to John*, p. 37.

3. Cf. Bultmann, *The Gospel of John*, p. 108; R.E. Brown, *The Gospel According to John*, pp. 74 & 77, and Barrett, *The Gospel According to St. John*, 2nd edn, p. 179.

4. Ernst Haenchen, *John (Hermeneia)*, vol. 1 (Philadelphia: Fortress Press, 1984), p. 158.

5. See Leon Morris, *The Gospel According to John*, p. 37; R.E. Brown, *The Gospel According to John*, vol. 29, pp. lxviii-lxix; R.H. Strachan, *The Fourth Gospel: Its Significance and Environment*, 3rd edn (London: SCM,

1941), p. 110; B.W. Bacon, 'New and Old in Jesus' Relation to John', *Journal of Biblical Literature* 48 (1929), pp. 40-81.

6. 'The Greek mss. read "his two disciples"; but the position of "his" varies so much that it is probably to be considered a later scribal clarification' (R.E. Brown, *The Gospel According to John*, vol. 29, p. 74).

7. The word ἀκολουθέω is essentially restricted to the Gospels and seems to have been carried over from its usage in the Rabbinic world to depict the teacher-pupil relationship in which the pupil 'follows after' (הלר אהרי) the Rabbi, 'The simple *akoloutheo* is never used metaphorically in the NT. The semi-literal sense of 'going behind' remains even in the special sense. . . On the other hand, *akoloutheo* is always used (except in Jn 21.19ff. and Rev. 14.4) with reference to the earthly Jesus'; C. Blendinger, 'Disciple', *The New International Dictionary of New Testament Theology*, vol. 1, ed. Colin Brown, (Grand Rapids: Zondervan, 1975), p. 482.

8. Bernard, *op. cit.*, p. 54. Note that Bernard, then, does not consider Jn 1.35-51 as an account of the calling of the disciples. It is legitimate to question his assertion that the aorist *only* indicates 'action at one definite moment'—cf. the use of the ingressive aorist in Jn 1.14 (ἐγένετο) and Jn 4.52 (ἔσχεν).

9. I.e. 1.37, 38, 40, 43; 6.2; 8.12; 10.4, 5, 27; 11.31; 12.26; 13.36(2X), 37(2X); 18.15; 20.6; 21.19, 20, 22.

10. I.e. 1.43; 8.12; 10.4, 5, 27; 12.26; 21.19, 22.

11. So Haenchen, *John*, p. 158.

12. '. . . Their following is the first step to faith on the part of two disciples; it leads to 'remaining' with Jesus, not just that day (v. 39) but in permanent fellowship with him'. Schnackenburg, *The Gospel According to St. John*, vol. 1, p. 308.

13. Morris, *The Gospel According to John*, p. 156.

14. R.F. Collins, 'The Representative Figures of the Fourth Gospel—II', p. 127.

15. Bultmann, *The Gospel of John*, pp. 101-102.

16. Maynard hints that in this reference we see no more than a deference to tradition; 'The Role of Peter in the Fourth Gospel', p. 532.

17. Cf. Lindars, *The Gospel of John*, p. 114.

18. We have the same style of anticipatory descriptions displayed in Jn 11.1-2 with reference to Lazarus, Mary and Martha.

19. I.e. Matthew, 3 times; Mark, once; Luke, 2 times.

20. J.K. Elliot, 'Κηφᾶς· Σίμων Πέτρος· ὁ Πέτρος: An Examination of New Testament Usage', *Novum Testamentum* 14 (1972), p. 243.

21. *Ibid.*, p. 242. On five occasions of textual variation, Elliot summarily rejects or accepts the variant most suitable to his thesis with no consideration of the quality of external evidence.

22. Mahoney, *Two Disciples at the Tomb*, p. 251 n. 86.

23. These particular occurrences of the full name will be discussed in more detail later in their respective sections of this work.

24. Mahoney has built the case that the Beloved Disciple serves as a 'prop' or an 'other-directed function within the Gospel'; *op. cit.*, p. 300; see also pp. 287-301. If indeed the Beloved Disciple is here in 1.40 serving in his typical fashion, then as Lindars says, it is 'possible that he is left unnamed because John's narrative did not require further mention of him'; *The Gospel of John*, p. 114.

25. Maynard, 'The Role of Peter in the Fourth Gospel', p. 533.

26. R.E. Brown, *The Gospel According to John*, vol. 29, p. 73.

27. Compare the name given to Simon's father in these two places with that in Mt. 16.17 (βαριωνᾶ). According to Schnackenburg, this suggests an independent perhaps original tradition; *The Gospel According to St. John*, vol. 1, n. 86, p. 311.

28. Schnackenburg, *The Gospel According to St. John*, vol. 1, p. 313; M.-É. Boismard, 'Les traditions johanniques concernant le Baptiste', *Revue Biblique* 7 (1963), pp. 39-42; Spitta, *Das Johannesevangelium als Quelle der Geschichte Jesu* (1910), p. 56f.

29. Boismard, 'Les traditions johanniques concernant le Baptiste', p. 41.

30. *Ibid.* p. 42. See below for further discussion regarding the interpretation of πρῶτον.

31. R.E. Brown, *The Gospel According to John*, vol. 29, p. 74.

32. Boismard, 'Les traditions johanniques concernant le Baptiste', p. 42.

33. Schnackenburg, *The Gospel According to St. John*, vol. 1, p. 312; Boismard also makes this case, and like Schnackenburg, he hesitates to make much of this hypothesis of redactional activity. Nevertheless, he does conclude, 'L'hypothèse d'une origine rédactionelle du v. 43 ne doit pas être exclue, ce qui rendrait évidemment plus facile l'identification du deuxième disciple de 1, 35 ss avec Philippe'; 'Les traditions johanniques concernant le Baptiste', p. 42.

34. *Ibid.*

35. This may mean that Andrew 'first of all' went to find Peter before going to see where Jesus was staying (vv. 38-39), so that Peter would have been present from v. 39 and on in the narrative. Lindars describes this as 'certainly awkward, and the difficulty was felt from the beginning'; *The Gospel of John*, p. 114. The inherent difficulty of such a reading attests to its genuineness.

36. So Edwin A. Abbot, *Johannine Grammar* (London: A & C Black, 1906), section 1901[b]; also Cullmann, *Peter: Disciple, Apostle, Martyr*, 2nd edn (London: SCM Press, 1957), p. 75.

37. Cullmann, *Peter*, p. 28.

38. Haenchen, *John*, p. 164. Haenchen does not point out, however, that in all of the Gospel of John, James is never named before his brother—in fact, the two of them are never named, except by the phrase 'the sons of

Zebedee', in 21.2. One should not transfer the practice of the Synoptists over to the Fourth Evangelist. Perhaps it is wisest not to 'permit the thought patterns of the early church' to influence even one's counter-arguments.

39. Bultmann, *The Gospel of John*, p. 101, n. 3.

40. Cf. Lindars, *The Gospel of John*, p. 115.

41. Bernard, *op. cit.*, p. 58.

42. Lindars, *The Gospel of John*, p. 115.

43. E.g. p^{66}, p^{75}, $\aleph^c$, B, f^1, f^{13}, cop, arm, geo, syr^r, it^a, A.

44. R.E. Brown, *The Gospel According to John*, vol. 29, p. 75.

45. If we were to try and harmonize this with the Synoptic account, we would then have trouble identifying this disciple with one of the Zebedee brothers.

46. Snyder, 'Jn 13.16 and the Anti-petrinism of the Johannine Tradition'. *Biblical Research* 16 (1971), p. 10.

47. See Chapter 7.D.

48. Bernard, *op. cit.*, p. 59. Bernard carries on the description '. . . as the novelty of their intercourse with Jesus passed away,. . . [this enthusiasm] did not become a reasoned conviction until later'; *ibid.*

49. Peter F. Ellis, *The Genius of John: A Composition-Critical Commentary on the Fourth Gospel* (Collegeville: The Liturgical Press, 1984), p. 32.

50. R.E. Brown, *The Gospel According to John*, vol. 29, p. 80.

51. *Both* evangelists may have taken the event out of its original setting for their own purposes.

52. So Schnackenburg, *The Gospel According to St. John*, p. 312. Cf. also Cullmann, *Peter*, p. 21; and J.N. Sanders and B.A. Mastin, *A Commentary on the Gospel According to St. John* (London: Adam & Charles Black, 1969), p. 100.

53. Bultmann, *The Gospel of John*, p. 101.

54. *Ibid.*

55. Cf. Mt. 1.21, 5.43, 5.48 for other examples of this use of the future tense.

56. R.E. Brown, *The Gospel According to John*, vol. 29, p. 80.

57. It is not sufficient to ascribe John's inclusion of the naming of Peter to a 'reluctant submission' to a well-known tradition, as Haenchen suggests; 'verse 42 is to be taken as a reflection of a pre-Johannine tradition that the narrator did not want to overlook'; *John*, p. 165. Close comparisons reveal that John does treat this pericope in his own way, for his own purposes.

58. Cf. also Jesus' words to Nathanael in 1.47-49. As Schnackenburg states, 'It appears from the scene with Nathanael that here too Jesus is meant to be seen as the possessor of divine knowledge. . . ', *The Gospel According to St. John*, vol. 1, p. 311.

59. E.g. Barrett, *op. cit.*, p. 182; Schnackenburg, *The Gospel According to St. John*, vol. 1, p. 311; Bernard, *op. cit.*, p. 59; and many others.

60. Bernard, *op. cit.*, p. 59. Cf. the use of this verb with the verb βλέπειν.

ἐμβλέπειν may be understood as signifying 'understanding gaze', 'looking intently upon', or even 'considering'; Bauer, Arndt and Gingrich, *A Greek-English Lexicon of the New Testament and Other Early Christian Literature* (Chicago: University of Chicago Press, 1957), p. 254.

61. Bultmann, *The Gospel of John*, p. 102, n. 1.

62. Schnackenburg, *The Gospel According to St. John*, vol. 1, p. 312.

63. Cecil Roth, 'Simon–Peter', *Harvard Theological Review* 54 (1961), pp. 96-97. Roth offers 15 examples to illustrate his point.

64. *Ibid.*, p. 97.

65. Joseph A. Fitzmyer, *Essays on the Semitic Background of the New Testament* (London: Geoffrey Chapman, 1971), p. 110.

66. Morris, *The Gospel According to John*, p. 161. Origen comments in his treatise *On Prayer*, that 'a "name" is a compendious appellation manifesting the individual quality of the being named... when the quality of Abram changed, he was called Abraham; and when Simon's, he was named Peter...'; *Alexandrian Christianity*, vol. 2. eds. and trans. J.E.L. Oulton and H. Chadwick (Philadelphia: The Westminster Press, 1954), p. 286.

67. Bernard, *op. cit.*, p. 60.

68. Among those who see this as reflective of Simon's innate personality are Lindars, *The Gospel of John*, p. 116; R.E. Brown, *The Gospel According to John*, vol. 29, p. 76; Bernard, *op. cit.*, p. 59. Those who see this as a reference to Peter's prospective *change* in character include Morris. *The Gospel According to John*, p. 161; Strachan, *op. cit.*, p. 119, '...Jesus recognized the possibilities (for a deepening and strengthening of character) from the first'.

69. B.F. Westcott, *The Gospel According to St. John* (London: John Murray, 1908), p. 25. Cf. also Schnackenburg, *The Gospel According to St. John*, vol. 1, p. 312. R.E. Brown cites Origen as an early example of this interpretation, criticising the approach as 'more a case of theologizing from general NT evidence than an exegesis of John'; *The Gospel According to John*, vol. 29, p. 80.

70. R.E. Brown, *The Gospel According to John*, vol. 29, p. 76.

71. Emil Gottlieb Kraeling, *The Brooklyn Museum Aramaic Papyri New Documents of the Fifth Century BC from the Jewish Colony at Elephantine* (New York: Rand McNally, 1969), p. 228 (8.10) which reads, in part, '...Witnesses hereto (are) "Atarmalki, son of QLQLN; Sinkishir, son of Shabbetai; witness: Aqab, son of Kepha"'.

72. Joseph A. Fitzmyer, 'Aramaic *Kepha*' and Peter's name in the New Testament', in *Text and Interpretation: Studies in the New Testament Presented to Matthew Black* eds. Ernest Best and R. McWilson (Cambridge Cambridge University Press, 1979), p. 130.

73. Barrett, *op. cit.*, p. 183.

74. Agourides, 'Peter and John in the Fourth Gospel', p. 3.

75. Maynard, 'The Role of Peter in the Fourth Gospel', p. 532.

76. Schnackenburg, *The Gospel According to St. John*, vol. 1, p. 312.

77. Beginning with the fourteenth-century writer Ludolphus; cf. Mary Shorter, 'The Position of Chapter VI in the Fourth Gospel', *The Expository Times* 84 (1974), p. 181.

78. Among the proponents of this transposition are Strathmann, Bultmann, Wikenhauser, Bernard, Schnackenburg, F.W. Lewis, Moffat and MacGregor. Among those who hold to the traditional order are Dodd, Barrett, Marsh, Strachan, D.M. Smith, R.E. Brown and Lindars.

79. *Ibid.*, p. 182.

80. Further, the eschatological discourse of ch. 6 becomes symbolically fulfilled in ch. 11, in the raising of Lazarus.

81. Strachan, *The Fourth Gospel: Its Significance and Environment*, p. 81.

82. However, evidence exists supporting the theory that Origen's version of the Gospel did not place ch. 6 in its present setting; Shorter, *op. cit.*, p. 1183.

83. Bultmann, *The Gospel of John*, p. 285.

84. Dwight Moody Smith, jr. *The Composition and Order of the Fourth Gospel: Bultmann's Literary Theory* (New Haven: Yale University Press, 1965), p. 152.

85. Barrett postulates that John is dependent upon the Synoptics at these points, *loc. cit.*

86. Schnackenburg, *The Gospel According to St. John*, vol. 2, pp. 69-70.

87. Cf. 1 Jn 2.19; see also Chapter 1.C above.

88. R.E. Brown, *The Gospel According to John*, vol. 29, p. 296.

89. Schnackenburg, *loc. cit.*

90. Barrett, *op. cit.*, p. 303.

91. *Ibid.*; also R.E. Brown, *The Gospel According to John*, p. 296.

92. For differing interpretations, cf. James D.G. Dunn, 'John VI—A Eucharistic Discourse?', *New Testament Studies* 17 (1971), p. 330, and R.E. Brown, *The Community of the Beloved Disciple*, p. 74.

93. See the previous discussion of Jn 1.42; 2.C above.

94. Leon Morris argues this is meant to be a cause for greater offence; *The Gospel According to John*, pp. 383-84. On the other hand, Schnackenburg, *The Gospel According to St. John*, vol. 2, p. 71, and Marcus Dods, *The Gospel of John: The Expositors Greek Testament*, vol. 1 (Grand Rapids: Wm B. Eerdmans, 1976), p. 759, both argue that Jesus was saying this to encourage the faith of his disciples.

95. Barrett, *op. cit.*, p. 305.

96. For detailed discussions on this hermeneutical challenge, cf. R.E. Brown, *The Gospel According to John*, vol. 29, p. 298; Lindars, *The Gospel of John*, p. 273; Morris, *The Gospel According to John*, p. 385; Schnackenburg, *The Gospel According to St. John*, vol. 2, p. 273; Barrett, *op. cit.*, pp. 304-305; Dunn, 'John VI—A Eucharistic Discourse?', p. 332.

97. Cf. Jn 1.14 and 3.6.

98. I.e. 35-50 or 51-58, or *both*, as the present writer postulates.

99. ῥήματα need not refer exclusively to the words of the preceding discourse; all the words of the incarnate Christ may be meant, and John no doubt does not forget that Jesus himself is the creative word of God (1.1)'; Barrett, *loc. cit.*

100. Schnackenburg, *The Gospel According to St. John*, vol. 2, p. 73.

101. Barrett, *op. cit.*, p. 305.

102. Ibid. Yet, of course, one must regard the disciples on a higher level of faith than the 'Jews' or the crowd. 'While he criticizes "the Jews" without qualification, however, for their unbelief (cf. 36), he says to "the disciples" only that "some" among them do not believe'; Schnackenburg, *The Gospel According to St. John*, vol. 2, p. 73.

103. Barrett, *loc. cit.*

104. Marcus Dods, *op. cit.*, p. 759.

105. R.E. Brown, *The Gospel According to John*, vol. 29, p. 297.

106. John 6.65 is obviously closely related to both 6.37 and 44 (R.E. Brown calls v. 65b a 'composite' of the two; *The Gospel According to John*, vol. 29, p. 297). Could something similar to what we have in John have been expanded by Matthew to create his own version? Certainly this would be much more true of Mt. 11.27.

107. Cf. Jn 19.12

108. R.E. Brown, *The Gospel According to John*, vol. 29, p. 301.

109. R.E. Brown, *The Community of the Beloved Disciple*, p. 74, n. 131.

110. This is due to Luke's omission of Mk 6.45-8.2. In Mark, the confession follows the feeding of the four thousand, a request for a sign and a discourse on heaven.

111. See the following discussion on 6.69, 2.C.

112. Lindars, *The Gospel of John*, p. 275.

113. See Chapter 1.F above.

114. As discussed, *ibid.*

115. Morris, *The Gospel According to John*, p. 388.

116. Cf. the ὑπάγειν of 6.67 and the strong words of Jesus to Peter in Mk 8.33; ὕπαγε ὀπίσω μοῦ, Σατανᾶ. Cf. also Jn 18.6.

117. So Dods, *op. cit.*, p. 760.

118. Schnackenburg, *The Gospel According to St. John*, vol. 2, p. 75.

119. *Ibid.*

120. Dods, *op. cit.*, p. 760.

121. Schnackenburg, *The Gospel According to St. John*, vol. 2, p. 75.

122. Barrett makes special note that the phrase here in 68 describing the words is anarthrous, postulating that the use of the article 'would imply a formula' (*op. cit.*, p. 306). This argument is difficult to sustain, especially in light of the use of the article in both vv. 60 and 63 to describe the teaching of Jesus.

123. Schnackenburg, *The Gospel According to St. John*, vol. 2, p. 75.
124. Lindars, *The Gospel of John*, p. 275.
125. Cf. Jn 17.8; 8.31, 32; 18.38; 16.30; 1 Jn 4.16.
126. Hoskyns sees development on the part of Peter and the other disciples here: 'The emphasis on the knowledge of the disciples, contrasted with their belief, preserves the climax of Peter's confession in the synoptic gospels. This belief, which in 1.35-45, 49 is inadequate, now becomes knowledge'; *The Fourth Gospel*, p. 343.
127. Many commentators, however, qualify this understanding of their synonymity with the observation that Jesus, while described as knowing God the Father, is never said to believe in Him.
128. Schnackenburg, *The Gospel According to St. John*, vol. 2, p. 77.
129. Mk 1.42, par. Lk. 4.34.
130. Snyder, 'Jn 13.16 and the Anti-Petrinism of the Johannine Tradition', p. 11. Cf. also, Maynard 'The Role of Peter in the Fourth Gospel'; 'There are no demons in the Fourth Gospel, so their supernatural testimony about Jesus' divine origin is here made by Peter'; p. 534.
131. *Ibid.*
132. *Ibid.*
133. Bultmann, *The Gospel of John*, p. 451, n. 1.
134. Schnackenburg, *The Gospel According to St. John*, vol. 2, p. 78.
135. Joachim Jeremias asserts that διάβολος is part of a later stratum of gospel tradition than σατανᾶς, thus concluding that the Synoptics reflect an older form of the saying than that which is found in John: *The Parables of Jesus*, 2nd edn (New York: Charles Scribners Sons, 1963), p. 81.
136. Lindars, *The Gospel of John*, p. 275.
137. Barrett, *op. cit.*, p. 308.
138. Lindars, *The Gospel of John*, p. 276. Cf. also Jn 13.2.
139. Although the choice of the Twelve is not recorded in John as it is in the Synoptics, the fact that Jesus chose his own followers is repeated in Jn 13.18 and 15.16.
140. Schnackenburg, *The Gospel According to St. John*, vol. 2, p. 78.
141. Cf. 6.61, 64 and 65.

Notes to Chapter 3

1. As do C.K. Barrett, R.E. Brown, C.H. Dodd and Schnackenburg.
2. Cf. C.H. Dodd, *The Interpretation of the Fourth Gospel* (Cambridge: Cambridge University Press, 1963), part III; and R.E. Brown, *The Gospel According to John*, vol. 29, p. 38.
3. Cf. Jn 13.1.
4. R.E. Brown, *The Gospel According to John*, vol. 29A, p. 18.
5. R.E. Brown, *The Community of the Beloved Disciple*, p. 191.

6. Lindars, *The Gospel of John*, p. 457.

7. Paul S. Minear, 'The Beloved Disciple in the Gospel of John: Some Clues and Conjectures', pp. 116-17. Minear sees this as a pattern that recurs in other narratives.

8. Cf. 13.2—καὶ δείπνου γινομένου.

9. Cf. Mk 14.12-16 and parallels; Mk 14.23-25 and parallels.

10. R.E. Brown, *The Gospel According to John*, vol. 29A, p. 558.

11. Lindars, *The Gospel of John*, p. 444.

12. J.H. Bernard, *A Critical and Exegetical Commentary on the Gospel According to St. John*, vol. 2, p. 470.

13. R.E. Brown, *The Gospel According to John*, vol. 29A, p. 577.

14. Lindars, *The Gospel of John*, p. 458.

15. Mahoney, *Two Disciples at the Tomb*, p. 90, n. 103.

16. The *prominence* of the position will be elaborated upon in the following discussion.

17. Francis J. Moloney, 'Jn 1.18: "In the Bosom of" or "Turned Towards" the Father?' *Australian Biblical Review* 31 (1983), p. 65.

18. *Ibid., p.* 66.

19. Lorenzen, *Der Lieblingsjünger im Johannesevangelium*, p. 41; Minear, 'The Beloved Disciple in the Gospel of John: Some Clues and Conjectures', pp. 116-17, interprets the phrase as suggesting 'intimacy of vision and knowledge that qualifies a person to mediate divine grace and truth'; Jürgen Roloff, 'Der johanneische "Lieblingsjünger" und der Lehrer der Gerechtigkeit', *New Testament Studies*, 15 (1968), p. 138; E.L. Allen, 'On This Rock', *Journal of Theological Studies* 5 (1954), p. 62; H. Strathmann, 'Die Stellung des Petrus in der Urkirche', *Zeitschrift für Systematische Theologie* 20 (1943), p. 266; Maynard, 'The Role of Peter in the Fourth Gospel', p. 536.

20. Sanders and Mastin, *The Gospel According to St. John*, p. 313, n. 1.

21. Rudolf Meyer, 'κολπος', *Theological Dictionary of the New Testament*, vol. 3, ed. Gerhard Kittel, trans. Geoffrey Bromiley (Grand Rapids: Eerdmans, 1965), p. 825.

22. *Ibid.*, p. 824.

23. J.A. Motyer, 'Body', *The New International Dictionary of New Testament Theology* vol. 1, ed. Colin Brown (Grand Rapids: Zondervan, 1975), p. 240.

24. Bernard, *op. cit.*, p. 471 and Barrett, *op. cit.*, p. 446.

25. Lindars, *The Gospel of John*, p. 458.

26. R.E. Brown, *The Gospel According to John*, vol. 29A, p. 574 and Bernard, *loc. cit.*

27. Lindars, *The Gospel of John*, p. 458.

28. Sanders and Mastin, *loc. cit.*

29. R.E. Brown, *The Gospel According to John*, vol. 29A, p. 574.

30. *Ibid.*, p. 575.

31. Bruce M. Metzger, *A Textual Commentary on the Greek New*

Testament (New York: United Bible Societies, 1971), p. 240.

32. Marie-Emile Boismard, Problèmes de critique textuelle concernant le Quatrième Evangile', *Revue Biblique* 60 (1953), pp. 357-59.

33. K.G. Kuhn, 'The Lord's Supper and the Communal Meal at Qumran', *The Scrolls and the New Testament*, ed. Krister Stendahl, (New York: Harper, 1957), p. 69.

34. Barrett, *op. cit.*, p. 447.

35. Cf. the various theories on the composition of the Gospel of John. Proponents of the theory of the progressive development of the Gospel suggest that the bulk of this material, esp. chs. 15-17, were later insertions of liturgical or kerygmatic material.

36. Especially in light of v. 14—'If I, then, your Teacher and Lord, have washed your feet, you also ought to wash one another's feet'.

37. Maynard, 'The Role of Peter in the Fourth Gospel', p. 535.

38. *Ibid*. Maynard describes Peter as 'near the borderline of exclusion from the group', p. 534.

39. Snyder, 'Jn 13.16 and the Anti-Petrinism of the Johannine Tradition', p. 9.

40. Agourides, 'Peter and John in the Fourth Gospel', p. 4; apart from other problems there may be in Agourides' interpretation, to describe Peter's 'final wholehearted acceptance' of Jesus' washing as a prefiguring of apostolic restoration is to attach more positive value to Peter's eagerness than the evangelist himself does.

41. Hawkin, 'The Function of the Beloved Disciple Motif in the Johannine Redaction', p. 143.

42. Mahoney, *op. cit.*, p. 93.

43. *Ibid.*, p. 95.

44. Pamment, 'The Fourth Gospel's Beloved Disciple', p. 306.

45. Neirynck, '"The Other Disciple Disciple" in Jn 18, 15-16', p. 141.

46. Barrett, *loc. cit.*

47. Gunther, 'The Relation of the Beloved Disciple to the Twelve', p. 129.

48. R.E. Brown, *The Gospel According to John*, vol. 29A, p. 578. Some scholars (e.g. Loisy, W. Baur) attach theological significance to this action, since the word ψωμίον also had been used to designate the eucharistic host. Because Judas received without discernment he condemned himself (cf. 1 Cor. 11.29) and thus Satan entered him (Jn 13.27). If this is how the evangelist intended the actions of Jesus to be understood, then why did he omit the words of the institution?

49. Lindars, *The Gospel of John*, p. 458.

50. N.E. Johnson, 'The Beloved Disciple and the Fourth Gospel', p. 287.

51. Sanders and Mastin, *op. cit.*, p. 314. Cf. also Bernard, *op. cit.*, p. 474.

52. R.E. Brown, *The Gospel According to John*, vol. 29A, p. 578.

53. Cf. Jn 3.18-20; 6.28; 12.48—note the emphasis that it is *man's* choice to remain in darkness rather than light.

54. Cf. Jn 3.19, also 1 Jn 1.4, 1 Jn 2.8-9.

55. 'In its circumstantiality, the verse resembles 13.23-25 above' (Mahoney, *op. cit.*, p. 93).

56. Lindars, *The Gospel of John*, p. 460.

57. R.F. Collins, 'The Representative Figures of the Fourth Gospel—II', pp. 119-20.

58. Cf. R.E. Brown, *The Gospel According to John*, vol. 29A, p. 575; Lightfoot, *St. John's Gospel* (Oxford: Clarendon Press, 1956), p. 265f.; Barrett also insists that the Beloved Disciple must have understood. Because of the inconsistency of the passage he then relays his doubt of the historicity of the narrative; *op. cit.*, p. 447.

59. Sanders and Mastin, *loc. cit.*

60. Mahoney, *loc. cit.*

61. *Ibid.*, p. 95.

62. Note that Jn 13.1, 2 has already set this stage.

63. *Ibid.*, p. 304.

64. Lindars, *The Gospel of John*, p. 457.

65. Barrett, *op. cit.*, p. 438.

66. Snyder, *op. cit.*, p. 12.

67. See Chapter 1.F above.

68. Maynard, 'The Role of Peter in the Fourth Gospel', pp. 536-37.

69. Hawkin, *op. cit.*, p. 143.

70. R.E. Brown, *The Gospel According to John*, vol. 29A, p. 577.

71. Maynard, 'The Role of Peter in the Fourth Gospel', p. 537. Cf. also Barrett, *op. cit.*, pp. 377-78 and Sanders and Mastin, *op. cit.*, p. 313, n. 1.

Notes to Chapter 4

1. As in Jn 18.1.

2. With words connected by καί, 'When the subject consists of sing. + sing. or of sing. + plur. the verb agrees with the first subject if the verb stands before it. . .', Blass, Debrunner and Funk, *A Greek Grammar of the New Testament and Other Early Christian Literature* (Chicago: University of Chicago Press, 1961), section 135. Cf. also, E. Kautzsch and A.E. Cowley, *Gesenius' Hebrew Grammar*, 2nd English edn (Oxford: Clarendon, 1910), pp. 489-92.

3. P. Benoit, *The Passion and Resurrection of Jesus Christ* (New York: Herder and Herder, 1969), p. 58.

4. See Chapter 1.B above.

5. R.E. Brown, *The Gospel According to John*, vol. 29A, p. 823.

6. Bultmann, *The Gospel of John*, p. 645, n. 5.

7. Lorenzen, *Der Lieblingsjünger im Johannesevangelium: Eine redaktions-geschichtliche Studie*, p. 32.

8. Anton Dauer, *Die Passionsgeschichte im Johannesevangelium* (München: Kösel-Verlag, 1972), pp. 75-76.

9. John does use this term in describing Peter's second and third denials; 18.25, 27.

10. Barrett, *op. cit.*, p. 525.

11. This relatively rare word is found 6 times in the NT (3 times in John). In Jn 18.18 it is used rather redundantly of Peter and the guards.

12. Boismard, *L'Evangile de Jean: Etudes et Problemes* (Paris: Editions du Cerf, 1958), pp. 240-43.

13. R.E. Brown, *The Gospel According to John*, vol. 29A, p. 825.

14. Aor, ptc. of περιάπτω—'kindle'.

15. Lk. 22.59; Mk 14.71; Mt. 26.74.

16. N.B. αὐλήν, παιδίσκη, ὑπηρέται, θερμαινόμενος and ἀλέκτωρ ἐφώνησεν.

17. Barrett, *op. cit.*, p. 525.

18. Bultmann, *The Gospel of John*, p. 645, n. 4.

19. Nearly all other manuscripts *except* P[60vid], P[66], B, א*, A, D[suppl], W, and ψ have the article.

20. Lindars, *The Gospel of John*, p. 548.

21. Gunther, 'The Relation of the Beloved Disciple to the Twelve', p. 147.

22. Haenchen, *John* (Hermeneia), vol. 2, p. 167.

23. Dauer, *Die Passionsgeschichte im Johannesevangelium*, pp. 74-75.

24. Barrett, *loc. cit.*

25. Potter, *op. cit.*, p. 295.

26. Dauer, *Die Passionsgeschichte im Johannesevangelium*, p. 75.

27. R.A. Edwards, *The Gospel According to St. John: Its Criticism and Interpretation* (Philadelphia: Fortress Press, 1954), p. 137; J.H. Bernard, *St. John*, vol. 2, p. 593; and John Marsh, *The Gospel of St. John* (Middlesex: Penguin, 1968), p. 588.

28. B. Weiss, *Das Johannes-Evangelium* (Göttingen: Vandenhoeck und Ruprecht, 1902), p. 480 and W. Sanday, *The Criticism of the Fourth Gospel* (Oxford: Oxford University Press, 1905), p. 101.

29. Adolf Schlatter, *Der Evangelist Johannes*, 2nd edn (Stuttgart: Calwer, 1960), p. 332.

30. Barrett, *op. cit*, pp. 525-26.

31. Dauer, *Die Passionsgeschichte im Johannesevangelium*, p. 75.

32. Neirynck, 'The "Other Disciple" in Jn 18, 15-16', p. 114.

33. Gunther, *op. cit.*, pp. 146-47. Gunther's dramatic description of the dastardly character and scheming of the anonymous disciple runs on at length.

34. Charles Homer Giblin, 'Confrontations in Jn 18, 1-27', *Biblica* 65 (1984), p. 228.

35. R.E. Brown makes this assumption: 'Again, only in the fourth gospel does "another disciple" have a role in the drama of Peter's denial (18.15, presumably "the disciple whom Jesus loved")', 'The Passion According to John: Chapter 18 and 19', *Worship* 49 (1975), p. 128.

36. B.F. Westcott, *The Gospel According to St. John*, p. 255.

37. Neirynck, 'The "Other Disciple" in Jn 18, 15-16', p. 141.

38. *Ibid.*

39. The issue is not whether or not φιλεῖν and ἀγαπᾶν are to be distinguished in meaning. The question is whether or not they come from the same hand.

40. Boismard, *L'Evangile de Jean: Etudes et problèmes*, pp. 240-43.

41. R.E. Brown, *The Gospel According to John*, p. 983.

42. Cf. Collins' summary: 'Thus both by reason of the mention of the "other disciple" in Jn 18, 15, and of the Johannine tendency to place the Beloved Disciple alongside the more traditional figure of Peter, we have every reason to think that the other disciple who brought Peter into the court of the high priest (Jn 18.15-16) is the Beloved Disciple'; *op. cit.*, p. 129.

43. Giblin, *op. cit.*, p. 228. Haenchen, Barrett, Bultmann and others maintain this same perspective, cf. n. 22 above.

44. Note that γνωστός here governs a genitive, while in the preceding verse the equivalent phrase was in the dative. 'There is no apparent difference of meaning, but perhaps a different hand (the redactor) added the parenthetical clarification here', R.E. Brown, *The Gospel According to John*, vol. 29A, p. 824.

45. Bultmann cites Matthew Black, *An Aramaic Approach to the Gospels and Acts*, 2nd edn (Oxford: Clarendon Press, 1954), p. 192f., in support of his thesis; *op. cit.*, p. 64, n. 4.

46. See n. 8 above.

47. J.H. Moulton and W.F. Howard, *A Grammar of New Testament Greek*, vol. 1 (Edinburgh: T & T Clark, 1929), p. 192.

48. Agourides, 'Peter and John in the Fourth Gospel', p. 5.

49. Walter Grundmann, 'Das Wort von Jesu Freunden (Joh. xv, 13-16) und das Herrenmahl', *Novum Testamentum* 3 (1959), p. 65, n. 1.

50. E.g. Jn 18.5-6.

51. H.G. Liddell and R. Scott, *A Greek-English Lexicon*, rev. edn, vol. 1 (Oxford: Clarendon Press, 1940), p. 140.

52. As Schnackenburg notes, '21.9 does not need, on that account, to come from the same hand', *The Gospel According to St. John*, vol. 3 (New York: Crossroad, 1982), p. 445, n. 52.

53. R.E. Brown, *The Gospel According to John*, vol. 29A, p. 791.

54. *Ibid.* But cf. M. Goguel, 'Did Peter Deny His Lord?' *Harvard Theological Review* 25 (1932), pp. 1-27, who argues that the whole scene is a

fabrication based upon words of Jesus spoken, 'in a moment of fear', to the effect that 'even Peter himself would not wait for the cock to crow three times before denying him'; p. 27.

55. Barrett, *op. cit.*, p. 527.

56. Note the uses of ἑστώς and θερμαινόμενος.

57. Cf. the Synoptics, where in Matthew and Mark the accuser is still a servant-girl; Luke has a single 'other' (ἕτερος) accuser.

58. Barrett, *op. cit.*, p. 529.

59. R.E. Brown, *The Gospel According to John*, vol. 29A, p. 828.

60. Having said this, we must bear in mind that there is nothing mutually exclusive between the second and third possible interpretations. That is, an account of an actual event may be infused with a theological function.

61. Thereby giving the Johannine narrative much more coherence than Barrett recognizes; cf. n. 55 above.

62. Benoit, *The Passion and Resurrection of Jesus Christ*, p. 69.

63. 'He impetuously tried to come to the aid of his Lord, but he so misunderstood that his actions were wrong and he is rebuked. The Fourth Evangelist has deliberately associated this failure with Peter'; Maynard, 'The Role of Peter in the Fourth Gospel', p. 539. Cf. also Agourides, 'Peter and John in the Fourth Gospel', p. 5; 'We must not overlook the fact that according to the narrative in the Fourth Gospel, it is Peter again who misunderstands the deliverance of Jesus to his enemies. The Synoptic writers avoid any reference to Peter in relation to the mutilation of the slave of the High Priest'.

64. Neirynck, 'The "Other Disciple" in Jn 18, 15-16', p. 134.

65. *Ibid.*

66. R.E. Brown, *The Gospel According to John*, vol. 29A, p. 827.

67. Maynard, 'The Role of Peter in the Fourth Gospel', p. 538.

68. I.e. 'Simon Peter said to him "Lord, where are you going?" Jesus answered, "Where I am going you cannot follow me now; but you shall follow me afterward"'.

69. J.C. Fenton, *The Passion According to John* (London: SPCK, 1961), p. 26.

70. R.E. Brown, *The Gospel According to John*, vol. 29A, p. 482.

71. Agourides, 'Peter and John in the Fourth Gospel', p. 5. Cf. also Barrett, who writes regarding the Beloved Disciple, 'Here with Mary, he is the sole representative of the associates of Jesus; even Peter, with whom he appears elsewhere, is absent'; *The Gospel According to St. John*, p. 552.

72. Bultmann, *The Gospel According to John*, p. 673. Others who transfer the symbolism of Jewish Christianity from Peter to Mary for their interpretation of this passage are: Loisy, Schulz, Pamment, Minear and Gunther.

73. Cf. Bultmann, *The Gospel of John*, pp. 515, 520, and Dauer, 'Das Wort des Gekreuzigten an Seine Mutter und den Jünger den er liebte. Eine

traditionsgeschichtliche und theologische Untersuchung zu Joh 19, 25-27',
Biblische Zeitschrift 11 (1967)', pp. 224-25.

74. Dauer, 'Das Wort des Gekreuzigten', p. 225.

75. I.e. Mary Magdalene, Mary the mother of James and Joseph and
Salome (Mk 15.40) the mother of the sons of Zebedee (Mt. 27.56).

76. I.e. 'the mother of Jesus, his mother's sister, Mary of Clopas and Mary
Magdalene', Jn 19.25. As R.E. Brown notes, 'the sentence structure would
seem to favour four women; "A and B, C and D"'; *The Gospel According to
John*, vol. 29A, p. 904.

77. Morris, *The Gospel According to John*, p. 811. Most interpreters have
adopted this position. Cf. Westcott, *op. cit.*, p. 275; Hoskyns, *The Fourth
Gospel*, p. 530; Barrett, *op. cit.*, p. 551; Sanders and Mastin, *The Gospel
According to St. John*, p. 408; R.E. Brown, *The Gospel According to John*,
vol. 29A, p. 904, and others.

78. Cf. Westcott, *op. cit.*, p. 275. Cf. also Schnackenburg, *The Gospel
According to St. John*, vol. 3, p. 276.

79. R.E. Brown, *The Gospel According to John*, vol. 29A, p. 906.

80. παρά may not necessarily refer to 'immediately beside', but perhaps
'by' in a more general sense. Cf. Sanders and Mastin, *op. cit.*, p. 408.
However, according to John they would have had to have been close enough
to carry on a conversation with Jesus.

81. R.E. Brown, *The Gospel According to John*, vol. 29A, p. 904.

82. Bultmann, *The Gospel of John*, p. 520.

83. Ethelbert Stauffer, *Jesus and His Story*, 1st American edn (New York:
Alfred A. Knopf, 1960), p. 179, n. 1. Barrett also adds *T. Gittin* 7.1.; *Y. Gittin*
7, 48c, 39; and *Baba Metzia* 83b; *ibid.*

84. Barrett, *op. cit.*, p. 551.

85. *Ibid.*

86. Bultmann, *The Gospel of John*, p. 672.

87. Cf. the Church Fathers Athanasius, Epiphanius, Hilary. Also, Westcott,
op. cit., p. 276 ('the last office of filial piety'); Bernard, *op. cit.*, p. 633; Dods,
op. cit., p. 858; Barclay, *The Gospel of John*, vol. 2, pp. 255-57; Dodd, *The
Interpretation of the Fourth Gospel*, p. 428; Sanders and Mastin, *op. cit.*,
p. 408; Morris, *The Gospel According to John*, p. 812; Bruce, *The Gospel of
John* (Grand Rapids: Eerdmans, 1983), p. 372.

88. Sanders and Mastin, *op. cit.*, p. 408. Cf. also Bernard, who states 'John
was nephew to Mary and in sympathy he was nearer to her than these
stepsons', *op. cit.*, p. 633.

89. O'Grady, 'The Role of the Beloved Disciple', p. 61.

90. R.E. Brown, *The Gospel According to John*, vol. 29A, p. 923.

91. Barrett, *op. cit.*, p. 552.

92. R.E. Brown, *The Gospel According to John*, vol. 29A, p. 923.

93. For a concise synopsis and further references, see R.F. Collins,
'Representative Figures of the Fourth Gospel—II', pp. 121-22. He divides

scholars who interpret Mary in the Fourth Gospel from a symbolical perspective into three groups: 1) Those who see her as a representation of Jewish Christianity (e.g. Loisy, Bultmann, Schulz); 2) Those, particularly from a strong Roman Catholic tradition, who see Mary as the representative of the community of believers, i.e. the Church (e.g. Schürmann, Dauer, Balducci, Feuillet, de la Potterie); 3) Those who see Mary as the model for all Christians through her faith response (e.g. Uzin, Crossan). Cf. also R.F. Collins, 'Mary in the Fourth Gospel. A Decade of Johannine Studies', *Louvain Studies* 3 (1970), pp. 99-142; and Schnackenburg, *The Gospel According to St. John*, vol. 3, pp. 279-82 and p. 457, n. 31.

94. In addition to those listed in the preceding note is E.F. Scott, *The Fourth Gospel: Its Purpose and Theology*, 2nd edn (Edinburgh: T & T Clark, 1920).

95. Schnackenburg, *The Gospel According to St. John*, vol. 3, p. 278; Gunther, *op. cit.*, p. 131 and Collins, 'Representative Figures of the Fourth Gospel—II', p. 122.

96. Minear, 'The Beloved Disciple in the Gospel of John: Some Clues and Conjectures', p. 119-20.

97. R.E. Brown, *The Gospel According to John*, vol. 29A, p. 926.

98. *Ibid.*

99. *Ibid.*

100. Snyder, 'John 13.16 and the Anti-Petrinism of the Johannine Tradition', p. 12.

101. Lindars, *The Gospel of John*, p. 580.

102. *Ibid.*

103. *Ibid.*, pp. 179-80. Somewhat related to this interpretation is that of Barrett, who sees a stress on the *unity* of the church. 'The Christian receives in the present age houses and brothers and sisters and mothers and children and lands (Mk 10.30)'; *op. cit.*, p. 552.

104. E.L. Titus, *The Message of the Fourth Gospel* (New York: Abingdon, 1957), p. 230.

105. Dauer, 'Das Wort des Gekreuzigten', pp. 236-37.

106. Snyder, *op. cit.*, p. 13.

107. Maurice Goguel, *The Birth of Christianity* (London: George Allen & Unwin, 1963), pp. 110-14.

108. *Ibid.*, p. 113. Goguel cites Eduward Meyer and Johannes Weiss as precedents for this approach, *loc. cit.*, n. 1.

109. *Ibid.*, p. 114.

110. Maynard, 'The Role of Peter in the Fourth Gospel', p. 539.

111. Barrett, *op. cit.*, p. 552, and Dauer, 'Das Wort des Gekreuzigten', p. 81.

112. R.E. Brown, *The Gospel According to John*, vol. 29A, p. 923. In criticism of the 'adoption formula' Brown argues, 'seemingly there is no precise parallel where the mother is addressed first. In fact, the adoption

formulas we find in Scripture generally have a 'you are. . . ' pattern, unlike John's "here is. . . "', *ibid*, p. 907.

113. M. de Goedt, 'Un schème de révélation dans le quatrième évangile', *New Testament Studies* 8 (1963), 277-285.

114. Minear, 'The Beloved Disciple in the Gospel of John: Some Clues and Conjectures', p. 119.

115. 'He who saw it has borne witness—his testimony is true and he knows that he tells the truth—that you may also believe'. The vast majority of scholars take this to be a reference to the Beloved Disciple (cf. Jn 21.24), although a less likely possibility is that it is a reference to one of the soldiers.

116. Maynard, 'The Role of Peter in the Fourth Gospel', p. 539. It is interesting to note that here Maynard has no hesitation in understanding Peter as a *representative disciple*, whereas in other discussions he is quick to focus on Peter *the individual*.

117. However, it will be noted that the Beloved Disciple follows at least a little further (19.24).

118. Snyder, *op. cit.*, p. 12.

119. Agourides, 'Peter and John in the Fourth Gospel', p. 5.

120. *Ibid.*

Notes to Chapter 5

1. Gunther, 'The Relation of the Beloved Disciple to the Twelve', p. 132. N.B. the confidence Minear expresses in his interpretation of 20.1-10: 'It is clear that a negative picture is again assigned to Peter in contrast to the positive picture of his rival'; 'The Beloved Disciple in the Gospel of John: Some Clues and Conjectures', p. 121.

2. F. Neirynck, 'John and the synoptics: The Empty Tomb Stories', *New Testament Studies* 30 (1984), p. 165.

3. As Schnackenburg comments, 'The problem of history of tradition for which the synoptic traditions and texts for comparisons are helpful, may not be ignored under any circumstances. The efforts of literary criticism, especially with Jn 20.1-18, have led to widely differing results; with the difficulty of the text before us, no certain conclusion satisfactory in all respects may be expected. The main purpose remains for us a more exact definition of the intention behind the evangelist's statement'. *The Gospel According to St. John*, vol. 3, p. 301; '. . . speculation on common sources of Mark and John is certainly not the most promising way of interpreting Jn 20'; Neirynck, *ibid*.

4. Even Jn 20.2 reports her as saying 'We. . . '.

5. Mark reports that the women did not say anything to anyone 'for they were afraid' (Mk 16.8).

6. I.e., D, it $^{a\ b\ d\ e\ l\ r\ syr\ pal\ mss}$; Marcion and Diatessaron.

7. See the discussion following on the relationship between Lk. 24.12 and 24.

8. R.E. Brown, *The Gospel According to John*, vol. 29A, p. 995.

9. B.F. Westcott and F.J.A. Hort, *The New Testament in the Original Greek*, vol. 2, *Introduction and Appendix* (Cambridge: Macmillan, 1881), pp. 134f. Cf. also, R.E. Brown, *The Gospel According to John*, pp. 969, 1000.

10. Schnackenburg, *The Gospel According to St. John*, vol. 3, p. 309.

11. Mahoney, *op. cit.*, p. 59.

12. *Ibid.*

13. *Ibid.*, p. 68.

14. Mahoney, who does not accept Lk. 24.12 as original to the text, nevertheless says the text 'especially in the light of p^{75}, retains such weight that we are unable to pass certain judgment against it'; *loc. cit.* cf. also Fitzmyer, *The Gospel According to Luke X-XXIV*, vol. 28A (Garden City, NY: Doubleday, 1985), pp. 130-31, 1547.

15. Cf. a similar use of the plural in Lk. 21.5 (as compared to Mk 13.1) and Acts 17.28.

16. Neirynck, 'John and the Synoptics: The Empty Tomb Stories', p. 173.

17. J. Muddiman, 'A note on Reading Luke xxiv. 12', *Ephemerides Theologicae Louvanienses* 48 (1972), p. 547.

18. Cf. R.J. Dillon, *From Eye-Witnesses to Ministers of the Word: Tradition and Composition in Luke 24* (Rome: Pontifical Biblical Institute, 1978), pp. 64ff.

19. Grant R. Osborne, *The Resurrection Narratives: A Redactional Study* (Grand Rapids: Baker Book House, 1984), p. 114, n. 16.

20. Lk. 5.1-11 and parallels.

21. Dillon, *op. cit.*, p. 64 (cf. also n. 184).

22. '... its inclusion in the original text of the Lucan Gospel merits more than a D in the UBSGNT^3 rating'; Fitzmyer, *The Gospel According to Luke X–XXIV*, p. 1547.

23. Cf. Metzger, *Textual Commentary*, p. 184; I. Howard Marshall calls it a 'cross reference' to 24, *Commentary on Luke* (Grand Rapids: Eerdmans, 1978), p. 888; Jeremias, *The Eucharistic Words of Jesus* trans. A. Ehrhardt (London: SCM Press, 1966), pp. 149ff.; Dillon, *op. cit.*, p. 65; Fitzmyer, *The Gospel According to Luke X-XXIV*, p. 1547.

24. Robert Leaney, 'The Resurrection Narratives in Luke (XXIV.12-53)', *New Testament Studies* 2 (1956), p. 111.

25. ἔδραμεν is the 2nd aorist form of τρέχω. It is significant that the relatively unusual 'historical present' (βλέπει) is found in both accounts.

26. Schnackenburg, *The Gospel According to St. John*, vol. 3, p. 309; see also K. Peter Curtis, 'Luke xxiv, 12 and John xx, 3-10', *Journal of Theological*

Studies 22 (1971), pp. 512-15 and R.H. Fuller, *The Formation of the Resurrection Narratives* (New York: MacMillan, 1971), pp. 101-103.

27. I.e., ἀναστάς, θαυμάζειν with the accusative, and τὸ γεγονός.

28. B. Lindars, 'The Composition of John XX', *New Testament Studies* 7 (1961), p. 146.

29. Neirynck, 'John and the Synoptics: The Empty Tomb Stories', p. 175.

30. *Ibid.*

31. Joachim Jeremias, *The Eucharistic Words of Jesus*, p. 150.

32. Cf. J. Schniewind, *Die Parallelperikopen bei Lukas und Johannes* (Leipzig: A Deichert, 1914); and F. Hauck, *Das Evangelium des Lukas* (Leipzig: A. Deichert, 1934), p. 6f. n. 2.

33. Schnackenburg, *The Gospel According to St. John*, vol. 3, p. 307.

34. Fitzmyer, *The Gospel According to Luke X-XXIV*, p. 1542; Metzger, *Textual Commentary*, p. 184. For a full discussion of this, see also John E. Alsup, *The Post-Resurrection Appearance Stories of the Gospel-Tradition* (London: SPCK, 1975), pp. 95-100.

35. Leaney, *op. cit.*, p. 113. Schnackenburg characterizes the source behind the resurrection narrative of both Luke and John as having 'vivid description' and an 'apologetic tendency', *The Gospel According to St. John*, vol. 3, p. 307.

36. I.e., 1 Cor. 15.3-8.

37. Lindars, *The Gospel of John*, p. 597.

38. *Ibid.*, p. 1002.

39. For a discussion of this literary development, see Schnackenburg, *The Gospel According to St. John*, vol. 3, p. 309. See also Lindars, 'The Composition of John XX', pp. 142-47.

40. I.e., in this case, the theme of 'faith'.

41. Schnackenburg, *The Gospel According to St. John*, vol. 3, p. 314.

42. Lindars, *The Gospel of John*, p. 595.

43. Cf. Mk 16.2, Mt. 28.1 and Lk. 24.1.

44. Osborne, *The Resurrection Narratives: A Redactional Study*, p. 149. Cf. also Brown, *The Gospel According to John*, vol. 29A, p. 981; Schnackenburg, *The Gospel According to St. John*, vol. 3, p. 308.

45. Bernard, *St. John*, p. 702.

46. *Ibid.*, p. 703.

47. Paul S. Minear, '"We don't know where. . . " Jn 20.2', *Interpretation* 30 (1976), p. 126.

48. In all the citations Minear lists a personal pronoun is found, although only Jn 4.22 uses the pronoun in the nominative case for specific emphasis.

49. Lindars, *The Gospel of John*, p. 600.

50. R.E. Brown, *The Gospel According to John*, vol. 29A, p. 983.

51. As does Barrett, *The Gospel According to St. John*, p. 563.

52. So Bernard, *op. cit.*, p. 658.

53. Morris, *The Gospel According to John*, p. 832.

54. R.E. Brown, *The Gospel According to John*, vol. 29A, p. 985.

55. Lindars, *The Gospel of John, loc. cit.*

56. R.E. Brown, *The Gospel According to John*, p. 1007.

57. *Ibid.*, cf. also Hoskyns, *The Fourth Gospel*, p. 541.

58. R.E. Brown, *The Gospel According to John*, p. 1007.

59. Mahoney, *Two Disciples at the Tomb*, p. 248.

60. *Ibid.*, p. 307.

61. *Ibid.*, p. 250.

62. For a full discussion of the meaning of the phrase, see F. Neirynck, 'Parakypsas blepei: Lc 24, 12 et Jn 20, 5', *Ephemerides Theologicae Louvanienses* 53 (1977), pp. 113-152. See also Fitzmyer, *The Gospel According to Luke X-XXIV*, p. 1547.

63. Their significance will be discussed below (Chapter 5.B).

64. Morris, *The Gospel According to John*, p. 832.

65. Lindars, *The Gospel of John*, p. 601.

66. Hoskyns, *loc. cit.*

67. Hawkin, 'The Function of the Beloved Disciple Motif in the Johannine Redaction', p. 145.

68. Jacob Kremer, *Die Osterbotschaft der vier Evangelien* (Stuttgart: Katholisches Bibelwerk, 1968), pp. 90-91.

69. Schnackenburg, *The Gospel According to St. John*, vol. 3, p. 314. Cf. also Schnackenburg, 'Der Jünger, den Jesus liebte', *Evangelisch-Katholischer Kommentar zum Neuen Testament: Vorarbeiten*, vol. 2 (Zürich: Neukirchener Verlag, 1970), p. 104.

70. Cf. Mk 16.7 and Mt. 28.7.

71. Agourides, 'Peter and John in the Fourth Gospel', p. 6.

72. As Lorenzen suggests; *Der Lieblingsjünger im Johannesevangelium*, p. 32.

73. R.E. Brown, *The Gospel According to John*, vol. 29A, p. 1006.

74. Maynard, 'The Role of Peter in the Fourth Gospel', p. 540; cf. also, Barrett, *op. cit.*, p. 563.

75. Cf. John 11.31.

76. As noted in Chapter 2.B above, the metaphorical use of ἀκολουθέω is always used with reference to Jesus Christ.

77. Lightfoot, *op. cit.*, p. 332; cf. also Sanders, *op. cit.*, p. 420.

78. See Chapter 2.B above.

79. Mahoney, *loc. cit.*

80. L.H. Duparc, 'Le premier signe de la Résurrection chez saint Jean. Jean 20, 7', *Bible et Vie Chrétienne* 86 (1969), pp. 70-77, and F. Salvoni, 'The So-Called Jesus Resurrection Proof (Jn 20.7)', *Restoration Quarterly* 27 (1979), pp. 72-76.

81. Fitzmyer, *The Gospel According to Luke X-XXIV*, p. 1548.

82. Implying that Jesus took them off and folded them neatly; W.W. Reiser, 'The Case of the Tidy Tomb: The Place of the Napkins of Jn 11.44 and 20.7', *Heythrop Journal* 14 (1973), pp. 47-57.

83. R.E. Brown, *The Gospel According to John*, vol. 29A, p. 1008.

84. Cf. Lk. 24.12, 24 and Jn 20.2-10.

85. Mahoney, *op. cit.*, p. 282. Cf. also Gunther, 'Peter's role in this narrative is limited to entering the tomb in order to be the chief witness to conditions inside it'; 'The Relation of the Beloved Disciple to the Twelve', p. 132.

86. *Ibid.*

87. Lindars, *The Gospel of John*, p. 602.

88. Maynard, 'The Role of Peter in the Fourth Gospel', p. 540.

89. R.E. Brown, *The Gospel According to John*, vol. 29A, p. 987.

90. Minear, '"We don't know where. . ." Jn 20.2', p. 127.

91. *Ibid.*

92. See the following discussion on the reference to 'τὴν γραφήν' in v. 9.

93. *Ibid.*

94. Bultmann, *The Gospel of John*, p. 684.

95. Bultmann, *op. cit.*, p. 685; cf. also P. Benoit, *The Passion and Resurrection of Jesus Christ*, p. 64, and G. Hartmann, 'Die Vorlage der Osterberichte in Joh 20', *Zeitschrift für die Neutestamentliche Wissenschaft* 55 (1964), pp. 197-220.

96. If an individual scripture reference is meant here, it could have been Ps. 16.10.

97. *Ibid.*, p. 417. Cf. also R.E. Brown's evaluation, *The Gospel According to John*, vol. 29A, p. 988.

98. Haenchen, *John*, p. 208.

99. Lindars, *The Gospel of John*, *loc. cit.*

100. Bultmann, *loc. cit.* Also, Hawkin appears to accept Bultmann's argument here, *op. cit.*, p. 145.

101. Hoskyns, *op. cit.*, p. 540.

102. Barrett, *op. cit.*, p. 563.

103. R.E. Brown, *The Gospel According to John*, vol. 29A, p. 1005.

104. Haenchen, *op. cit.*, p. 208.

105. Lorenzen, *op. cit.*, p. 34, n. 38.

106. Gunther, 'The Relation of the Beloved Disciple to the Twelve', p. 133.

107. R.E. Brown, *The Gospel According to John*, p. 1005.

108. Lindars, *The Gospel of John*, *loc. cit.*

109. Osborne, *The Resurrection Narratives: A Redactional Study*, p. 147. Cf. also Collins, 'The Representative Figures of the Fourth Gospel—II', pp. 128, 130.

110. *Ibid.*, p. 153.

111. *Ibid.*, p. 154.

112. Mahoney, *op. cit.*, p. 260.
113. Maynard, 'The Role of Peter in the Fourth Gospel', p. 540. Haenchen also sees this section in John as a polemic not against Peter in particular, but against exclusive claims of the Twelve. He asserts that this passage claims 'apostolic succession' for *all* believers, or disciples; *op. cit.*, p. 216.
114. 'This he said about the Spirit, which those who believed on him were to receive, for the Spirit was not yet (given), because Jesus was not yet glorified'.

Notes to Chapter 6

1. Grant R. Osborne, 'John 21: A Test Case for History and Redaction in the Resurrection Narratives', *Gospel Perspectives II*, ed. R.T. France and D. Wenham (Sheffield: JSOT Press, 1981), pp. 317-18.
2. I.e., the reference to Peter's martyrdom and the death of the Beloved Disciple.
3. 'From textual evidence, including that of such early witnesses as p^{66} and Tertullian, the Gospel was never circulated without ch. xxi (A 5th or 6th century Syriac ms. [British Museum cat. add. no. 14453] that ends with Jn xx 25 has apparently lost the final folios)'; R.E. Brown, *The Gospel According to John*, vol. 29A, p. 1077.
4. Cf. Marie-Joseph Lagrange, *L'Évangile selon Saint Jean*, 8th edn (Paris: Gabalda, 1948), p. 522; William Temple, *Readings in St. John's Gospel* (Toronto: Macmillan, 1968), p. 377; Leon Morris, *The Gospel According to John*, p. 859; Stephen S. Smalley, 'The Sign in John xxi', *New Testament Studies* 29 (1974), pp. 273-88.
5. Hoskyns, *The Fourth Gospel*, p. 550. So also Temple, *Readings in St. John's Gospel*, p. 377 and Morris, *The Gospel According to John*, p. 859.
6. Hoskyns, *The Fourth Gospel*, p. 550; Morris, *The Gospel According to John*, p. 859.
7. Lagrange, *loc. cit.*
8. Marsh, *op. cit.*, p. 658.
9. Smalley, 'The Sign in John xxi', p. 276-77.
10. *Ibid.*
11. Paul S. Minear, 'The Original Functions of John 21', *Journal of Biblical Literature* 102 (1983), p. 91.
12. *Ibid.*, p. 92.
13. *Ibid.*, p. 93.
14. R.E. Brown, *The Gospel According to John*, vol. 29A, p. 1078.
15. Barrett, *The Gospel According to St. John*, p. 576.
16. It should be noted that it is possible to maintain the *supplementary* nature of ch. 21 and still hold to a common authorship of 1-20 and 21. Cf. Marcus Dods, *The Gospel of John*, vol. 1, p. 867; Bernard, *St. John*, vol. 2,

pp. 687-88; Lightfoot, *St. John's Gospel: A Commentary*, p. 339; Sanders and Mastin, *The Gospel According to St. John*, p. 441-42; Lindars, *The Gospel of John*, pp. 621-22; Mahoney, *Two Disciples at the Tomb*, pp. 36-38.

17. C.H. Dodd, *The Interpretation of the Fourth Gospel*, p. 431.

18. *Ibid.*

19. Bultmann, *The Gospel of John*, p. 702.

20. *Ibid.*, pp. 701-702.

21. Alan Shaw, 'Image and Symbol in John 21', *Expository Times* 86 (1975), p. 311.

22. Lindars, *The Gospel of John*, p. 618. So also Pamment, 'The Fourth Gospel's Beloved Disciple', p. 366.

23. Cf. Lightfoot, *St. John's Gospel*, p. 279ff; Dods, *op. cit.*, p. 867; Bernard, *op. cit.*, p. 688; Hoskyns, *The Fourth Gospel*, p. 561; Sanders and Mastin, *op. cit.*, pp. 441-42; Lindars, *The Gospel of John*, p. 621; Morris, *The Gospel According to John*, p. 859; Mahoney, *op. cit.* (although Mahoney involves an editor—see following discussion), pp. 36-38.

24. Dods, *op. cit.*, p. 867.

25. Sanders and Mastin, *op. cit.*, pp. 441-42.

26. Mahoney, *op. cit.*, p. 38; Mahoney's reconstruction is to be differentiated from those which hold that the editor of ch. 21 added material which had not come directly from the evangelist responsible for John 1-20.

27. For a list of these, see Barrett, *op. cit.*, p. 576; Moffat, *An Introduction to the Literature of the New Testament* (Edinburgh: T & T Clark, 1927), p. 57; and Bultmann, *the Gospel of John*, p. 710.

28. M.E. Boismard, 'Le Chapitre XXI de Saint Jean. Essai de critique littéraire', *Revue Biblique* 54 (1947), pp. 473-501. Cf. also W.J. Tobin, 'The Petrine Primacy Evidence of the Gospels', *Lumen Vitae* 23 (1968), p. 59.

29. G.W. Broomfield, *John, Peter and the Fourth Gospel*, pp. 147ff.

30. B. de Solages, and J.M. Vacherot, 'Le Chapitre XXI de Jean est-il de la même plume que le reste de l'Evangile?' *Bulletin de Littérature Ecclésiastique* 80 (1979), pp. 96-101.

31. Of course, this raises the possibility that the writer of 1 John was the same person responsible for the final editing of the Gospel; cf. J. Terence Forestell, *The Word of the Cross* (Rome: Biblical Institute Press, 1974), p. 168.

32. R.E. Brown, *The Gospel According to John*, vol. 29A, p. 1080.

33. *Ibid.*, p. 1094.

34. Reflecting a minority perspective, Osborne suggests that the two narratives, i.e. Lk 5.1-11 and Jn 21.1-14, are based on separate incidents; 'John 21: A Test Case for History and Redaction in the Resurrection Narratives'.

35. Lindars is a minority voice against this view: 'It is probably a mistake to suppose that the story is a fusion of traditions. The theme of the meal, in which Jesus himself provides the food (vv. 9, 12a, 13), is not a separate story,

but a new feature introduced specially to lead into the theme of feeding in vv. 15-17'; *The Gospel of John*, pp. 622-23.

36. Cf. R.E. Brown: 'These stories had already been combined long before they came to the redactor responsible for ch. xxi'; *The Gospel According to John*, vol. 29A, p. 1094; Smalley suggests that John consciously combined the two stories, 'The Sign in John xxi', p. 287. Perhaps Barrett's statement is to be preferred: 'whether they [*the traditional narratives*] were combined by the author of ch. 21, or were found by him in their present state, cannot be determined'; *op. cit.*, p. 578.

37. N.E. Johnson, 'The Beloved Disciple and the Fourth Gospel', p. 290.

38. Smalley, 'The Sign in John xxi', p. 287. So also Sanders and Mastin, *op. cit.*, p. 450; Barrett, *op. cit.*, p. 578.

39. For example, seven disciples are described in 1-14 while only two are mentioned in 15-23; 1-14 speaks symbolically of fish while 15-23 speaks of sheep. Cf. discussion in R.E. Brown, *The Gospel According to John*, vol. 29A, p. 1084.

40. R.E. Brown, *The Gospel According to John*, vol. 29A, p. 1095. Cf. also Barrett, *op. cit.*, p. 578.

41. Mahoney, *op. cit.*, p. 39.

42. N.E. Johnson, *op. cit.*, p. 284.

43. R.E. Brown, *The Gospel According to John*, vol. 29A, p. 1082.

44. Cf. the use of the verb in Luke (3X) and the other Gospels (no occurrences).

45. Osborne, 'John 21: A Test Case for History and Redaction in the Resurrection Narratives', p. 299.

46. Snyder, 'Jn 13.16 and the Anti-Petrinism of the Johannine Tradition', p. 13.

47. J.F. O'Grady, 'The Role of the Beloved Disciple', *Biblical Theology Bulletin* 9 (1979), pp. 60-61.

48. Mahoney, *op. cit.*, p. 293.

49. Marsh, *op. cit.*, p. 87.

50. R.E. Brown, *The Community of the Beloved Disciple*, p. 87. Cf. also, Temple, *Readings in St. John's Gospel*, p. 377.

51. R.E. Brown, *The Gospel According to John*, vol. 29A, p. 1071.

52. Lindars, *The Gospel of John*, p. 625.

53. Schnackenburg surveys and summarizes the various interpretations, *The Gospel According to St. John*, vol. 3, pp. 357-58. More recently, two more gematriacal solutions have been presented; cf. N.J. McEleney, '153 Great Fishes (Jn 21, 11)—Gematriacal Atbash', *Biblica* 58 (1977), pp. 411-17 and J.A. Romeo 'Gematria and Jn 21.11—The Children of God', *Journal of Biblical Literature* 97 (1978), pp. 263-64.

54. R.E. Brown, *The Gospel According to John*, vol. 29A, p. 1076; also Barrett, *op. cit.*, p. 581.

55. Morris, *The Gospel According to John*, p. 867.

56. Grant Osborne, 'John 21: A Test Case for History and Redaction in the Resurrection Narratives', pp. 302-303.

57. Lindars, *The Gospel of John*, p. 629. Cf. also, R.E. Brown, *The Gospel According to John*, vol. 29A, p. 1075; Schnackenburg, *The Gospel According to St. John*, vol. 3, p. 358; Barrett, *op. cit.*, p. 581.

58. Lindars, *The Gospel of John*, p. 629. It is interesting to note that Morris interprets the unbroken net symbolically even though he hesitates to interpret the actual number of the fish symbolically, *The Gospel According to John*, pp. 867-68.

59. Schnackenburg, *The Gospel According to St. John*, vol. 3, p. 538. Luke appears to be mainly concerned with missionary activity and not Church unity as in John.

60. Osborne, 'John 21: A Test Case for History and Redaction in the Resurrection narratives', p. 303.

61. Temple, *Readings in St. John's Gospel*, p. 398.

62. See Chapter 1.B above.

63. Maynard, 'Peter in the Fourth Gospel', pp. 544-45. Schuyler Brown writes (p. 476), 'In ch. 21, however, the contrast between Peter and the beloved disciple is no longer so disadvantageous for the former', 'Apostleship in the New Testament as an Historical and Theological Problem'.

64. E.g. Snyder, *op. cit.*, p. 13.

65. Agourides, 'Peter and John in the Fourth Gospel', p. 7.

66. *Ibid.*

67. Bernard, *op. cit.*, p. 691.

68. 'The double name 'Simon Peter' is only to be expected with a narrator from Johannine circles', Schnackenburg, *The Gospel According to St. John*, vol. 3, p. 353.

69. Bernard, *op cit.*, p. 694.

70. See 2.B above.

71. Maynard, 'Peter in the Fourth Gospel', p. 544.

72. Lindars, *The Gospel of John*, p. 625. Morris cautiously states: '. . . the general impression left is that of men without a purpose'; *The Gospel According to John*, p. 862.

73. Edward A. McDowell, Jr. 'Lovest Thou Me?' *Review and Expositor* 32 (1935), p. 434.

74. *Ibid.*

75. Sanders and Mastin, *op. cit.*, p. 443.

76. Morris, *The Gospel According to John*, p. 861.

77. Schnackenburg, *The Gospel According to St. John*, vol. 3, p. 353.

78. E.g., Jn 3.3-8 (ἄνωθεν, πνεῦμα); see also E. Richard, 'Expressions of Double Meaning and their Function in the Gospel of John', *New Testament Studies* 31 (1985), pp. 96-112.

79. So Barrett, *op. cit.*, p. 579.

80. *Ibid.*

81. Snyder, *op. cit.*, p. 13.

82. *Ibid.*

83. So Marinus de Jonge, *Jesus: Stranger from Heaven and Son of God* (Missoula, Montana: Scholars Press, 1977), p. 212; and Gunther, 'The Relation of the Beloved Disciple to the Twelve', p. 133.

84. Tobin, *op. cit.*, p. 61.

85. *Ibid.*

86. E.A. Abbot, *Diatessarica: Johannine Vocabulary*, p. 2999; cf. also Bernard, *op. cit.*, vol. 2, p. 698, n. 1.

87. Bauer, Arndt and Gingrich, *op. cit.*, p. 284.

88. R.E. Brown, *The Gospel According to John*, vol. 29A, p. 1072.

89. Cf. Liddell and Scott, *A Greek English Lexicon* (Oxford: Clarendon Press, 1940), p. 362; cf. also Brown, *The Gospel According to John*, pp. 864-65; Dods, *op. cit.*, p. 868 (he cites Aristophanes, *Clouds*, 480, in support); Bultmann, *The Gospel of John*, p. 708.

90. R.E. Brown, *The Gospel According to John*, vol. 29A, p. 1072.

91. Lagrange, *op. cit.*, p. 525.

92. '. . . where men are naked, neither greeting, nor reading, nor prayer is in order. . . ' *T. Berakoth* 2.20 (5).

93. Barrett, *op. cit.*, p. 581.

94. Gunther, 'The Relation of the Beloved Disciple to the Twelve', p. 133.

95. Agourides, 'Peter and John in the Fourth Gospel', p. 6.

96. We have a hint of this evaluation of Peter's actions in Morris' statement: Peter's example of diving into the water was not followed'; *The Gospel According to John*, p. 865.

97. I.e., Questions and Answers on Genesis, V 22.

98. Agourides, 'Peter and John in the Fourth Gospel', p. 6. Others who hint at the 'penitential' or 'purifying' nature of the swim include: Gunther, 'The Relation of the Beloved Disciple to the Twelve', p. 133; Tobin, *op. cit.*, p. 61.

99. Cf. Jn 9.7; 13.5-10.

100. Lars Hartman, 'An Attempt at a Text-Centered Exegesis of John 21', *Studia Theologica* 38 (1984), p. 39.

101. M. Goguel, *The Birth of Christianity*. Cf. also F. Spitta, *Das Johannesevangelium als Quelle der Geschichte Jesu*, 1910.

102. Bultmann, *The Gospel of John*, p. 712.

103. R.E. Brown, *The Gospel According to John*, vol. 29A, p. 1111.

104. Chapter 3.C above.

105. For a discussion of the significance of the number of fish, see pp. 135f. above.

106. See Chapter 6.B above.

107. F.M. Braun, 'Quatre "Signes" Johanniques de l'Unité Chrétienne', *New Testament Studies* 9 (1963), pp. 153-55.

108. Cf. also Jn 6.44 for a similar use of the verb.

109. Osborne, 'John 21: A Test Case for History and Redaction in the Resurrection Narratives', p. 303.

110. Osborne, 'John 21: A Test Case for History and Redaction in the Resurrection Narratives', p. 308. Cf. also Lindars, *The Gospel of John*, p. 635, and R.E. Brown, *The Gospel According to John*, vol. 29A, pp. 1103f.

111. So Agourides, 'The Purpose of John 21', p. 7.

112. Mt. 26.33 and Mk 14.26-31.

113. Osborne, 'John 21: A Test Case for History and Redaction in the Resurrection Narratives', p. 325, n. 77.

114. 'Jesus was asking Peter to leave behind attachments to other people and follow him'; Osborne, 'John 21: A Test Case for History and Redaction in the Resurrection Narratives', p. 308.

115. Maynard, 'The Role of Peter in the Fourth Gospel', p. 542. Cf. also Spicq, C, *Agapè dans le Nouveau Testament. Analyse des Textes* (Paris: Gabalda et Cie., 1959), pp. 230-37, and Tobin, *op. cit.*, p. 63.

116. I.e. *Agapè dans le Nouveau Testament. Analyse des Textes*.

117. Spicq, *op. cit.*, p. 233.

118. Tobin, *op. cit.*, p. 63.

119. Gunther refers to the 'heavenly quality' of ἀγαπᾶν, 'The Relation of the Beloved Disciple to the Twelve', p. 133.

120. Spicq, *op. cit.*, p. 234.

121. Gunther, 'The Relation of the Beloved Disciple to the Twelve', p. 133.

122. Tobin, *loc. cit.*

123. Osborne, 'John 21: A Test Case for History and Redaction in the Resurrection Narratives', p. 308.

124. Maynard, 'The Role of Peter in the Fourth Gospel', p. 542.

125. Spicq, *op. cit.*, p. 234.

126. K.L. McKay, 'Style and Significance in the Language of Jn 21.15-17', *Novum Testamentum* 4 (1985), pp. 319-33.

127. McKay, *op. cit.*, p. 321.

128. *Ibid.*

129. *Ibid.*, p. 322.

130. Osborne, 'John 21: A Test Case for History and Redaction in the Resurrection Narratives', p. 308.

131. I.e., how would the switch in verbs be meaningful even for the writer and readers if Peter is reported to be in agreement with Jesus while at the same time changing the sense of the question?

132. So McKay, *op. cit.*, p. 332, who describes the variations as 'gently significant'.

133. Osborne, 'John 21: A Test Case for History and Redaction in the Resurrection Narratives', p. 308.

134. Paul Gaechter, 'Das dreifache, "Weide meine Lämmer"', *Zeitschrift für Katholische Theologie* 69 (1947), p. 329.

135. R.E. Brown, *The Gospel According to John*, vol. 29A, p. 1106.

136. Gaechter, *op. cit.*, p. 343-44.

137. Brown, Donfried and Reumann, *Peter in the New Testament*, p. 143, n. 304.

138. I.e. 'This was the *third* time that Jesus was revealed to the disciples after he was raised from the dead (Jn 21.14)'.

139. Agourides, 'Peter and John in the Fourth Gospel', p. 6. He goes on to link the schematisation of triads to John 1 and the account of the first three days of Jesus' ministry, thereby linking the opening and closing of the Gospel, *ibid*.

140. J.F.X. Sheehan, 'Feed My Lambs', *Scripture* 16 (1964), p. 27.

141. Osborne, 'John 21: A Test Case for History and Redaction in the Resurrection Narratives', pp. 308-309.

142. *Ibid*.

143. Gaechter calls them 'völlig synonym'; *op. cit.*, p. 331.

144. So Bultmann, *The Gospel of John*, p. 713 and Schnackenburg, *The Gospel According to St. John*, vol. 3, p. 366.

145. So Cullmann; *Peter: Disciple, Apostle, Martyr*, p. 65; and R.E. Brown, *The Gospel According to John*, vol. 29A, p. 1113.

146. Gunther, 'The Relation of the Beloved Disciple to the Twelve' p. 140. To be accurate, it needs to be said that Gunther does suggest this in the context of the *irony* of the situation as he understands the relationship between Peter and the Johannine community. For more on the role of Peter as a protector from hereby, see also Donfried, et al. *Peter in the New Testament* (New York: Paulist Press, 1973), p. 142.

147. McKay, *op. cit.*, p. 332. Cf. also Hartman, *op. cit.*, p. 32.

148. Osborne, 'John 21: A Test Case for History and Redaction in the Resurrection Narratives', p. 312.

149. Snyder, *loc. cit.*

150. Agourides, 'Peter and John in the Fourth Gospel', p. 7.

151. O'Grady, 'The Role of the Beloved Disciple', p. 60.

152. *Ibid.*, p. 63.

153. Pamment, *op. cit.*, p. 367. Cf. also Bultmann, *The Gospel of John*, p. 701.

154. Osborne, 'John 21: A Test Case for History and Redaction in the Resurrection Narratives', p. 302.

155. *Ibid*.

156. Marinus de Jonge, *Jesus: Stranger from Heaven and Son of God*, p. 212. Cf. also, Gunther, 'The Relation of the Beloved Disciple to the Twelve', p. 133.

157. O'Grady, 'The Role of the Beloved Disciple', p. 60.

158. R.F. Collins, 'The Representative Figures of the Fourth Gospel—II', p. 131.

159. O'Grady, 'The Role of the Beloved Disciple', p. 60.

160. Cf. Dodd, 'A Note on John 21, 24', *Journal of Theological Studies* 4 (1953), pp. 212-13; J. Chapman, 'We Know That His Testimony is True', *Journal of Theological Studies* 31 (1930), pp. 379-87 and Maynard, 'The Role of Peter in the Fourth Gospel', pp. 531-48.

161. O'Grady, 'The Role of the Beloved Disciple', p. 61; Osborne, 'John 21: A Test Case for History and Redaction in the Resurrection Narratives', p. 302.

162. Osborne, 'John 21: A Test Case for History and Redaction in the Resurrection Narratives', p. 313.

163. Ibid., p. 326, n. 99.

164. de Jonge, *Jesus: Stranger from Heaven and Son of God*, pp. 211-12.

165. See Chapter 1.B above.

166. Pamment, *op. cit.*, p. 367.

167. Some Scholars discern a difference in the portrayal of Beloved Disciple here in ch. 21, as an active and involved character in the narrative. 'No longer is the beloved disciple present and absent; he is really present and affects the behaviour of Peter'; Pamment, *op. cit.*, p. 367.

168. Forestell, *op. cit.*, p. 134.

169. Bernard, *op. cit.*, vol. 2, p. 692.

170. Bultmann, *The Gospel of John*, p. 715.

171. A.T. Robertson, *A Grammar of the Greek New Testament in the Light of Historical Research* (5th edn; New York, Hodder & Stoughton, 1931), pp. 1009-10.

172. Schnackenburg, *The Gospel According to St. John*, vol. 3, p. 370. Similarly, Brown suggests that the witness and tradition of perfect discipleship of which the Beloved Disciple is the type and origin remains with all believers through the Paraclete; *The Gospel According to John*, vol. 29A, p. 1122.

173. Agourides, 'Peter and John in the Fourth Gospel', p. 6.

174. Gunther, 'The Relation of the Beloved Disciple to the Twelve', p. 133.

175. *Ibid.*

176. Osborne, 'John 21: A Test Case for History and Redaction in the Resurrection narratives', p. 302.

177. Hartman, *op. cit.*, p. 38.

178. Cf. Collins, 'The Representative Figures of the Fourth Gospel—II', p. 129: 'Vv. 20-23 indicate that even the Beloved Disciple follows after Jesus and his friend, Peter,...'

179. Lindars, *The Gospel of John*, p. 622.

180. Snyder, *op. cit.*, p. 13. Another who evaluates Peter's martyrdom similarly is Agourides, 'Peter and John in the Fourth Gospel', p. 7.

181. See the discussion of Peter's martyrdom earlier in this chapter, ßC.

182. Schuyler Brown, 'Apostleship in the New Testament as an Historical and Theological Problem', p. 476.

183. Agourides, 'Peter and John in the Fourth Gospel', p. 7.

184. R.E. Brown, *The Gospel According to John* vol. 29A, p. 1110.

185. Lindars, *The Gospel of John*, p. 618, and Pamment, *op. cit.*, p. 366.

186. Maynard, 'The Role of Peter in the Fourth Gospel', p. 545. Maynard cites Snyder, Schmithals, Barrett and Klein as proponents of this view.

187. Cf. Chapter 1.C above.

188. Cf. O'Grady, 'The Role of the Beloved Disciple', pp. 62-63 and Maynard, *loc. cit.*

189. O'Grady, 'The Role of the Beloved Disciple', pp. 62-63. Cf. also P. le Fort, *Les Structures de l'Eglise militante selon saint Jean. Etude d'ecclésiologie concrète appliquée au IVe évangile et aux épîtres johanniques* (Geneva: Labor & Fides, 1970), p. 145.

190. Minear, 'The Original Functions of John 21', pp. 94-95.

Notes to Chapter 7

1. Mahoney, *Two Disciples at the Tomb*, pp. 7-8.

2. Mahoney, *op. cit.*, pp. 282-83.

3. See Chapter 1.C.

4. I.e. 'The Book of Signs' (Jn 1–12) and 'the Book of Glory' (Jn 13–20). The prologue (Jn 1.1-18) is another distinguishable section in the structure of the Gospel; cf. Chapter 3.A.

5. Cf. Chapter 6.A.

6. See below.

7. 'Where I am going you cannot follow me now; but you shall follow me afterward'.

8. Brevard Childs, *The New Testament as Canon: An Introduction*, 1st edn (Philadelphia: Fortress, 1985), p. 119.

9. In the *Acts of Peter and the Twelve Apostles*, the author, speaking as Peter, describes an anonymous 'young disciple' who was following Jesus at a time when the other disciples, including Peter, did not recognize either Jesus Christ or his companion (VI, 1, 8-9). James M. Robinson, ed., *The Nag Hammadi Library* (Leiden: E.J. Brill, 1977, pp. 268-69.

10. See Chapter 1.E above. The anonymity may have a symbolic, representative function. But it may also point to the second-generation context of his readership; see Kurt Aland, 'The Problem of Anonymity and Pseudonymity in the New Testament in Christian Literature of the First Two Centuries', in *The Authorship and Integrity of the New Testament* (London: SPCK, 1965).

11. Compare Jn 1.18, which speaks of the Son εἰς τὸν κόλπον τοῦ πατρός, and Jn 13.23, which speaks of the Beloved Disciple ἐν τῷ κόλπῳ τοῦ Ἰησοῦ.

12. See Chapter 4.D above.

13. See 6.D above.

14. Collins, 'The Representative Figures of the Fourth Gospel - II', p. 131.

15. Schuyler Brown, *The Origins of Christianity*, p. 142.

16. I.e. 'This is the disciple who is bearing witness to these things, and who has written these things; and we know that his testimony is true'.

17. I.e. 'He who saw it has borne witness—his testimony is true, and he knows that he tells the truth—that you may also believe'.

18. Potter, 'The Disciple whom Jesus Loved', *Life of the Spirit* 16 (1962), p. 297.

19. John does not include something simply because it was already in the Synoptic tradition. He is selective in his use of material. For instance, in ch. 13 we find the footwashing episode, in which Peter is highlighted, instead of the institution of the Lord's Supper.

20. I.e. at Caesarea Philippi (Mk 8.29 and parallels). Chapter 2.B above.

21. See Chapter 2.C above.

22. Maynard, 'The Role of Peter in the Fourth Gospel', p. 543.

23. See Chapter 6.C above.

24. See Chapter 5.B above. Cf. also Mk 16.7 and 1 Cor. 15.5. In one way or another, these passages point to the central role Peter played as witness. This is not to suggest that the Johannine 'empty tomb' scene is to be equated with the resurrection appearances.

25. *Contra* Maynard; 'Peter in the Fourth Gospel, pp. 544-45. See also, Chapter 1.B and Chapter 6.C above.

26. Osborne, 'John 21: Test Case for History and Redaction in the Resurrection Narratives', pp. 317-18.

27. Agourides, 'Peter and John in the Fourth Gospel', p. 5.

28. For a summary of work in the area of the Johannine community, see the text and references in Chapter 1.C.

29. Raymond E. Brown and John P. Meier, *Antioch and Rome: New Testament Cradles of Catholic Christianity* (New York: Paulist Press, 1983), p. 214.

30. E.g., 'They went out from us,. . . ' (1 Jn 2.19).

31. O'Grady, 'The Role of the Beloved Disciple', p. 63.

32. Schuyler Brown, *The Origins of Christianity*, p. 117. See also R.E. Brown, '"Other Sheep Not of this Fold': The Johannine Perspective on Christian Diversity in the Late First Century', *Journal of Biblical Literature* 97 (1978), pp. 5-22.

33. O'Grady, 'The Role of the Beloved Disciple', p. 63.

34. Painter, *op. cit.*, pp. 525-26.

35. Patristic evidence suggests that the two streams co-existed in tension for some time, probably in Asia Minor, before the community of the Beloved Disciple became an indistinguishable part of the greater tradition. See Raymond Brown and John P. Meier, *Antioch and Rome: New Testament and Rome: New Testament Cradles of Catholic Christianity* (New York: Paulist, 1983), p. 214.

BIBLIOGRAPHY

Commentaries

Barclay, W. *The Gospel of John*, The Daily Study Bible: 2 vols.; rev. edn; Toronto: G.R. Welch, 1975.

Barrett, C.K., *The Gospel According to St. John*, 2nd edn; Philadelphia: Westminster, 1978.

Becker, J. *Das Evangelium nach Johannes*, Gütersloh: Gütersloher Verlagshaus, 1979.

Bernard, J.H., *A Critical and Exegetical Commentary on the Gospel According to St. John*, 2 vols.; Edinburgh: T & T Clark, 1928.

Boice, James Montgomery, *The Gospel of John*, 5 vols.; Grand Rapids: Zondervan, 1979.

Boismard, M.-E. & A. Lamouille, *L'Evangile de Jean*, vol. 3; Louvain: Desclée de Brouwer, 1958.

Brown, R. E., *The Gospel According to John*, The Anchor Bible, vols. 29-29A; Garden City: Doubleday, 1970.

Bruce, F.F., *The Gospel of John*, Grand Rapids: Eerdmans, 1983.

Bultmann, R. *The Gospel of John: A Commentary*, trans. G.R. Beasley-Murray; Oxford: Basil Blackwell, 1971.

Calvin, J. *The Gospel According to St. John*, New York: Harper & Row, 1959.

Dods, M. *The Gospel of John*, The Expositor's Greek Testament, 1; Grand Rapids: Eerdmans, 1976.

Ellis, P F. *The Genius of John: A Composition—Critical Commentary on the Fourth Gospel*, Collegeville, Minnesota: The Liturgical Press, 1984.

Filson, F. V. *The Gospel According to John*, Richmond: John Knox, 1963.

Fitzmyer, J.A., *The Gospel According to Luke X-XXIV*, Anchor Bible 28A; Garden City, NY: Doubleday, 1985.

Godet, F. L. *Commentary on John's Gospel*, Grand Rapids: Kregel, 1978.

Haenchen, E. *Das Johannesevangelium: ein Kommentar*, Tübingen: Mohr, 1980. ET *John*, Hermeneia 1-2; Philadelphia: Fortress, 1984.

Hauck, F., *Das Evangelium des Lukas*, Leipzig: A. Deichert, 1934.

Henstenberg, W., *Commentary on the Gospel of St. John*, 2 vols.; Minnesota: Klock & Klock, 1980.

Hoskyns, E. C. *The Fourth Gospel*, 2nd edn; ed. N. Davey; London: Faber & Faber, 1947.

Howard, W.F., *The Gospel According to St. John*, The Interpreter's Bible 8; New York: Abingdon, 1952.

Lagrange, M. J. *Évangile selon Saint Jean*, 8th edn; Paris: Gabalda, 1948.

Lightfoot, R. H. *St. John's Gospel: A Commentary*, Oxford: Clarendon, 1956.

Lindars, B. *The Gospel of John*, Grand Rapids: Eerdmans, 1981.

Loisy, A. *Le Quatrième Evangile*, 2nd edn; Paris: Nourry, 1921.

Lüthi, W., *St. John's Gospel: An Exposition*, Richmond: John Knox, 1960.

Macgregor, G.H.C., *The Gospel of John*, The Moffat New Testament Commentary; New York: Harper & Brothers, 1928.

Marshall, I. Howard, *Commentary on Luke*, Grand Rapids: Eerdmans, 1978.

Marsh, J. *Saint John*, London: SCM, 1977.

Mears, E. *The Gospel of St. John*, London: John Murray, 1930.

Michaels, J. R. *John*, A Good News Commentary; New York: Harper & Row, 1981.

Morris, L. *The Gospel According to John*, The New International Commentary on the New Testament; Grand Rapids: Eerdmans, 1971.

Plummer, A., *The Gospel According to St. John*, Grand Rapids: Baker Book House, 1981.

Sanders, J.N. & B.A. Mastin, *The Gospel According to St. John*, London: A. & C. Black, 1968.

Schlatter, A. *Der Evangelist Johannes*, 3rd edn; Stuttgart: Calwer, 1960.

Schnackenburg, R. *The Gospel According to St. John*, 3 vols.; New York: Crossroads, 1980-82.

Tasker, R.V.G., *The Gospel According to St. John*, Tyndale Commentaries, vol. 4; Grand Rapids: Eerdmans, 1960.

Tenney, M. C., *John: The Gospel of Belief*, Grand Rapids: Eerdmans, 1953.

Weiss, B. *Das Johannes-Evangelium*, Göttingen: Vandenhoeck & Ruprecht, 1928.

Westcott, B.F., *The Gospel According to St. John*, 2 vols. London: Murray, 1908.

Wikenhauser, A. *Das Evangelium nach Johannes*, 3rd edn; Regensburg: Pustet, 1961.

Zahn, T. *Das Evangelium des Johannes ausgelegt*, Leipzig: Deichert, 1921.

Books

Abbot, E. A., *Johannine Grammar*, London: A & C Black, 1906.

—*Johannine Vocabulary*, London A & C Black, 1906.

Alsup, John E., *The Post-Resurrection Appearance Stories of the Gospel Tradition*, London: SPCK, 1975.

Bacon, B. W. *The Fourth Gospel in Research and Debate*, New Haven: Yale University Press, 1918.

Bauer, W. *Orthodoxy and Heresy in Earliest Christianity*, ed. Kraft, R. & G. Krodel; Philadelphia: Fortress, 1971.

—Arndt, W.F. & F.W. Gingrich, *A Greek-English Lexicon of the New Testament and Other Early Christian Literature*, 3rd edn; Chicago: University of Chicago Press, 1957.

Beker, J. *Auferstehung der Toten im Urchristentum*, Stuttgart: Katholisches Bibelwerk, 1976.

Benoit, P., *The Passion and Resurrection of Jesus Christ*, New York: Herder & Herder, 1969.

Bergmeier, R. *Glaube als Gabe nach Johannes*, Stuttgart: Kohlhamer, 1980.

Black, M. *An Aramaic Approach to the Gospels and Acts*, 2nd edn; Oxford: Clarendon, 1954.

Blass, F. & A. Debrunner, *A Greek Grammar of the New Testament and Other Early Christian Literature*, trans. R. Funk; Chicago: Chicago University Press, 1961.

Bligh, J. *The Sign of the Cross. The Passion and Resurrection of Jesus according to St. John*, Slough: St. Paul, 1975.

Bode, E. L. *The First Easter Morning*, Rome: Biblical Institute Press, 1970.

Bogart, J., *Orthodox and Heretical Perfectionism in the Johannine Community*, Missoula: Scholars Press, 1977.

Boismard, M. E. *L'Evangile de Jean: Etudes et Problèmes*, Paris: Editions du Cerf, 1958.

Bornkamm, G. *Jesus of Nazareth*, trans. McLuskey & Fraser; New York: Harper & Row, 1960.

Braun, F. M. *Jean le théologien et son Evangile dans l'Eglise Ancienne*, vol. 1. Paris: Gabalda, 1959.

—*Jean le théologien: Les grandes traditions d'Israël et l'accord des Ecritures selon le Quatrième Evangile*, vol. 2.; Paris: Gabalda, 1964.

Broomfield, G.W., *John, Peter and the Fourth Gospel*, London: SPCK, 1934.

Brown, R. E. and J. P. Meier, *Antioch and Rome: New Testament Cradles of Catholic Christianity*, New York: Paulist, 1983.

—*The Community of the Beloved Disciple*, New York: Paulist, 1979.

—et al., eds. *Mary and the New Testament*, Philadelphia: Fortress, 1978.

—Donfried, K.P. & J. Reumann eds., *Peter in the New Testament*, New York: Paulist, 1973.

Brown, S. *The Origins of Christianity: A Historical Introduction to the New Testament*, Oxford: Oxford University Press, 1984.

Brownlee, W.H., *John and Qumran*, ed. J. H. Charlesworth; London: Geoffrey Chapman, 1972.

Bruce, F.F., *Peter, Stephen, James and John: Studies in Non-Pauline Christianity*, Grand Rapids: Eerdmans, 1979.

Bruns, J. E. *The Christian Buddhism of St. John*, Toronto: Paulist, 1971.

Childs, B. S., *The New Testament as Canon: An Introduction*, Philadelphia: Fortress, 1985.

Colson, J., *L'Enigme du disciple que Jésus aimait*, Paris: Beauchesne, 1969.

Colwell, E.G. & E.L. Titus, *The Gospel of the Spirit: A Study in the Fourth Gospel*, New York: Harper & Brothers, 1953.

Cross, F.L., ed., *Studies in the Fourth Gospel*, London: Mowbray, 1957.

Cullmann, O. *The Johannine Circle*. London: SCM, 1976.

—*Peter: Disciple, Apostle, Martyr*, London: SCM, 1953.

Culpepper, R. Alan, *The Johannine School*, Missoula: Scholars, 1975.

Dauer, A. *Die Passionsgeschichte im Johannesevangelium*, München: Kösel, 1972.

Delling, G. *Die Taufe im Neuen Testament*, Göttingen: Vandenhoeck & Ruprecht, 1963.

—*Wort und Werk Jesus im Johannes Evangelium*, Göttingen: Vandenhoeck & Ruprecht, 1966.

Dibelius, M., *From Tradition to Gospel*, London: Ivor Nicolson & Watson, 1934.

Dillon, R.J., *From Eye-Witnesses to Ministers of the Word: Tradition and Composition in Luke 24*, Rome: Pontifical Biblical Institute, 1978.

Dodd, C.H., *Historical Tradition in the Fourth Gospel*, New York: Cambridge University Press, 1963.

— *The Interpretation of the Fourth Gospel*, Cambridge: Cambridge University Press, 1963.

Dunn, J. D.G., *Unity and Diversity in the New Testament*, London: SCM, 1977.

Edwards, R.A., *The Gospel According to St. John: Its Criticism and Interpretation*, Philadelphia: Fortress, 1954.

Fenton, J.C., *The Passion According to John*, London: SPCK, 1961.

Fitzmyer, J.A., *Essays on the Semitic Background of the New Testament*, London: Geoffrey Chapman, 1971.

Forestell, J. T. *The Word of the Cross*, Rome: Biblical Institute Press, 1974.

Fort, P. le, *Les Structures de l'Eglise militante selon saint Jean. Etude d'ecclésiologie concrète appliquée au IVe évangile et aux épîtres johanniques*, Geneva: Labor & Fides, 1970.

Fortna, R.T., *The Gospel of Signs*, Cambridge: Cambridge University Press, 1970.

Freyne, S. *The Twelve: Disciples and Apostles. A Study in the Theology of the First Three Gospels*, London: Sheed & Ward, 1968.

Fuller, R. H. *The Formation of the Resurrection Narratives*, New York: Macmillan, 1971.

Glasson, T.F., *Moses in the Fourth Gospel*, London: SCM, 1963.

Goguel, M. *The Birth of Christianity*, New York: Macmillan, 1954.

Goodspeed, E. J., *The Twelve: The Story of Christ's Apostles*, Philadelphia: J.C. Winston, 1957.

Grass, H. *Ostergeschehen und Osterberichte*, Göttingen: Vandenhoeck & Ruprecht, 1970.

Grundmann, W., *Zeugnis und Gestalt des Johannesevangeliums. Eine Studie zur denkerischen Leistung des vierten Evangelisten*, Stuttgart: Calwer, 1961.

Guenther, H. O., *The Footprints of the Twelve in Early Christian Traditions: A Study in the Meaning of Religious Symbolism*, New York: Peter Lang, 1985.

Hahn, F. *Christologische Hoheitstitel*, 3rd edn; Göttingen: Vandenhoeck & Ruprecht, 1963.

— *Mission in the New Testament*, London: Lutterworth, 1965.

Heise, J., *Bleiben: μενειν in den Johanneischen Schriften*, Tübingen: Mohr, 1967.

Hoskyns, E. C. and F. N. Davey, *The Riddle of the New Testament*, London: Faber & Faber, 1958.

Howard, W.F., *Christianity According to St. John*, London: Duckworth, 1943.

— *The Fourth Gospel in Recent Criticism and Interpretation*, 4th edn; London: Epworth, 1955.

Hunter, A.M., *According to John*, London: SCM, 1968.

Jeremias, J. *The Eucharistic Words of Jesus*, trans. A. Ehrhardt, London: SCM, 1966.

— *New Testament Theology*, vol. 1; New York: Scribners, 1971.

Jonge, M. de, *Jesus: Stranger from Heaven and Son of God*, Missoula, Montana: Scholars, 1977.

— *L'Évangile de Jean: Sources, Rédaction, Théologie*, Leuven: Leuven University Press, 1977.

Karrer, O. *Peter and the Church: An Examination of Cullmann's Thesis*, Freiburg: Herder, 1963.

Käsemann, E. *Exegetische Versuche und Besinnungen*, vol. 1; 2nd edn; Göttingen: Vandenhoeck & Ruprecht, 1964.

— *The Testament of Jesus*, London: SCM, 1968.

Kautzsch, E and A.E. Cowley, *Gesenius' Hebrew Grammar*, 2nd English edn; Oxford: Clarendon, 1910.

Kegel, G. *Auferstehung Jesu—Auferstehung der Toten. Eine traditionsgeschichtliche Untersuchung zum Neuen Testament*, Gütersloh: Gerd Mohn, 1970.

Koester, H. *Einführung in das Neue Testament*, Berlin: de Gruyter, 1980.

Kraeling, E. G. *The Brooklyn Museum Aramaic Papyri: New Documents of the Fifth Century B.C. from the Jewish Colony at Elephantine*, New York: Rand McNally, 1969.

Kraft, H. *Die Entstehung des Christentums*, Darmstadt: Wissenschaftliche Buchgesellschaft, 1981.

Kragerud, A., *Der Lieblingsjünger im Johannesevangelium: Ein exegetischer Versuch*, Hamburg: Grosshaus Wegner, 1959.

Kremer, J. *Die Osterbotschaft der vier Evangelien*, Stuttgart: Katholisches Bibelwerk, 1968.

Kuhl, J., *Die Sendung Jesus und der Kirche nach dem Johannes-Evangelium*, St. Maurice, Switzerland: St. Augustin, 1967.

Kümmel, W. G. *Introduction to the New Testament*, rev. edn; trans. Howard Clark Kee; London: SCM, 1975.

Kysar, R. *The Fourth Evangelist and his Gospel*, Minneapolis: Augsburg, 1975.

— *John: The Maverick Gospel*, Atlanta: John Knox Press, 1976.

Langbrandtner, W., *Weltferner Gott oder Gott der Liebe*, Frankfurt: Lang, 1977.

Lattke, M. *Einheit im Wort*, München: Kösel, 1975.

Leon-Dufour, X. *The Resurrection of Jesus and the Message of Easter*, trans. R.N. Wilson; New York: Holt, Rinehart and Winston, 1974.

Liddell, H.G. and R. Scott, *A Greek-English Lexicon*; rev. edn; vol. 1.; Oxford: Clarendon, 1940.

Lindars, B., *Behind the Fourth Gospel*, London: SPCK, 1976.

Lofthouse, W.F., *The Disciple Whom Jesus Loved*, London: Epworth, 1936.

Lorenzen, T. *Die Bedeutung des Lieblingsjüngers für die johanneische Theologie*, Rüschlikon, 1969.

— *Der Lieblingsjünger im Johannesevangelium: Eine redaktionsgeschichtliche Studie*, Stuttgart: Katholisches Bibelwerk, 1971.

Mahoney, R. K., *Two Disiples at the Tomb*, Frankfurt: Lang, 1974.

Martyn, J. L. *The Gospel of John in Christian History*, New York: Paulist, 1979.

Marxsen, W. *The Resurrection of Jesus of Nazareth*, London: SCM, 1970.

Maynard, A.H., 'The Function of Apparent Synonyms and Ambiguous Words in the Fourth Gospel' (Dissertation, University of Southern California).

Metzger, B. M., *A Textual Commentary on the Greek New Testament*, New York: United Bible Societies, 1971.

— *The Early Versions of the New Testament*, Oxford: Clarendon, 1977.

Miranda, J. P. *Der Vater, der mich gesandt hat*, Frankfurt: Lang, 1972.

Moffat, J. *An Introduction to the Literature of the New Testament*, Edinburgh: T & T Clark, 1927.

Mohr, T. A. *Marcus- und Johannespassion*, Zürich: Theologischer Verlag, 1982.

Morris, L. *Studies in the Fourth Gospel*, Grand Rapids: Eerdmans, 1969.

Moule, H.C.F., *Jesus and the Resurrection. Expository Studies on St. John XX. XXI*; London: Seeley, 1893.

Moulton, J.H. & W.F. Howard, *A Grammar of New Testament Greek*, vol. 1; Edinburgh: T & T Clark, 1929.

Müller, H.B., *Die Geschichte der Christologie in der johanneischen Gemeinde*, Stuttgarter Bibelstudien, 77, Stuttgart: Katholisches Bibelwerk, 1975.

Mussner, F. *Petrus und Paulus—Pole der Einheit. Eine Hilfe für die Kirchen*; Quaestiones Disputatae, 76; Freiburg: Herder, 1976.

Neirynck, F. *Jean et les synoptiques*, Leuven: Leuven University Press, 1979.

Olsson, B., *Structure and Meaning in the Fourth Gospel*, Lund: Lund University Press, 1974.

Osborne, G. R., *The Resurrection Narratives*, Grand Rapids: Baker, 1984.

Otto, H.P., 'Funktion und Bedeutung des Leiblingsjüngers im Johannes-Evangelium (Unpublished Dissertation cited by Thyen, 1971, p. 343, n. 2).

Oulton, J.E.L., and H. Chadwick, eds. and trans. *Alexandrian Christianity*, vol. 2; Philadelphia: Westminster, 1954, p. 286.

212   *Peter and the Beloved Disciple*

Painter, J. *John. Witness and Theologian*, London: SPCK, 1975.

Pallis, A., *Notes on St. John and the Apocalypse*, London: 1928.

Pancaro, S. *The Law in the Fourth Gospel: The Torah and the Gospel, Moses and Jesus, Judaism and Christianity According to John*; Leiden: Brill, 1975.

Perrin, N. *The Resurrection according to Matthew, Mark and Luke*, Philadelphia: Fortress, 1977.

Pesch, R. *Der reiche Fischfang (Lk 5, 1-11/Jo 21, 1-15). Wundergeschichte-Berufungsgeschichte-Erscheinungsbericht*, Düsseldof: Patmos, 1969.

— *Simon-Petrus*, Stuttgart: Hiersmann, 1980.

Pollard, T.E., *Johannine Christology and the Early Church*, Cambridge: Cambridge University Press, 1970.

Robertson, A.T., *A Grammar of the Greek New Testament in the Light of Historical Research* 5th edn; New York: Hodder & Stoughton, 1931.

Robinson, J. M., ed., *The Nag Hammadi Library: In English*, New York: Harper & Row, 1977.

Ruckstuhl, E. *Die literarische Einheit des Johannesevangeliums*, Freiburg: Paulus, 1951.

Schnackenburg, R. *The Church in the New Testament*, trans. O'Hara, W.J.; New York: Seabury, 1965.

Schnackenburg, R. et. al., *Die Kirche des Anfangs: Festschrift für Heinz Schürmann*, Freiburg: Herder, 1975.

Schnider, F. and W. Stenger, *Die Ostergeschichten der Evangelisten*, München: Kösel, 1969.

Schniewind, J., *Die Parallelperikopen bei Lukas und Johannes*. Leipzig: Deichert, 1914.

Schweizer, E. *Church Order in the New Testament*, London: SCM, 1961.

Scott, E.F., *The Fourth Gospel: Its Purpose and Theology*, 2nd edn; Edinburgh: T & T Clark, 1920.

Segovia, F. F., *Love Relationships in the Johannine Tradition: Agape/Agapan in 1 John and the Fourth Gospel*, Missoula: Scholars, 1982.

Smith, D. M. Jr., *The Composition and Order of the Fourth Gospel*, New Haven: Yale University Press, 1965.

— *Johannine Christianity*, Columbia: University of South Carolina Press, 1984.

— *John*, Proclamation Commentaries; Philadelphia: Fortress, 1976.

Spicq, C., *Agapé dans le Nouveau Testament. Analyse des Textes*, Paris: Gabalda, 1959.

Spitta, F., *Das Johannesevangelium als Quelle der Geschichte Jesu*, 1910.

Strachan, R. H., *The Fourth Gospel: Its Significance and Environment*, 3rd edn; London: SCM, 1941.

Stauffer, E. *Jesus and his Story*, New York: Knopf, 1960.

Taylor, M. J., *John: The Different Gospel*, New York: Alba House, 1983.

Temple, S. *The Core of the Fourth Gospel*, London: Mowbrays, 1975.

Temple, W. *Readings in St. John's Gospel*, New York: St. Martin's, 1968.

Titus, E.L., *The Message of the Fourth Gospel*, New York: Abingdon, 1957.

Westcott, B.F. and F.J.A. Hort, *The New Testament in the Original Greek*; vol. 1, *Text*; vol. 2, *Introduction and Appendix*, Cambridge: Macmillan, 1881.

Whiteacre, R. *Johannine Polemic*, Chico: Scholars, 1982.

Woll, D. B. *Johannine Christianity in Conflict*, Chico, CA: Scholars, 1981.

Articles

Ackroyd, P.R., 'The 153 Fishes in John xxi. 11—A Further Note', *Journal of Theological Studies* 10 (1959), p. 94.

Agnew, F., 'Vocatio primorum discipulorum in traditio synoptics', *Verbum Domini* 46 (1968), pp.129-47.

Agourides, S., 'Peter and John in the Fourth Gospel', *Studia Evangelica* 4; ed. F.L. Cross; Berlin: Akademie, 1968.

— 'The Purpose of John 21', *Studies in the History and the Text of the New Testament*, ed. B.L. Daniels & M.J. Suggs; Salt Lake City: University of Utah Press, 1967.

Aland, Kurt, 'The Problem of Anonymity and Pseudonymity in Christian Literature of the First Two Centuries', in *The Authorship and Integrity of the New Testament*, London: SPCK, 1965.

Allen, E.L., 'On this Rock', *Journal of Theological Studies* 5 (1954), pp. 59-62.

Arnenillas, P., 'El discipulo amado, modelo perfecto de discipulo de Jesus, segun el IV Evangelio', *Ciencia Tomista* 89 (1962), pp. 3-68.

Bacon, B. W. 'The Motivation of John 21.15-25', *The Journal of Biblical Literature* 50 (1931), pp. 71-80.

— 'New and Old in Jesus' Relation to John', *Journal of Biblical Literature* 48 (1929), pp. 40-81.

Bakker, J.T., ' " De Moeder van Jezus was daar": Ein reactie', *Homiletica en Biblica* 21 (1962), pp. 51-54.

Balague, M., 'La prueba de la Resurreccion (Jn 20, 6-7)', *Estudios Biblicos* 25 (1966), pp. 169-92.

Bassler, J.M., 'The Galileans: A Neglected Factor in Johannine Community Research', *Catholic Biblical Quarterly* 43 (1981), pp. 243-57.

Bauder, W., 'Disciple', *The New International Dictionary of New Testament Theology*, vol. 1; ed. Colin Brown: Grand Rapids: Zondervan, 1976, pp. 487-94.

Becker, J. 'Aus der Literatur zum Johannesevangelium (1978-80)', *Theologische Rundschau* 47 (1982), pp. 305-47.

Benoit, P., 'Marie-Madeleine et les Disciples au Tombeau selon Joh 20.1-18', *Judentum, Urchristentum und Kirche* (1960), pp. 141-52.

Bishop, E.F.F., ' "He that eateth bread with me hath lifted up his heel against me"—Jn xiii 18 (Ps xli 9)', *Expository Times* 70 (1959), pp. 331-33.

Bligh, J. 'Jesus in Galilee', *The Heythrop Journal* 5 (1964), pp. 18-26.

Boismard, M. E. 'Le chapitre xxi de saint Jean. Essai de critique littéraire', *Revue Biblique* 54 (1947), pp. 473-501.

— 'Les traditions johanniques concernant le Baptiste', *Revue Biblique* 70 (1963), pp. 5-42.

— 'Problèmes de critique textuelle concernant le Quatrième Evangile', *Revue Biblique* 60 (1953), pp. 357-59.

Boxel, P. van, 'Glaube und Liebe. Die Aktualität des johanneischen Jünger-modells', *Geist und Leben* 48 (1975), pp. 18-28.

Braun, F.-M. 'Apostolique et pnuematique selon saint Jean', *Revue Thomiste* 71 (1971), pp. 451-62.

— 'Quatre "signes" johanniques de l'unité chrétienne', *New Testament Studies* 9 (1963), pp. 147-55.

Brown, R. E., 'Johannine Ecclesiology—The Community's Origins', *Interpretation* 31 (1977), pp. 379-93.

— 'John 21 and the First Appearance to Peter', in *Resurrexit*, ed. E. Dhanis; Rome: Biblical Institute Press, 1974.

— '"Other Sheep Not of This Fold": The Johannine Perspective on Christian Diversity in the Late First Century', *Journal of Biblical Literature* 97 (1978), pp. 5-22.

— 'The Passion According to John: Chapters 18-19', *Worship* 49 (1975), p. 126-34.

Brown, S. 'Apostleship in the New Testament as an Historical and Theological Problem', *New Testament Studies* 30 (1984), pp. 474-80.

Bruce, F.F., 'St. John at Ephesus', *Bulletin of the John Rylands Library, University of Manchester* 60 (1978), pp. 339-61

Bruns, J. E. 'Ananda: The fourth evangelist's model for "the disciple whom Jesus loved"?', *Studies in Religion/Sciences Religieuses* 3 (1983), pp. 236-43.

Carson, D. A., 'Recent Literature on the Fourth Gospel: Some Reflections', *Themelios* 9 (1983), pp. 8-18.

Ceroke, C.P., 'Mary's Maternal Role in John 19, 25-27', *Marian Studies* 11 (1960), pp. 123-51.

Chapman, J., 'We Know That His Testimony is True', *Journal of Theological Studies* 31 (1930), pp. 379-87.

Charpentier, E.,'Jour de pâques: Le tombeau vide (Jn 20.1-9)', *Esprit et Vie* 79 (1969), pp. 262-66.

Chevallier, M.-A., 'La Fondation de l'Église dans le quatrième évangile: Jn 19/25-30' *Etudes Théologiques et Religieuses* 58 (1983), pp. 343-53.

Collins, A. Y. 'Crisis and Community in John's Gospel', *Currents in Theology and Mission* 7 (1980), pp. 196-204.

Collins, R.F., 'Mary in the Fourth Gospel. A Decade of Johannine Studies', *Louvain Studies* 3 (1970), pp. 99-142.

— 'The Representative Figures of the Fourth Gospel—I' *Downside Review* 94 (1976), pp, 26-46.

— 'The Representative Figures of the Fourth Gospel—II' *Downside Review* 94 (1976), pp. 118-32.

Cousar, C. B., 'John, 1.29-42', *Interpretation* 31 (1977), pp. 401-406.

Craig, W.L., 'The Historicity of the Empty Tomb of Jesus', *New Testament Studies* 31 (1985), pp. 39-67.

Cribbs, F. L. 'St. Luke and the Johannine Tradition', *Journal of Biblical Literature* 90 (1971), pp. 422-50.

Curtis, K. P. G., 'Luke xxiv, 12 and John xx, 3-10', *Journal of Theological Studies* 22 (1971), pp. 512-15.

— 'Three Points of Contact Between Matthew and John in the Burial and Resurrection Narratives', *Journal of Theological Studies* 23 (1972), pp. 440-44.

Dauer, A. 'Das Wort des Gekreuzigten an seine Mutter und den "Jünger den er liebte". Eine traditionsgeschichtliche und theologische Untersuchung zu Joh 19, 25-27', *Biblische Zeitschrift* 11 (1967), pp. 222-39.

Derret, J.D.M., '"Domine, tu mihi lavas pedes?" (Studios su Giovanni 13, 1-30)', *Bibbia e Oriente* 21 (1979), pp. 13-42.

Dingler, E., 'Die Petrus-Rom-Frage: Ein Forschungsbericht', *Theologische Rundschau* 25 (1959), pp. 189-230, 289-335.

Dodd, C.H., 'A note on John 21, 23', *Journal of Theological Studies* 4 (1953), pp. 212-13.

— 'The Appearance of the Risen Christ', in *Studies in the Gospels. Essays in Memory of R.H. Lightfoot*, ed. D.E. Wineham; Oxford: Basil Blackwell, 1967.

Domeris, W.R., 'The Johannine Drama', *Journal of Theology for Southern Africa* 42 (1983), pp. 29-35.

Duparc, L.H., 'Le premier signe de la Résurrection chez saint Jean. Jean 20, 7', *Bible et Vie Chrétienne* 86 (1969), pp. 70-77.

Dupont, L., et al., 'Recherche sur la structure de Jean 20', *Biblica* 54 (1973), pp. 482-98.

Dunn, J. D.G., 'John VI—A Eucharistic Discourse', *New Testament Studies* 17 (1971), pp. 328-38.

Elliott, J.H., 'Ministry and Church Order in the NT: A Traditional Historical Analysis (1 Pt. 5, 1-5 and plls.)', *Catholic Biblical Quarterly* 32 (1970), pp. 367-81.

Elliot, J.K., 'Κηφᾶς· Σίμων Πέτρος· ὁ Πέτρος: An Examination of New Testament Usage', *Novum Testamentum* 14 (1972), pp. 241-56.

Emerton, J.A., 'The Hundred and Fifty-Three Fishes in John xxi.11', *Journal of Theological Studies* 9 (1958), pp. 86-89.

— 'Some New Testament Notes', *Journal of Theological Studies* 11 (1960), pp. 329-36.

Ferraro, G., '"Pneuma" in Giov. 13.21', *Rivista Biblica* 28 (1980), pp. 185-211.

Feuillet, A., 'Le découverte du tombeau vide en Jean 20, 3-10 et la Foi au Christ ressuscité', *Esprit et Vie* 87 (1977), pp. 256-66.

— 'L'heure de la femme (Jn 16, 21) et l'heure de la Mère de Jésus (Jn 19, 25-27)', *Biblica* 47 (1966), pp. 169-84.

Fitzmyer, J. A., 'Aramaic *Kepha*' and Peter's Name in the New Testament', in *Text and Interpretation: Studies in the New Testament Presented to Matthew Black*, ed. Best, Ernest and Robert McL. Wilson; Cambridge: Cambridge University Press, 1979.

Fisher, L.R., '"Betrayed by Friends": An Expository Study of Ps. 22', *Interpretation* 18 (1964), pp. 20-38.

Flowers, H.J., 'The Calling of Peter and the Restoration of Peter', *Anglican Theological Review* (1922), pp. 234-39.

Fortna, R.T., 'Jesus and Peter at the High Priest's House: A Test Case for the Relation between Mark's and John's Gospels', *New Testament Studies* 24 (1978), p. 371-83.

Fuller, R.H., 'The "Thou Art Peter" Pericope and the Easter Appearances', *McCormick Quarterly* 20 (1967), pp. 309-315.

Gaechter, Paul, 'Das dreifache "Weide meine Lämmer"', *Zeitschrift für Katholische Theologie* 69 (1947), pp. 328-44.

Gewalt, D., 'Die Verleugnung des Petrus', *Linguistica Biblica* 43 (1978), pp. 13-44.

Giblin, C. H. 'Confrontation in John 18, 1-27', *Biblica* 65 (1984), pp. 210-32.

Glombitza, O., 'Petrus—der Freund Jesu. Überlegungen zu Joh xxi 15ff.', *Novum Testamentum* 6 (1963), pp. 277-85.

Gnidovec, F., '"Introivit ... er vidit er credidit' (Jn 20, 8)', *Estudios Biblicos* 41 (1983), pp. 137-55.

Goedt, M. de, 'Un Schème de Révélation dans le Quatrième Evangile', *New Testament Studies* 8 (1963), pp. 277-85.

Goguel, Maurice, 'Did Peter Deny His Lord? A Conjecture', *Harvard Theological Review* 25 (1932), pp. 1-27.

Grassi, Joseph A., 'The Role of Jesus' Mother in John's Gospel: A Reappraisal', *The Catholic Biblical Quarterly* 48 (1986), pp. 67-80.

Griffith, B.G., 'The Disciple Whom Jesus Loved', *Expository Times* 32 (1921), p. 379.

Grigsby, B.H., 'Gematria and John 21.11—Another Look at Ezekiel 47.10', *Expository Times* 95 (1984), p. 177-78.

Grundmann, Walter, 'Das Wort von Jesu Freunden (Joh XV, 13-16) und das Herrenmahl', *Novum Testamentum* 3 (1959), pp. 62-69.

— 'Verständnis und Bewegung des Glaubens im Johannes-Evangelium', *Kerygma und Dogma* 6 (1960), pp. 143-50.

Gryglewicz, F. "'Niewiasta' i 'uczén, Horego milowal Jezus (La "femme" et le 'disciple que Jésus aimait')', *Roczniki Teologiczno-Kanoniczne* 14 (1967), pp. 39-48.

Gunther, J.J., 'Early Identifications of Authorship of the Johannine Writings', *Journal of Ecclesiastical History* 31 (1980), pp. 407-27.

—'The Relation of the Beloved Disciple to the Twelve', *Theologische Zeitschrift* 37 (1981), pp. 129-48.

Haenchen, Ernst, 'Petrus-Probleme', *New Testament Studies* 7 (1961), pp. 187-97.

Hahn, F. 'Die Jüngerberufung Joh 1, 35-51', in *Neues Testament und Kirche. Für Rudolf Schnackenburg*, ed. J. Gnilka; Freiburg: Herder, 1974.

— 'Sehen und Glauben im Johannesevangelium', in *Neues Testament und Geschichte. Historisches Geschehen und Deutung im Neuen Testament. Oscar Cullmann zum 70. Geburtstag*, ed. H. Baltenweiler & B. Reicke; Zürich: Theologischer Verlag, 1972.

Halsema, J.H. van, 'De moeder van Jezus was daar', *Homiletica en Biblica* 21 (1962), pp. 25-28.

Hanhart, K. 'The Structure of John 1, 35—4, 54'. In *Studies in John Presented to Professor H.N. Sevenster on the Occasion of his Seventieth Birthday*, Leiden: Brill, 1970.

Hartman, L. 'An Attempt at a Text-Centered Exegesis of John 21', *Studia Theologica* 38 (1984), pp. 29-45.

Hartmann, G., 'Die Vorlage der Osterberichte in Joh 20', *Zeitschrift für die neutestamentliche Wissenschaft* 55 (1964), pp. 197-220.

Hawkin, D. J., 'The Function of the Beloved Disciple Motif in the Johannine Redaction', *Laval Théologique et Philosophique* 33 (1977), pp. 135-50.

Heyraud, L.,'Judas et la nouvelle alliance dans le cène selon saint Jean', *Bible et Vie Chrétienne* 44 (1962), pp. 39-48.

Hudry-Clergeon, C., 'Le quatrième évangile indique-t-il le nom de son auteur?', *Biblica* 56 (1975), pp. 545-49.

Hullen, A.B., 'The Call of the Four Disciples in John 1'. *Journal of Biblical Literature* 67 (1948), pp. 153-57.

Jiminez, F. M. 'El discipulo de Jesucristo, segun el evangelio de S. Juan', *Estudios Biblicos* 30 (1971), pp. 269-311.

Johnson, L. 'The Beloved Disciple—A Reply', *Expository Times* 77 (1966), p. 380.

— 'What was the Beloved Disciple?', *Expository Times* 77 (1966), pp. 157-58.

Johnson, N.E., 'The Beloved Disciple and the Fourth Gospel', *Church Quarterly Review* 167 (1966), pp. 278-91.

Jonge, M. de, 'The Beloved Disciple and the Date of the Gospel of John', *Text and Interpretation*, ed. E. Best & R. McL. Wilson, Cambridge: Cambridge University Press, 1979, pp. 100-101.

Joubert, H.L.N., 'The Holy One of God (John 6.69), *Neotestamentica* 2 (1968), pp. 57-69.

Karrer, O., 'Simon Petrus, Jünger, Apostel, Felsenfundament', *Bibel und Kirche* 23 (1968), pp. 37-43.

Kemp, I. S., 'Peter's Denial and the Question of Mimesis (Mk. 14.66-72)', *Notre Dame English Journal* 14 (1982), pp. 177-89.

Kerrigan, A., 'Jn 19, 25-27 in the Light of Johannine Theology and the Old Testament', *Antonianum* 35 (1960), pp. 369-416.

Kilmartin, E.J., 'The Mother of Jesus was There. (The Significance of Mary in Jn 2, 3-5 and Jn 19, 25-27)', *Sciences Ecclésiastiques* 15 (1963), pp. 213-26.

King, J.S., 'R.E. Brown on the History of the Johannine Community', *Scripture Bulletin* 13 (1983), pp. 26-30.

— 'E.F. Scott: "The Fourth Gospel"—75 Years On', *Expository Times* 94 (1983), pp. 359-63.

— 'Is Johannine Archaeology Really Necessary?' *Evangelical Quarterly* 56 (1984), pp. 203-211.

Klein, G., 'Die Verleugnung des Petrus. Eine traditionsgeschichtliche Untersuchung', *Zeitschrift für Theologie und Kirche* 58 (1961), pp. 285-328.

Kruse, H., 'Magni Pisces Centum Quinquaginto Tres (Jo 21, 11)', *Verbum Domini* 38 (1960), pp. 129-48.

Kuhn, K.G., 'The Lord's Supper and the Communal Meal at Qumran', *The Scrolls and the New Testament*, ed. Krister Stendahl; New York: Harper, 1957.

Kysar, Robert, 'Community and Gospel: Vectors in Fourth Gospel Criticism', *Interpretation* 31 (1977), pp. 355-66.

Lampe, G.W.H., 'St. Peter's Denial', *Bulletin of the John Rylands Library*, University of Manchester 5 (1973), pp. 346-68.

Langkammer, H., 'Christ's "Last Will and Testament" (Jn 19.26, 27) in the Interpretation of the Fathers of the Church and the Scholastics', *Antonianum* 43 (1968), pp. 99-109.

Leaney, R. 'The Resurrection Narratives in Luke (XXIV. 12-53)', *New Testament Studies* 2 (1956), pp. 110-14.

Leibig, J. E., 'John and the Jews: Theological Antisemitism in the Fourth Gospel', *Journal of Ecumenical Studies* 20 (1983), pp. 209-34.

Léonard, J.-M., 'Notule sur l'Evangile de Jean. Le disciple que Jésus aimait et Marie', *Etudes Théologiques et Religeuses* 58 (1983), pp. 355-57.

Lindars, B. 'The Composition of John XX', *New Testament Studies* 7 (1961), pp. 142-47.

Manns, F., 'Le lavement des pieds. Essai sur la structure et la Signification de Jean 13', *Revue des Sciences Religieuses* 55 (1981), pp. 149-69.

Masson, P. C., 'Le reniement de Pierre Mk 14.66-72; Matt 26.69-75; Lk 22.56-62; Jn 18.18-27', *Revue d'Histoire et de Philosophie Religieuses* 37 (1957), pp. 24-35.

Maynard, A. H., 'The Role of Peter in the Fourth Gospel', *New Testament Studies* 30 (1984), pp. 531-48.

McDowell, Edward A., Jr., '"Lovest Thou Me?" A Study of John 21.15-17', *Review and Expositor* 32 (1935), pp. 422-41.

McEleney, N.J., '153 Great Fishes (John 21, 11)—Gematriacal Atbash', *Biblica* 58 (1977), pp. 411-17.

McHugh, J., 'The Glory of the Cross: The Passion According to St. John', *Clergy Review* 67 (1982), pp. 79-83.

McKay, K.L., 'Style and Significance in the Language of John 21.15-17', *Novum Testamentum* 4 (1985), pp. 319-33.

Meeks, W. A., 'The Man from Heaven in Johannine Sectarianism', *Journal of Biblical Literature* 91 (1972), pp. 44-72.

Mercier, R., 'Lo que "el otro discipulo" vio en la tumba vacia. Juan 20.5-7', *Revue Biblique* 43 (1981), pp. 3-32.

Merkel, H., 'Peter's Curse', *The Trial of Jesus: Festschrift for C.F.D. Moule*; London: SCM, 1970.

Meyer, R., 'κολπος', *Theological Dictionary of the New Testament*, vol. 3; ed. Gerhard Kittel, trans. Geoffrey Bromiley; Grand Rapids: Eerdmans, 1965, pp. 824-25.

Michel, O. 'Ein johanneischer Osterbericht', *Studien zum Neuen Testament und zur Patristik*, Berlin: Akademi, 1961.

Minear, P. S., 'The Beloved Disciple in the Gospel of John: Some Clues and Conjectures', *Novum Testamentum* 19 (1977), pp. 105-23.

— 'The Original Functions of John 21', *Journal of Biblical Literature* 102 (1983), pp. 85-98.

—'"We don't know where. . . " John 20.2, *Interpretation* 30 (1976), pp. 125-39.

Mollat, D. 'La découverte du tombeau vide Jn 20, 1-9', *Assemblées du Seigneur* 21 (1969), pp. 90-100.

Moloney, F.J., 'John 1.18, "In the Bosom of" or "Turned towards" the Father?', *Australian Biblical Review* 31 (1983), pp. 63-71.

—'Revisiting John', *Scripture Bulletin* 11 (1980), pp. 9-15.

Moreton, M.B., 'The Beloved Disciple Again', *Studia Biblica II*, ed. E.A. Livingstone, Sheffield: JSOT, 1980.

Motyer, J.A., 'Body', *The New International Dictionary of New Testament Theology* vol. 1; Grand Rapids: Zondervan, 1975.

Muddiman, J., 'A note on Reading Luke xxiv. 12', *Ephemerides Theologicae Lovanienses* 48 (1972), pp. 542-48.

Neirynck, F. '*Apélthen pros heauton*. Lc 24, 12 et Jn 20, 10', *Ephemerides Theologicae Lovanienses* 54 (1978), pp. 104-18.

—"EIS TA IDIA; Jn 19, 27 (et 16, 32)', *Ephemerides Theologica Lovanienses* 59 (1979), pp. 356-65.

—'John and the Synoptics: The Empty Tomb Stories', *New Testament Studies* 30 (1984), pp. 161-87.

— 'The "Other Disciple" in Jn 18, 15-16', *Ephemerides Theologicae Lovanienses* 51 (1975), pp. 113-41.

— 'Parakypsas blepei: Lc 24, 12 et Jn 20, 5', *Ephemerides Theologicae Lovanienses* 53 (1977), pp. 113-52.

Niccacci, A., 'L'unita letteraria di Gv 13, 1-38', *Euntes docete* 29 (1976), pp. 291-323.

O'Grady, J., 'Individualism and Johannine Ecclesiology', *Biblical Theology Bulletin* 5 (1975), pp. 227-61.

— 'Johannine Ecclesiology: A Critical Evaluation'. *Biblical Theology Bulletin* 5 (1977), pp. 36-44.

— 'The Role of the Beloved Disciple', *Biblical Theology Bulletin* 9 (1979), pp. 58-65.

O'Rourke, J.J., 'Asides in the Gospel of John', *Novum Testamentum* 21 (1979), pp. 210-19.

Osborne, B., 'A Folded Napkin in an Empty Tomb: John 11.44 and 20.7 Again', *Heythrop Journal* 14 (1973), pp. 437-40.

Osborne, G. R., 'John 21: A Test Case for History and Redaction in the Resurrection Narratives'. *Gospel Perspectives II*, ed. R.T. France & D. Wenham; Sheffield: JSOT, 1981.

Osty, E., 'Les points de contact entre le récit de la passion dans saint Luc et dans saint Jean', *Recherches de Science Religieuse* 39 (1951), pp. 146-54.

Painter, J., 'Christology and the History of the Johannine Community in the Prologue of the Fourth Gospel', *New Testament Studies* 30 (1984), pp. 460-74.

— 'The Farewell Discourses and the History of Johannine Christianity', *New Testament Studies* 27 (1981), pp. 526, 528, 530-34.

— 'Glimpses of the Johannine Community in the Farewell Discourses', *Australian Biblical Review* 28 (1980), pp. 21-38.

— 'The "Opponents" in I John', *New Testament Studies* 32 (1986), pp. 48-71.

Pamment, M. 'The Fourth Gospel's Beloved Disciple', *Expository Times* 94 (1983), pp. 363-67.

Parker, P., 'John and John Mark', *Journal of Biblical Literature* 79 (1960), pp. 97-110.

— 'John and the Son of Zebedee and the Fourth Gospel', *Journal of Biblical Literature* 81 (1962), pp. 35-43.

— 'Luke and the Fourth Evangelist', *New Testament Studies* 9 (1963), pp. 317-36.

Patterson, David, 'Before the Cock Crows Twice [Peter's Despair]', *Epiphany* 3 (1983), pp. 98-101.

Perry, M.C., 'The Other of the Two: A Fresh Look at John 1.35ff.', *Theology* 64 (1961), pp. 153-54.

Pfnitzner, V.C., 'The Coronation of the King—Passion Narrative and Passion Theology in the Gospel of St. John', *Lutheran Theological Journal* 10 (1976), p. 1-12.

Philips, G. A., 'This is a Hard Saying. Who Can be a Listener to It? Creating a Reader in John 6', *Semeia* 26 (1983), pp. 23-56.

Porter, J.R., 'Who was the Beloved Disciple?', *Expository Times* 77 (1966), p. 213.

Potter, R., 'The Disciple whom Jesus Loved', *Life of the Spirit* 16 (1962), pp. 293-97.

Potterie, I. de la, 'Genèse de la foi pascale d'après Jn. 20', *New Testament Studies* 30 (1984), pp. 26-49.

— 'La Parole de Jésus "Voici ta Mère" et l'accueil du Disciple (Jn 19, 27b)', *Marianum* 36 (1974), pp. 1-39.

Refoulé, F., 'Primauté de Pierre dans les évangiles', *Revue de Sciences Religieuses* 38 (1964), pp. 1-41.

Reiser, W.W., 'The Case of the Tidy Tomb: The Place of the Napkins of John 11.44 and 20.7', *Heythrop Journal* 14 (1973), pp. 47-57.

Richard E., 'Expressions of Double Meaning and their Function in the Gospel of John', *New Testament Studies* 31 (1985), p. 96-112.

Rigg, H., 'Was Lazarus "the Beloved Disciple"?', *Expository Times* 33 (1922), pp. 232-34.

Rogers, A.D., 'Who was the Beloved Disciple?', *Expository Times* 77 (1966), p. 214.

Roloff, J. 'Der johanneische "Lieblingsjünger" und der Lehrer der Gerechtigkeit', *New Testament Studies* 15 (1968), p. 129-51.

Romeo, J.A., 'Gematria and John 21.11—The Children of God', *Journal of Biblical Literature* 97 (1978), pp. 263-64.

Roth, C. 'A Further Discussion', *Harvard Theological Review* 57 (1964), pp. 60-61.

— 'Simon-Peter', *Harvard Theological Review* 54 (1961), pp. 91-97.

Ruckstuhl, E. 'Die johanneische Menschensohnforschung 1957-1969', *Theologische Berichte*, ed. Pfammater und Furgen; Zürich: Benziger Verlag, 1972.

Rush, F.A., 'The Signs and the Discourse—The Rich Theology of John 6', *Currents in Theology and Mission* 5 (1978), pp. 386-90.

Russel, R., 'The Beloved Disciple and the Resurrection', *Scripture* 8 (1956), pp. 57-62.

Salas, A., 'Apacienta mis Corderas (Jn 21, 15-17)', *Ciudad de Dios* 179 (1966), pp. 672-80.

Salvoni, F., 'The So-Called Jesus Resurrection Proof (John 20.7)', *Restoration Quarterly* 27 (1979), pp. 72-76.

Sanders, J.N., 'Those Whom Jesus Loved', *New Testament Studies* 1 (1955), pp. 29-41.

— 'Who was the Disciple whom Jesus Loved?' *Studies in the Fourth Gospel*, ed. F.L. Cross; London: Mowbray, 1975.

Soards, M.L., 'τὸν ἐπενδύτην διεζώσατο, ἦν γὰρ γυμνός', *Journal of Biblical Literature* 102 (1983), pp. 283-84.

Schnackenburg, R. 'Der Jünger, den Jesus liebte', *Evangelisch-Katholischer Kommentar zum Neuen Testament: Vorarbeiten*, vol. 2; Neukirchen-Vluyn: Neukirchener Verlag, 1970, pp. 97-117.

—'On the Origin of the Fourth Gospel', *Perspective* 11 (1970), pp. 239-40.

— 'The Disciple Whom Jesus Loved', *The Gospel According to St. John*, vol. 1; New York: Crossroads, 1980-82, 375-88.

Schneiders, S. M., 'The Face Veil: A Johannine Sign (John 20.1-10', *Biblical Theology Bulletin* 13 (1983), pp. 94-97.

Schwank, B., 'Christi Stellvertreter: Jo 21, 15-25', *Sein und Sendung* 29 (1964), pp. 531-42.

— 'Das leere Grab: Jo 20, 1-18', *Sein und Sendung* 29 (1964), pp. 388-400.

— 'Der geheimnisvolle Fischfang: Jo 21, 1-14', *Sein und Sendung* 29 (1964), pp. 484-98.

— 'Die ersten Gaben des erhöhten Königs: Jo 19, 23-30', *Sein und Sendung* 29 (1964), pp. 292-309.

— '"Einer von euch wird mich verraten': Jo 13, 18-30', *Sein und Sendung* 28 (1963), pp. 52-66.

— 'Petrus Verleugnet Jesus (Jo 18.12-27)', *Sein und Sendung* 29 (1964), pp. 51-65.

Shaw, A. 'The Breakfast by the Shore and the Mary Magdalene Encounter as Eucharistic Narratives', *Journal of Theological Studies* 25 (1974), pp. 12-26.

— 'Image and Symbol in John 21', *Expository Times* 86 (1975), p. 311.

Sheehan, J.F.X., 'Feed My Lambs', *Scripture* 16 (1964), pp. 21-27.

Shepherd, M.H., 'The Twelve', *The Interpreters Dictionary of the Bible*, vol. 4; New York: Abingdon, 1962, p. 719.

Shorter, M. 'The Position of Chapter VI in the Fourth Gospel', *Expository Times* 84 (1973), p. 181-83.

Smalley, S.S., 'Diversity and Development in John', *New Testament Studies* 17 (1971), pp. 276-92.

— 'The Sign in John xxi', *New Testament Studies* 20 (1964), pp. 273-88.

Smereka, L., 'Ecce Mater Tua', *Ruch Biblijny I Liturgiczny* 9 (1956), pp. 244-61.

Smith, D. M. Jr, 'Johannine Christianity: Some Reflections on its Character and Delineation', *New Testament Studies* 20 (1975), pp. 222-48.

Smith, R., 'Books Worth Discussing: J. Louis Martyn. History and Theology in the Fourth Gospel. The Gospel of John in Christian Tradition. Raymond E. Brown. The Community of The Beloved Disciple', *Currents in Theology and Mission* 8 (1981), pp. 41-44.

Snyder, G. F., 'John 13.16 and the Anti-Petrinism of the Johannine Tradition', *Biblical Research* 16 (1971), p. 5-15.

Solages, B. de, & J.M. Vacherot, 'Le Chapitre XXI de Jean est-il de la même plume que le reste de l'Évangile?' *Bulletin de Littérature Ecclésiastique* 80 (1979), pp. 96-101.

Spaemann, H. 'Stunde des Lammes. Meditationen über die ersten Jüngerberufungen (Joh 1, 35-51)', *Bibel und Leben* 7 (1966), pp. 58-68.

Stenger, W., '"Der Geist ist es, der lebendig macht, das Fleisch nützt Nichts" (Joh 6, 63)', *Trierer Theologische Zeitschrift* 85 (1976), pp. 116-22.

Strathmann, H., 'Die Stellung des Petrus in der Urkirche', *Zeitschrift für Systematische Theologie* 20 (1943), pp. 129-39.

Strecker, G. 'Die Anfänge der johanneischen Schule', *New Testament Studies* 32 (1986), pp. 31-47.

Sturch, R.L., 'The Alleged Eyewitness Material in the Fourth Gospel', *Studia Biblica II* ed. E.A. Livingstone, Sheffield: JSOT, 1980.

Talavero, S., 'Problematica de la unidad en Jn 18-20', *Salamanticensis* 19 (1972), pp. 513-75.

Temple, S. 'The Two Traditions of the Last Supper, Betrayal and Arrest', *New Testament Studies* 7 (1960), p. 77-85.

Thyen, H., 'Entwicklungen innerhalb der johanneischen Theologie und Kirche im Spiegel von Joh 21 und den Lieblingsjüngertexte des Evangeliums', *Bibliotheca ephemeridum theologicarum Lovaniensium* 44; Louvain: 1977.

— *Tradition und Glaube: Festschrift für K.G. Kuhn*. Göttingen: Vandenhoeck & Ruprecht, 1971.

Thyes, A., 'Jean 19, 25-27 et la Maternité spirituelle de Marie', *Marianum* 18 (1956), pp. 80-117.

Titus, E.L., 'The Identity of the Beloved Disciple', *Journal of Biblical Literature* 69 (1950), pp. 323-28.

Tobin, W.J., 'The Petrine Primacy Evidence of the Gospels', *Lumen Vitae* 23 (1968), pp. 27-70.

Torrey, C.C., 'The Name "Iscariot"', *Harvard Theological Review* 36 (1943), pp. 51-62.

Trudringer, L.P., 'A propos de pêche (Jean 20.31-21.3)', *Foi et Vie* 74 (1975), pp. 55-57.

— 'Subtle Word-Plays in the Gospel of John and the Problem of Chapter 21', *Journal of Religious Thought* 28 (1971), pp. 27-31.

Turner, C.N., 'Transpositions of Text in St. John's Gospel. 2. St. John xviii 13-25', *Journal of Theological Studies*, 1901, pp. 141-42.

Voigt, S., 'O Discipulo Amado Recebe a Mae de Jesus "Eis Ta Idia": Velada Apologia de Joao em Jo 19, 27?', *Revista Eclesistica Braslieira* 35 (1975), pp. 771-82.

Watty, W.W., 'The Significance of Anonymity in the Fourth Gospel', *Expository Times* 90 (1979), pp. 209-12.

Wilckens, U., 'Der Paraklet und die Kirche', *Kirche: Festschrift für Günther Bornkamm*, ed. D. Lührmann & G. Strecker; Tübingen: Mohr, 1980.

Wilcox, M., 'The Composition of John 13.21-30', *Neotestamentica et Semitica: Studies in Honour of Matthew Black*, ed. E.E. Ellis & M. Wilcox; Edinburgh: T & T Clark, 1969, pp. 143-56.

Wind, A., 'Destination and Purpose of the Gospel of John', *Novum Testamentum* 14 (1972), pp. 26-69.

Wojciechowski, M., 'Certains aspects algébriques de quelques nombres symboliques de la Bible (Gen 5; Gen 14, 14; Jn 21, 11)', *Biblische Notizen* 23 (1984), pp. 29-31.

Wulf, F., 'Das marianische Geheimnis der Kirche im Licht des Johannsevangeliums', *Geist und Leben* 50 (1977), pp. 326-34.

Zelzer, K., '"*Oudepo gar edeisan*—den bisher hatten sie nicht verstanden", Zu Übersetzung und Kontextbezug von Joh 20, 9', *Bibel und Liturgie* 53 (1980), pp. 104-106.

INDEXES

INDEX OF BIBLICAL REFERENCES

Genesis
17.5   37, 39
17.15   37
32.28   38, 39

Ruth
2.14   64

2 Kings
10.11   79
23.34   38
24.17   38

Psalms
38   92
38.11   92
54.14   79

Isaiah
62.2   39
65.15   39

Matthew
4.18-22   27
7.15   147
11.20-28 47
11.20-24 47
11.27   47
13.54-58 43
16   36
16.13-20 27
16.16   43
16.17   47
16.18-19 122
16.23   51
18.18   122
19.26   37
26.21   43
26.51   87
26.69   72
27.55   90
28.9-10   102

Mark
1.16-20   27
1.16-18   36
1.17   28
3.16   36
3.31-35   93
6.1-6   43
8.27-33   51
8.27-30   27
8.29   35, 43
8.33   51
9   152
9.1   137
10.21   37
13   152
14.18   43
14.20   64
14.47   87
14.66   72
15.40   90, 91
16   102, 106

Luke
4.16-30   43
5.6   136
5.1-11   27, 131
8.51   33
9.18-21   27
9.20   43
9.28   33
10.1   44
13.23-26 108
20.17   37
22.50   87
22.21   43
22.55   74
22.56   72
22.58   83
23.49   90-92
23.53   107
24   105, 131
24.1-12   104

24.4-6   118
24.12   102-107, 116,
          119, 164
24.24   102-106, 164
24.30   131
24.31   131
24.34   105, 164
24.42   131
24.43   131
24.46   118

John
1-20   97, 125, 128-
          31, 133, 138
1-12   53, 55, 158
1   165
1.1-18   55
1.1   46
1.14   110
1.18   58, 160
1.19-51   36
1.25-51   32
1.29   34
1.35-51   32
1.35-50   45
1.35-43   31
1.35-42   27, 163
1.35-39   31
1.35   27, 30, 34
1.36   37
1.37   28
1.39-42   41
1.37-39   32
1.40-42   29, 32
1.40   30
1.41-50   36
1.41   30, 32, 35
1.42   36-38
1.43   21, 29, 32-
          35
1.44   31, 32
1.45   32

John (cont.)					
1.47	37	6.67	48	13.11	142
2	130	6.68	21, 49	13.16	62, 161
2.1	32	6.68-69	51	13.18	56
2.24	37	6.69	49, 50	13.19	56
3.11	110	6.70	46	13.20	61
3.16-21	65	7	42	13.21-30	56, 57, 61,
3.16-17	14	7.1	44, 126		63, 67, 160,
3.19	143	7.3	44		165
4	130	7.5	93	13.21-22	57
4.1	44	7.39	122	13.22	63
4.17-19	37	7.43	137	13.23-25	63, 66, 67,
4.22	110	8.20	46		81
4.29	82	9	130	13.23	55, 58, 109,
5-7	43	9.16	137		154
5	42	9.31	110	13.24	69, 167
5.1	126	9.35-38	49	13.25	56
6	22, 42, 43,	10	147	13.26	63, 64
	48	10.1	72	13.27-30	66
6.1	126	10.11	147	13.27	66
6.20	50	10.16	72, 169	13.28	63, 66, 67
6.22	81	10.19	137	13.29	63, 66
6.24	44	10.21	42	13.30	66
6.35-47	46	10.22	42	13.31-17.26	56
6.35	46, 50	10.34	120	13.36-38	69, 143, 147,
6.36	46	11	130		148, 163
6.37	46	11.26-27	49	13.36	69, 88, 158,
6.41	44	11.31	28, 71		164
6.45	46	11.52	136	13.37	149
6.48	50	12	43	13.38	127
6.51-58	43, 45	12.6	66	14-16	60
6.51	50	12.14-16	119	14.21-24	145
6.60-71	27, 41, 43,	12.32	143	14.26	15
	48, 52, 53,	12.42	78	15.25-26	15
	55, 158, 163,	12.43	143	16.7	15, 73
	168	12.47	14	16.13	15
6.60-69	24	13-21	21, 54, 163	16.27	145
6.60-66	50	13-20	55, 158, 159	17	136
6.60	44, 46	13	43, 55, 58,	17.9-14	14
6.61	45		82, 98, 108,	17.11	51
6.62	45		109, 143,	17.21	169
6.63-65	46		149, 158-160,	18-20	130
6.63	43, 45, 46,		166	18-19	158
	50	13.1-20	61, 63	18	77, 78, 80,
6.64	46, 47	13.1	55		84, 85, 109,
6.65-66	47	13.2	56, 57, 66		142, 143,
6.65	46, 47	13.6-9	163		148, 150,
6.66-71	44	13.6	21, 56, 61		158, 164-66
6.66-67	44	13.7-10	61	18.1-12	87
6.66	47	13.7	56	18.3	74
6.67-71	48	13.9	30, 116	18.5	83, 85
		13.10	56, 62	18.8	83

John (cont.)		20.1-18	101, 106				97, 124-138,
18.10	21, 86, 98,	20.1-10	101-108, 122,				142, 143,
	163		123, 164				148, 149,
18.11	87, 98	20.1-9	114				150, 152,
18.12	74	20.1	34, 103, 109				153, 155,
18.15-18	71, 163	20.2-10	31, 88, 160,				156, 158,
18.15-17	77, 127, 165		162, 165				159, 162,
18.15-16	64, 80, 81,	20.2	21, 81, 103,				164-67
	89, 111, 161		108-110, 154		21.1-25	55
18.15	31, 71, 72,	20.3-10	77, 80, 81,		21.1-23	77, 129
	76, 78, 80,		108		21.1-14	131, 132,
	81, 109	20.3-8	80			134, 135
18.16-17	76	20.3	80, 81, 102,		21.1	126, 134
18.16	21, 72, 73,		103, 105, 110		21.2	138
	80, 82	20.4-8	167		21.3	22, 30, 116,
18.17	73, 76, 83,	20.4	81, 101, 105,			135, 138,
	85		111, 112,			139, 163
18.18	74, 75, 84,		114, 121		21.6	143
	85, 143	20.5-8	113		21.7	22, 30, 116,
18.18-27	89, 165	20.5	80, 102, 103,			132, 134,
18.19-24	75, 84, 85		113, 116			140, 150,
18.25-27	71, 75, 163	20.6	80, 101-103,			154, 160,
18.25	75, 76, 82,		105, 113,			161, 163
	83, 143		116, 155		21.8	142
18.26-27	87	20.7	22, 105, 116,		21.9	84, 142
18.26	75, 76, 82,		121		21.10-14	165
	84, 86	20.8	49, 80, 81,		21.10	118
18.27	75, 87, 110		103, 105,		21.11	22, 30, 116,
18.28	34		111, 115,			128, 135,
19	89, 158, 160,		117, 119,			136, 143,
	162, 165		121, 127, 161			163
19.21	85	20.9	103, 118-120		21.12	134
19.24-26	71	20.10	102, 106,		21.14	134, 146
19.24	90, 137		118, 122, 127		21.15-23	131, 132, 154
19.25-27	89, 90, 96,	20.11-18	134		21.15-19	137, 143, 164
	97	20.11-14	106		21.15-17	88, 127, 134,
19.25	90, 91	20.11	103, 110			142, 143,
19.26-27	91, 96, 111	20.17	156			145-48, 154,
19.26	49, 77, 89,	20.19-23	122			155, 163, 165
	91, 108, 154	20.20-23	136		21.15	22, 132
19.28	93	20.21	127, 128		21.18-23	132
19.35	97, 108, 129,	20.22-23	122		21.18-19	142, 149,
	161	20.24	48			155, 164, 165
20-21	120	20.29-30	126		21.18	142, 155
20	80, 81, 88,	20.29	126-28, 158,		21.19	143, 146,
	96, 102, 105,		161			148, 155, 164
	106, 109,	20.30-31	126, 129		21.20-23	17, 151, 155,
	118, 125,	20.30	126, 129			165
	126, 127,	20.31	126		21.20	150, 154,
	134, 158,	21	10, 16, 31,			155, 159, 160
	163		84, 88, 96,		21.21	153

John (cont.)		*Acts*		*3 John*	
21.22-24	151	1.15	137	5	156
21.22-23	101, 155	12.12	59		
21.22	128, 146,	20.28-30	147	*Revelation*	
	151, 159, 164			3.17-18	140
21.23	14, 130, 152,	*1 Corinthians*		16.15	140
	155, 156	15	134, 140	17.16	140
21.24-25	129, 130, 132				
21.24	9, 130, 131,	*1 John*			
	151, 153,	2.15-17	14		
	154, 161	2.19	15, 48		
21.25	129, 131, 133	5.13	126		

INDEX OF AUTHORS

Abbott, E.A. 178n36, 201n86, 208
Ackroyd, P.R. 213
Agnew, F. 213
Agourides, S. 40, 62, 89, 114, 138, 146,
  148, 166, 172nn9,16, 180n74,
  185n40, 188n48, 189n63, 189n71,
  192n119, 195n71, 200n65,
  201nn95,98, 202n111, 203nn139,151,
  204n173, 205n183, 206n33, 213
Aland, K. 19, 175n69, 205n10, 213
Allen, E.L. 95, 184n19, 213
Alsup, J.E. 194n34, 208
Arndt, W.F. 180n60, 201n87, 208
Arnenillas, P. 213

Bacon, B.W. 171n6, 177n5, 208, 213
Bakker, J.T. 213
Balague, M. 213
Barclay, W. 190n87, 207
Barrett, C.K. 40, 45, 46, 51, 60, 64, 68,
  76, 78, 91-93, 115, 120, 128, 139,
  141, 176n3, 179n59, 180n73,
  181nn78,85,90,95,96,
  182nn99,101,102,103,122,
  183nn137,1, 184n24, 185n34,46,
  186nn58,65,71, 187nn10,17,24,30,
  188n43, 189nn55,58,61,71,
  190nn77,84,85,91, 191nn103,111,
  194n51, 195n74, 196n102, 197n15,
  198n27, 199nn36,38,40,54,
  200nn57,79, 201n93, 205n186, 207
Bassler, J.M. 213
Bauder, W. 176n85, 213
Bauer, W. 179n60, 201n87, 208
Becker, J. 207, 213
Beker, J. 208
Benoit, P. 118, 186n3, 189n62, 196n95,
  208, 213
Bergmeier, R. 208
Bernard, J.H. 28, 29, 33, 34, 37, 38,
  109, 176n2, 177n8,
  179nn41,48,59,60, 180nn67,68,
  181n78, 184nn12,24, 185n51,

187n27, 190nn87,88, 194n45,
  195n52, 197n16, 198n23,
  200nn67,69, 201n86, 204n172, 207
Bishop, E.F.F. 213
Black, M. 188n45, 208
Blass, F. 186n2, 208
Bligh, J. 208, 213
Bode, E.L. 208
Bogart, J. 208
Boice, J.M. 207
Boismard, M.-E. 13, 31, 32, 74, 81, 106,
  130, 173nn30,34, 178nn29,30,32,
  185n32, 187n12, 188n40, 198n28,
  207, 209, 213
Bornkamm, G. 209, 221
Boxel, P. van 213
Braun, F.M. 11, 172n26, 201n107, 209,
  213
Broomfield, G.W. 17, 130, 175n63,
  198n29, 209
Brown, C. 176nn85,91, 177n7
Brown, R.E. 10, 11, 16, 18, 24, 32, 37,
  39, 45, 47, 65, 69, 72, 74, 81, 94,
  103, 112, 116, 118, 120, 127, 131,
  146, 155, 161, 167, 168, 172n24,
  173nn30,36, 174nn41,52,53,57,
  175nn61,75, 176nn87,88,89,90,3,5,6,
  178nn26,31, 179nn44,50,56,
  180nn68,69,70, 181nn78,88,91,92,96,
  182nn106,108,109, 183nn1,4,5,
  184nn10,13,26,29, 185n48,
  186nn52,58,70,5, 187n13,
  188nn35,41,44,53, 189nn59,66,70,
  190nn76,77,79,81,90,92,
  191nn97,98,112, 193nn8,9,
  194nn44,50, 195nn54,56,57,58,73,
  196nn83,89,97,103,107, 197nn3,14,
  198nn32,33,
  199nn36,39,40,43,50,51,54, 200n57,
  201nn88,103, 202n110,
  203nn135,137,145, 204n172,
  205n184, 206n35, 207, 209, 213,
  214, 217, 220

Brown, S. 10, 16, 18, 172n18, 173n33, 174nn40,49,51, 175nn59,67, 176n92, 200n63, 204n182, 206nn15,32

Brownlee, W.H. 209

Bruce, F.F. 190n87, 207, 209, 214

Bruns, J.E. 9, 172n13, 209, 214

Bultmann, R. 9, 21, 33, 36, 37, 43, 51, 73, 77, 82, 89-91, 92, 118, 119, 128, 142, 151, 171n7, 174n45, 176n3, 177n15, 179n39, 180n61, 181nn78,83, 183n133, 187nn6,18, 188nn43,45, 189nn72,73, 190nn82,86,93, 196nn94,95,100, 198nn19,27, 201nn89,102, 203nn144,153, 204n170, 207

Calvin, J. 207

Carson, D.A. 214

Ceroke, C.P. 214

Chadwick, H. 180n66, 211

Chapman, J. 204n160, 214

Charpentier, E. 214

Chevallier, M.-A. 214

Childs, B. 159, 205n8, 209

Collins, A.Y. 214

Collins, R.F. 10, 11, 29, 66, 161, 172nn19,23, 175n76, 177n14, 186n57, 188n42, 190n93, 196n109, 203n158, 204n178, 206n14, 214

Colson, J. 209

Colwell, E.G. 209

Cousar, C.B. 214

Cowley, A.E. 186n2, 210

Craig, W.L. 214

Cribbs, F.L. 214

Cross, F.L. 172n9, 209, 213, 220

Cullman. O. 11, 16, 21, 35, 172n27, 173n30, 174n55, 175nn61,77, 178n37, 179n52, 203n145, 209, 210, 216

Culpepper, R.A. 209

Curtis, K.P.G. 193n26, 214

Dauer, A. 73, 77-79, 82, 90, 95, 187nn8,23,26, 189n73, 190nn74,93, 191nn105,111, 209, 214

Davey, F.N. 171n5, 207, 210

Debrunner, A. 186n2, 208

Delling, G. 209

Derrett, J.D.M. 214

Dibelius, M. 175n75, 209

Dillon, R.J. 105, 193nn18,21, 209

Dingler, E. 214

Dodd, C.H. 128, 180n68, 183n1, 190n87, 197n16, 204n160, 209, 214

Dods, M. 49, 109n87, 129, 181n94, 182nn104,117,120, 197n16, 207

Domeris, W.R. 214

Donfried, K.P. 203n137, 203n146, 209

Dunn, J.D.G. 22, 176nn81,91, 181n96, 209, 215

Duparc, L.H. 195n80, 215

Dupont, L. 215

Edwards, R.A. 187n27, 209

Elliot, J.K. 30, 177n20, 215

Ellis, P.F. 36, 179n49, 207, 221

Emerton, J.A. 215

Fenton, J.C. 88, 189n69, 209

Ferraro, G. 215

Feuillet, A. 190n93, 215

Filson, F.V. 207

Fisher, F.V. 215

Fitzmyer, J.A. 38, 39, 116, 180nn65,72, 193nn14,23, 194n34, 195nn62,81, 207, 209, 215

Flowers, H.J. 215

Forestell, J.T. 198n31, 204n168, 209

Fort, P. le 205n189, 210

Fortna, R.T. 210, 215

Freyne, S. 210

Fuller, R.H. 194n26, 210, 215

Gaechter, P. 146, 203nn134,136,143, 215

Gewalt, D. 215

Giblin, C.H. 79, 188nn34,43, 215

Gingrich, F.W.180n60, 201n87, 208

Glasson, T.F. 210

Glombitza, O. 215

Gnidovec, F. 215

Godet, F.L. 207

Goedt, M. de 215

Goguel, M. 95, 96, 188n54, 191nn107,108,109, 201n101, 210, 215

Goodspeed, E.J. 210

Grass, H. 210

Grassi, J.A. 215

Griffith, B.G. 215

Grigsby, B.H. 215

Grundmann, W. 83, 188n49, 210, 215

Gryglewicz, F. 216

Guenther, H.O. 210
Gunther, J.J. 9, 10, 17, 64, 77, 79, 147,
    172nn15,17, 174n56, 175n70,
    176nn82,86, 185n47, 187nn21,33,
    189n72, 191n95, 192n1,
    196nn85,106, 201nn83,94,98,
    202nn119,121, 203nn146,156,
    204nn174,175, 209, 216

Haenchen, E. 28, 33, 77, 119, 120,
    176n4, 177n11, 178n38, 179n57,
    187n22, 188n43, 196nn97,98,104,
    197n113, 207, 216
Hahn, F. 210, 216
Halsema, J.H. 216
Hanhart, K. 216
Hartman, L. 142, 201n100, 203n147,
    204n177, 216
Hartmann, G. 118, 196n95, 216
Hauck, F. 194n32, 207
Hawkin, D.J. 68, 172n11, 175nn61,74,
    185n41, 186n69, 195n67, 196n100,
    216
Heise, J. 210
Henstenberg, W. 207
Heyraud, L. 216
Hort, F.J.A. 103, 193n9, 212
Hoskyns, E.C. 113, 120, 126-28, 171n5,
    183n126, 190n77, 195nn57,66,
    196n101, 197nn5,6, 198n23, 207,
    210
Howard, W.F. 188n47, 207, 208, 210,
    211
Hudry-Clergeon, C. 216
Hullen, A.B. 216
Hunter, A.M. 210

Jeremias, J. 104, 106, 183n135, 193n23,
    194nn31,32, 210
Jiminez, F.M. 216
Johnson, L. 216
Johnson, N.E. 13, 65, 132, 133, 173n35,
    185n50, 199nn37,42, 216
Jonge, M. de 150, 201n83, 203n156,
    204n164, 210, 216
Joubert, H.L.N. 216

Karrer, O. 210, 216
Käsemann, E. 210
Kautzsch, E. 186n2, 210
Kegel, G. 210

Kemp, I.S. 216
Kerrigan, A. 216
Kilmartin, E.J. 217
King, J.S. 173n36, 217, 219
Klein, G. 205n186, 217
Koester, H. 210
Kraeling, E.G. 180n71, 210
Kraft, H. 208, 210
Kragerud, A. 10, 172n21, 211
Kremer, J. 114, 195n68, 211
Kruse, H. 217
Kuhl, J. 211
Kuhn, K.G. 60, 185n33, 217, 221
Kümmel, W.G. 211
Kysar, R. 15, 174nn42,44, 211, 217

Lagrange, M.J. 126, 141, 197nn4,7,
    197n7, 201n91, 207
Lamouille, A. 173n34, 207
Lampe, G.W.H. 217
Langbrandtner, W. 173n30, 211
Langkammer, H. 217
Lattke, M. 211
Leaney, R. 105, 193n24, 194n35, 217
Leibig, J.E. 217
Léon-Dufour, X. 211
Léonard, J.-M. 217
Liddell, H.G. 84, 188n51, 201n89, 211
Lightfoot, H.G. 186n58, 195n77,
    197n16, 198n23, 207, 214
Lindars, B. 17, 46, 51, 55, 57, 66-68,
    77, 94, 106, 108, 111, 113, 129,
    135, 154, 155, 172n21, 173n34,
    175n60, 176n1, 177n17, 178n35,
    179nn40,42, 180n68, 181nn78,96,
    182n112, 183nn124,136,138,
    184nn6,11,14,25, 185n49, 186n56,64,
    187n20, 191n101, 194nn28,37,42,49,
    195nn55,65, 196n87,99,108,
    198n16,22,35, 199n52,
    200nn57,58,72, 202n110, 204n179,
    205n185, 207, 211, 217
Lofthouse, W.F. 211
Loisy, A. 185n48, 189n72, 190n93, 207
Lorenzen, T. 73, 120, 175nn58,75,
    184n19, 187n7, 195n72, 196n105,
    211
Lüthi, W. 207

MacGregor, G.H.C. 181n78, 208
Mahoney, R.K. 11, 57, 63, 64, 104, 112,

115, 130, 133, 157, 171n1, 173n28,
    177n22, 178n24, 184n15, 185n42,
    186nn55,60, 193nn11,12,13,14,
    195nn59,79, 197n112, 198nn23,26,
    199nn41,48, 205nn1,2, 211
Manns, F. 217
Marsh, J. 126, 181n78, 187n27, 197n8,
    208
Marshall, I.H. 193n23, 208
Martyn, J.L. 15, 173nn30,32,36,
    174nn42,46, 211, 220
Marxsen, W. 211
Masson, P.C. 217
Mastin, B.A. 92, 130, 179n52,
    184nn20,28, 185n51, 186nn59,71,
    190nn77,87,88, 198nn16,23,25,
    199n38, 200n75, 208
Maynard, A.H. 10, 40, 61, 68, 88, 115,
    117, 122, 172n20, 174n48, 177n16,
    180n75, 183n130, 184n19,
    185nn37,38, 186nn68,71,
    189nn63,67, 191n110, 192n116,
    195n74, 196n88, 197n113, 200n63,
    202nn115,124, 204n160, 205n186,
    206n22, 211, 217
McDowell, E.A. 139, 200n73, 217
McEleney, N.J. 199n53, 217
McHugh, J. 217
McKay, K.L. 145, 202nn126,132,
    203n147, 217
Mears, E. 208
Meeks, W.A. 217
Meier, J.P. 167, 206n35, 209
Mercier, R. 217
Merkel, H. 217
Metzger, B.M. 184n31, 193n23, 194n34,
    211
Meyer, R. 58, 184n21, 191n108, 217
Michaels, J.R. 208
Michel, O. 218
Minear, P.S. 9, 12, 55, 96, 110, 118,
    127, 156, 172n12, 173n29,
    174nn42,46, 184nn7,19, 189n72,
    191n96, 192nn114,1, 194nn47,48,
    196n90, 197n11, 205n190, 218
Miranda, J.P. 211
Moffat, J. 181n78, 198n27, 208, 211
Mohr, T.A. 211
Mollat, D. 218
Moloney, F.J. 58, 184n17, 218
Moreton, M.B. 218

Morris, L. 21, 29, 113, 135, 139,
    174n57, 175n78, 176nn2,5, 177n13,
    180nn66,68, 181nn94,96, 182n115,
    190nn77,87, 195nn53,64, 197nn4,6,
    198n23, 199n55, 200nn58,72,76,
    201nn89,96, 208, 211
Motyer, J.A. 184n23, 218
Moule, H.C.F. 211
Moulton, J.H. 188n47, 211
Muddiman, J. 193n17, 218
Müller, H.B. 211
Mussner, F. 211

Neirynck, F. 9, 64, 80, 81, 87, 104, 106,
    172n10, 185n45, 187n32,
    188nn37,38, 189n64, 192nn2,3,
    193n16, 194n29, 195n62, 211, 218
Niccacci, A. 218

O'Grady, J. 134, 149, 150, 156, 173n32,
    174n39, 190n89, 199n47,
    203nn151,152,157, 204nn159,161,
    205nn188,189, 206nn31,33, 218
O'Rourke, J.J. 218
Olsson, B.211
Osborne, G. 120, 121, 144, 147, 193n19,
    194n44, 196nn109,110,111, 197n1,
    198n34, 199n45, 200nn56,60,
    202nn109,110,113,123,130,133,
    203nn141,148,154,155,
    204nn162,163,176, 206n26, 211, 218
Osty, E. 218
Otto, H.P. 210, 211, 218
Oulton, J.E.L. 180n66, 211

Painter, J. 14, 15, 157, 173n37,
    174nn47,50, 212, 218
Pallis, A. 212
Pamment, M. 9, 64, 151, 152, 171n8,
    174n45, 175n66, 185n44, 189n72,
    198n22, 203n153, 204nn166,167,
    205n185, 219
Pancaro, S. 15, 174nn42,43,45, 212
Parker, P. 219
Patterson, D. 219
Perrin, N. 212
Perry, M.C. 219
Pesch, R. 212
Pfnitzer, V.C. 219
Philips, G.A. 219
Plummer, A. 208

Pollard, T.E. 212
Porter, J.R. 219
Potter, R. 78, 175n64, 187n25, 206n18, 219
Potterie, I. de la 191n93, 219

Refoulé, F. 219
Reiser, W.W. 196n82, 203n137, 219
Reumann, J. 209
Richard, E. 200n78, 219
Rigg, H. 219
Robertson, A.T. 204n171, 212
Robinson, J.M. 171n2, 205n9, 212
Rogers, A.D. 219
Roloff, J. 219
Romeo, J.A. 199n53, 219
Roth, C. 38, 180n63, 219
Ruckstuhl, E. 212, 219
Rusch, F.A. 219
Russel, R. 219

Salas, A. 219
Salvoni, F. 195n80, 219
Sanders, J.N. 58, 65, 67, 92, 130, 179n52, 184nn20,28, 185n51, 186nn59,71, 190nn77,87,88, 198nn16,23,25, 199n38, 200n75, 208, 219
Schlatter, A. 79, 187n29, 208
Schnackenburg, R. 11, 17, 31, 39, 44, 46, 49, 50, 104, 106, 108, 114, 136, 139, 152, 172n25, 173n34, 174n57, 175nn61,75, 176n2, 177n12, 178nn27,28,33,52, 179nn58,59, 180nn62,69, 181nn76,78,89,94,96, 182nn100,102,118,119,121, 183nn123,128,134,140,1, 188n52, 190nn93,95, 192n3, 193nn10,26, 194nn33,39,41,44, 195n69, 199n53, 200nn57,59,68,77, 203n144, 204n172, 208, 212, 216, 220
Schneiders, S.M. 220
Schnider, F. 212
Schniewind, J. 194n32, 212
Schwank, B. 220
Schweizer, E. 176n91, 212
Scott, E.F. 191n94, 212, 217
Scott, R. 84, 188n51, 201n89, 211
Segovia, F.F. 212
Shaw, A. 129, 198n21, 220
Sheehan, J.F.X. 203n140, 220

Shepherd, M.H. 176nn83,91, 220
Shorter, M. 42, 181nn77,79,82, 220
Smalley, S.S. 127, 132, 179n4, 197n9, 199nn36,38, 202
Smereka, L. 220
Smith, D.M. Jr. 43, 174n42, 181nn78,84, 212, 220
Smith, R. 220
Snyder, G.F. 8, 50, 51, 61, 62, 68, 94, 95, 171n4, 179n46, 183n130, 185n39, 186n66, 191nn100,106, 192n118, 199n46, 200n64, 201n81, 203n149, 204n180, 205n186, 220
Soards, M.L. 20
Solages, B. de 198n30, 220
Spaemann, H. 220
Spicq, C. 144, 145, 202n101, 212
Stauffer, E. 91, 190n83, 212
Stenger, W. 212, 220
Strachan, R.H. 42, 176n5, 181nn78,81, 212
Strathman, H. 181n78, 184n19, 221
Strecker, G. 221
Sturch, R.L. 220

Talavero, S. 221
Tasker, R.V.G. 208
Taylor, M.J. 212
Temple, S. 221
Temple, W. 15, 197n4, 199n50, 200n61, 212, 221
Tenney, M. 208
Thyen, H. 106, 175n58, 211, 221
Thyes, A. 221
Titus, E.L. 171n5, 191n104, 209, 212, 221
Tobin, W.J. 198n28, 201nn84,98, 202nn115,118,122, 221
Torrey, C.C. 221
Trudringer, L.P. 221
Turner, C.N. 221

Vacherot, J.M. 198n30, 220
Voigt, S. 221

Watty, W.W. 9, 20, 172nn14,16, 175nn65,72, 221
Weiss, B. 187n28, 208
Weiss, J. 191n108
Westcott, B.F. 39, 80, 103, 180n69, 188n36, 190nn36,77,87,

193n9, 208, 212
Whiteacre, R. 212
Wikenhauser, A. 181n78, 208
Wilckens, U. 221
Wilcox, M. 221
Wind, A. 221

Wojciechowski, M. 221
Woll, D.B. 212
Wulf, F. 221

Zahn, T. 208
Zelzer, K. 221

INDEX OF SUBJECTS

Andrew 29-36, 41, 162
anonymity, function of 10, 12, 16-20,
    29, 31, 40, 57, 63, 67, 72, 76-80,
    104, 109, 160, 169, 213, 221
another disciple 32, 35, 76, 78, 86, 98,
    162
apocryphal embellishments 16, 86
apostasy (see also 'falling away') 53
apostles 8, 22-24, 62, 128, 139, 144,
    155, 167, 210
apostleship 62, 156, 168, 214
Apostolic Christianity 8, 11, 16, 24, 47,
    48, 52, 70, 95, 120-22, 124, 137-40,
    149, 155, 161, 166-70
appendix (John 21) 17, 55, 124, 126,
    128, 137, 159, 212
ascension of Jesus 45, 55, 137
Augustine 118
authority (see also 'ecclesiastical
    authority')
    of the Beloved Disciple 11, 16, 20,
        57, 95-97, 121, 153, 155, 165-
        67
    of Peter (apostolic) 10, 11, 16, 20,
        40, 48, 96-97, 114, 121-22,
        133, 137, 146-49, 156, 166-67,
        173n31
    pneumatic 10, 14-15, 156
    crisis of (see crisis)
authorship
    of the Gospel 8, 19, 151, 213, 216
    of John 21 128-31, 151

Beloved Disciple 7-14, 16-25, 27, 31,
    41, 48, 49, 52-60, 63-71, 76-83, 85,
    86, 88-90, 92-99, 101, 102, 103,
    108-25, 127-34, 137, 140, 145, 148,
    149, 150-70, 209, 216, 218-21
Bethany 28, 66
betrayal by Judas (see also 'Judas') 43,
    44, 56, 57, 59, 64-70, 79, 96, 116,
    163, 221
bosom (κολπος) 58, 160, 218
breast (see 'bosom')

burial of Jesus 78, 107, 108, 113, 214

Caesarea Philippi 27, 35, 43, 48, 53
Cephas 29, 40, 79
charcoal fire 76, 84, 142
christology 13-16, 30, 38, 39, 41, 66, 67,
    75, 122, 134, 137, 158, 165, 166,
    212, 218
church (see also 'ecclesiology') 11, 12,
    15, 19, 20, 22, 24, 30, 33, 39, 40,
    48, 52, 62, 66, 68, 70, 89, 94, 96,
    97, 99, 107, 110, 114, 117, 122,
    134-38, 143, 147, 149, 150-56, 160,
    167, 168, 210, 212, 215-17
clothes, Peter's (see also 'grave clothes')
    103, 107, 108, 116, 121, 122, 141,
    142, 163
coal-fire (see charcoal fire)
cockcrow 88
commission 22, 127, 128, 133, 136, 146,
    147, 163
commissioning
    of the disciples 122, 126-28
    of Peter 88, 138, 142, 146, 148,
        153, 162
community, Johannine 8-17, 20-22, 24,
    41, 43, 44, 47-49, 52-54, 56, 57, 58,
    62, 70, 81, 82, 97, 110, 112, 117,
    118, 123, 124, 125, 129, 131, 132,
    134-38, 149-63, 165-70, 208, 209,
    213, 214, 217, 218, 220
community history, Johannine 12-14,
    16
competition (see 'rivalry')
confession of Andrew 35, 36
confession of Peter 21, 22, 27, 41-43,
    47-53, 88, 118, 144, 158, 162, 163
courtyard of the High Priest 72, 73, 76,
    78-81, 83, 87, 97, 98, 143, 160,
    161, 163, 166
crisis of authority (see also 'authority')
    14, 16, 39, 55, 65, 139, 156, 159,
    168, 214
cross (see also 'crucifixion') 89-93, 96,

97, 99, 158, 160, 162, 165, 208, 209, 231, 217, 220
crucifixion 55, 70, 88-93, 96, 99, 111
'crypto-Christians' 78

denial, Peter's 37, 62, 69-71, 73-76, 82-89, 96-98, 127, 137, 139, 142-44, 148, 162-64, 215-17
discipleship 8, 23, 28, 29, 31, 35, 41, 46, 52, 55-57, 62, 66-68, 71, 81, 83, 98, 109, 112, 121, 123, 124, 133-35, 142, 143, 148, 150, 154, 155, 164, 169

ear 76, 86, 87, 98
ecclesial 10, 62, 96, 133, 150, 151, 160
ecclesiastical authority 10, 11, 40, 53, 122, 133, 156
ecclesiology 12-14, 16, 122, 134, 165, 213, 218
editor (see also 'redactor') 12, 20, 108, 130, 131, 133, 149, 151, 156, 159, 168
epilogue of the Gospel 17, 126, 127, 158, 162, 164, 169
Epistles of John 14, 15, 52, 156, 167
eschatology of the Gospel 13, 128, 133, 152, 153
evangelist (author of the Gospel of John) 7, 8, 10, 12, 14, 15, 17, 20, 22, 24, 27-31, 33, 35-45, 48-53, 57, 59, 60, 63, 64, 66, 67-71, 74, 76-79, 82-85, 87, 89, 91-97, 101, 102, 106, 108-12, 114-22, 126, 127, 129, 130, 131, 137, 138, 157-59, 164, 167, 208, 211, 214, 219
eyewitness material 14, 65, 84, 86, 135, 220

faith 9-11, 14, 22, 24, 41, 44, 46-53, 55, 62, 93, 96, 97, 101, 104, 107-109, 111-13, 117-21, 123, 124, 134, 151, 158, 161-63, 165-69
falling away 44, 48, 49, 52, 163, 168
family of God 158, 160, 165
first-hand material (see also 'eyewitness') 84, 86, 138
fish 153 128, 135, 136, 143
    allegorical interpretations 129, 135
flesh 43, 45
flock 147, 148, 167, 169

follow (figurative of 'discipleship') 11, 28-31, 35, 41, 44, 53, 69, 70, 72, 76, 79, 87, 88, 89, 98, 99, 101, 113, 115, 117, 120, 123, 135, 140, 143, 145, 148, 155, 162-64, 167
footwashing 21, 56, 61, 62, 163

Galilee 28, 32, 42, 44, 47, 48, 52, 131, 135, 163, 213
garden of Gethsemane 76, 86, 87, 98, 164, 207
Gentile Christianity 9, 15, 89, 128, 151, 152
glorification of Jesus (see also 'hour') 67, 161, 163
Gnosticism 160, 168
grave clothes 103, 107, 116, 121-22, 164

high priest 21, 76, 78, 79, 82, 83, 86, 98, 143, 160, 215
Holy Spirit 15, 122
hour, Jesus' 57, 67, 69, 70, 158, 163-65

impetuosity, Peter's 115, 141, 153, 154
interrogation, Jesus' 75, 76, 82-85, 110, 111, 158, 160, 161
interrogation, Peter's 82-85, 143
intimacy between Jesus and the Beloved Disciple 7, 24, 57-58, 63, 67-70, 81, 160-62, 166, 167

Jewish Christianity 9, 89, 90, 151
Johannine Christianity 8, 52, 212, 218, 220
Johannine community (see 'community, Johannine')
Johannine school 15, 127, 131, 157, 209
John the Baptist 21, 27, 28, 31, 41, 162
Judaism (see also 'synagogue') 15, 94, 212
Judas 21, 43, 51, 52, 56, 57, 59, 61-68, 79, 85, 158, 165, 216

Kepha (see 'Cephas')

Last Supper 17, 55-57, 108, 162, 163, 221
linen clothes (see 'grave clothes')
love 11, 62, 65, 77, 88, 101, 109, 112, 120, 127, 135, 137, 141-46, 148, 149, 154, 156, 163, 164, 212

Magdalene 102, 103, 108-10, 118, 122, 220
Malchus 86
martyrdom 142, 148, 149, 155, 159, 164
Mary, mother of Jesus 21, 42, 59, 89, 90, 92-95, 97, 99, 102, 108-10, 111, 118, 120, 122, 160, 163, 165, 209, 214, 217, 220
mediator, Beloved Disciple as 31, 49, 68-69, 98, 140, 161

nakedness, Peter's 141
naming of Peter 18, 36-41, 86, 98, 162
Nazareth (see Galilee)
net 136, 140, 143, 150, 153, 160, 161, 163

'other' disciple (see also 'another disciple') 31, 53, 72, 73, 76-82, 86, 98, 112-14, 117, 218

Paraclete 14, 15
passion narrative 86, 89, 107, 219
pastor 153, 164
pastoral 10, 20, 133, 136, 147-49, 153, 155, 163-65
Peter 7-13, 16, 21, 22, 24, 25, 27-33, 35-44, 46-64, 66-90, 96-99, 101-105, 107-17, 119-21, 122-25, 127, 128, 131-34, 137-51, 153-70, 207, 209-11, 213-17, 219
Petrine 9, 10, 95, 122, 135, 138, 155, 162, 166, 167, 170, 221
Philip 21, 29, 31-34
prologue of the Gospel 42, 55, 127, 218
public ministry of Jesus 55

'race' to the tomb 101, 108, 111-14, 123
redactor (see also 'editor') 10, 22, 31, 43, 81, 106, 130-32, 138, 150, 156
remaining 29, 151, 153, 159
representative figures 10, 18, 20, 24, 62, 70, 160
restoration of Peter 62, 133, 137, 138, 146, 148, 162, 163, 215, 219
resurrection of Jesus 21, 55, 62, 88, 95, 96, 101-103, 107, 108, 111, 114, 116-21, 123, 126, 131, 134, 137, 139, 140, 146, 150, 160, 161, 165, 208, 210, 211, 212, 214, 217-19
resurrection narratives 102, 103, 107,

144, 210, 211, 214, 217, 218
revelation of Jesus 12, 42, 53, 55, 96, 97, 133, 134, 160, 163, 166
rivalry, Peter (Apostolic) vs. Beloved Disciple (Johannine) 7, 10-12, 69, 112, 120, 144, 154

Samaritan woman 21, 82
Satan 48, 51, 53, 56, 65-67, 163
schism within Johannine community 15, 16, 168
second-generation Christianity 17-20, 30, 138, 156, 167
sectarianism 14, 168
sheep 62, 133, 134, 147, 156, 163, 169, 214
shepherd 42, 120, 133, 135, 147, 169, 220
signs 21, 55, 127, 157, 160, 210, 219
Simon 10, 29-32, 34-41, 49, 51, 56, 60, 87, 105, 114, 116, 138, 144, 148, 162, 212, 216, 219
Simon Peter (full name) 10, 30, 36, 38, 39, 41, 49, 51, 56, 60, 87, 116, 138, 144, 148, 162
Spirit 14, 15, 19, 45, 49-51, 55, 122, 123, 153, 156, 161, 209, 219
spokesman, Peter as 11, 21, 22, 24, 41, 49, 53, 68-70, 163, 164, 167
symbolic 11, 17, 20, 21, 23, 28, 29, 35, 38, 39, 52, 53, 57, 63, 64, 66, 69, 93, 94, 111, 112, 114, 129, 130, 135, 136, 141, 142, 147, 148, 160, 163, 210
synagogue 15, 43, 110
synoptic Gospels 10, 21, 23, 27, 29, 36, 40, 43, 47, 51, 53, 56, 64, 65, 67, 70-72, 74-76, 80, 83, 84, 87, 88, 90, 91, 92, 97, 101-103, 106-108, 132, 137, 138, 158, 162-64

the disciple whom Jesus loved 20, 49, 55, 160, 211, 214, 215, 219, 220
the other disciple (see 'other disciple')
three-fold (see also 'denial' and 'restoration') 84, 88, 142, 143, 146, 163, 164
tomb 11, 49, 88, 96, 101-17, 119-23, 140, 158, 160, 161, 163-65, 167, 211, 214, 218, 219
triple 88, 127, 143, 164

Twelve 11, 16, 17, 19, 21-24, 41, 42, 44, 46-50, 52, 53, 63, 68-70, 78, 95, 121, 123, 131, 148, 155, 163, 210, 216, 220

unbelief 44, 46, 49, 50, 52, 56, 93

witness 9, 15, 16, 18, 20, 24, 28, 34, 49, 62, 69, 86, 96, 97, 107, 108, 117, 121, 123, 124, 129, 130, 133, 134, 148, 150, 151, 153-55, 158, 160-62, 164, 165, 212

women 22, 90-92, 102, 104, 107

Zebedee 14, 17, 33, 219

JOURNAL FOR THE STUDY OF THE NEW TESTAMENT
Supplement Series

1 THE BARREN TEMPLE AND THE WITHERED TREE
William R. Telford

2 STUDIA BIBLICA 1978
II. Papers on the Gospels
E.A. Livingstone (ed.)

3 STUDIA BIBLICA 1978
III. Papers on Paul and Other New Testament Authors
E.A. Livingstone (ed.)

4 FOLLOWING JESUS
Discipleship in Mark's Gospel
Ernest Best

5 THE PEOPLE OF GOD
Markus Barth

6 PERSECUTION AND MARTYRDOM IN THE
THEOLOGY OF PAUL
John S. Pobee

7 SYNOPTIC STUDIES
The Ampleforth Conferences 1982 and 1983
C.M. Tuckett (ed.)

8 JESUS ON THE MOUNTAIN
A Study in Matthean Theology
Terence L. Donaldson

9 THE HYMNS OF LUKE'S INFANCY NARRATIVES
Their Origin, Meaning and Significance
Stephen Farris

10 CHRIST THE END OF THE LAW
Romans 10.4 in Pauline Perspective
Robert Badenas

11 THE LETTERS TO THE SEVEN CHURCHES OF ASIA
IN THEIR LOCAL SETTING
Colin J. Hemer

12 PROCLAMATION FROM PROPHECY AND PATTERN
Lucan Old Testament Christology
Darrell L. Bock

13 JESUS AND THE LAWS OF PURITY
Tradition History and Legal History in Mark 7
Roger P. Booth

14 THE PASSION ACCORDING TO LUKE
The Special Material of Luke 22
Marion L. Soards

15 HOSTILITY TO WEALTH IN THE SYNOPTIC GOSPELS
T.E. Schmidt

16 MATTHEW'S COMMUNITY
The Evidence of his Special Sayings Material
S.H. Brooks

17 THE PARADOX OF THE CROSS IN
THE THOUGHT OF ST PAUL
A.T. Hanson

18 HIDDEN WISDOM AND THE EASY YOKE
Wisdom, Torah and Discipleship in Matthew 11.25–30
C. Deutsch

19 JESUS AND GOD IN PAUL'S ESCHATOLOGY
L.J. Kreitzer

20 LUKE: A NEW PARADIGM
M.D. Goulder

21 THE DEPARTURE OF JESUS IN LUKE–ACTS
The Ascension Narratives in Context
M.C. Parsons

22 THE DEFEAT OF DEATH
Apocalyptic Eschatology in 1 Corinthians 15 and Romans 5
M.C. De Boer

23 PAUL THE LETTER-WRITER
AND THE SECOND LETTER TO TIMOTHY
M. Prior

24 APOCALYPTIC AND THE NEW TESTAMENT:
Essays in Honor of J. Louis Martyn
J. Marcus & M.L. Soards

25 THE UNDERSTANDING SCRIBE
Matthew and the Apocalyptic Ideal
D.E. Orton

26 WATCHWORDS:
Mark 13 in Markan Eschatology
T. Geddert

27 THE DISCIPLES ACCORDING TO MARK:
Markan Redaction in Current Debate
C.C. Black

28 THE NOBLE DEATH:
    Greco-Roman Martyrology and Paul's Concept of Salvation
    D. Seeley

29 ABRAHAM IN GALATIANS:
    Epistolary and Rhetorical Contexts
    G.W. Hansen

30 EARLY CHRISTIAN RHETORIC AND 2 THESSALONIANS
    F.W. Hughes